GUNFIGHTER®

Advanced Pistol

Warm Ups, Drills, Exercises and Quals

NAME: _____ UNIT: _____

www.GUNFIGHTERSERIES.com ©

Weapon Conditions

- Condition 4: No mag inserted. Slide forward on empty chamber. Hammer forward (if applicable). Weapon on safe (if applicable).

- Condition 3: Loaded mag inserted. Slide forward on empty chamber. Hammer forward (if applicable). Weapon on safe (if applicable).

- Condition 2: Loaded mag inserted. Slide forward with round in chamber. Hammer forward (if applicable). Weapon on safe (if applicable).

- Condition 1: Loaded mag inserted. Slide forward with round in chamber. Hammer cocked (if applicable). Weapon on safe (if applicable).

Always know the condition of your weapon!

Safety

- Treat every weapon as if it were loaded.

- Never point your weapon at anything you do not intend to shoot/destroy.

- Know your target and it's background.

- Keep your finger off the trigger until you intend to fire.

- Keep your weapon on safe until you are ready to fire.

- Always wear eye and ear protection, and proper protective clothing.

- Never shoot faster than you can effectively keep rounds on target.

- Be extremely cautious with back splatter and ricochets when shooting steel.

Warning

Perform these drills at your own risk. Only perform these drill in a safe manner which do not violate your range rules. Consult range staff for rules and regulations regarding drawing from a holster, rapid fire and multiple target engagements.

GUNFIGHTER is not responsible for any injury or death that may occur due to the use of this book. We recommend never shooting alone and under supervision of trained safety officers.

Table Of Contents:

Admin and Logistics.

Warm Up Dry Drills.
- By Pass
- Front One
- Over The Center
- Reorient
- Aftermath

Manipulations Drills.
- Hand Loader
- Rack Baby Rack
- Everybody Gets A Rack
- So You Had A Bad Day
- Jammin

Accuracy Drills.
- Warm Brass
- Wow
- Triggered
- Gut Check
- Long Arm
- Breaking Bad

Draw Drills.
- Close Encounter
- Frontal
- Side Shot
- Turn Left & Turn Right
- In A World Of Hurt

Positional Drills.
- Double Kneeling
- Supine
- Urban Prone

Movement Drills
- Stepping Out
- Sarg
- Pistol Sprints
- Shield
- Zig Zag

Recoil Management Drills.
- Elbows
- 2 To 5
- Multiplicity
- Test Yourself

Gunfighter Skills.
- Protector
- Too Busy
- Car Jack Right & Left
- Gundo Reload
- Crap Shoot
- Lean Into It

Advanced Course Of Fire Quals.
- Gunfighter Standard 3
- Gunfighter Standard 4

Custom Drill

Notes

Class Contacts and Names

How to use this book:

This book offers a carefully crafted catalog of training drills and is designed to log and track training progression as well as shot pattern placement analysis. **All targets may be downloaded for free** of our www.GunfighterSereis.com website and printed at home for free with the exception of the JD-QUAL1 target which may be purchased at numerous online retailers. The JD-Qual1 target may also be substituted with a cardboard IPSC with a rectangular body A zone.

For best results, conduct and record every drill at least once starting at the beginning. The more data you collect the better your results will be.

Most drills offer defensive time and scoring goals to achieve. Competitive shooters may set different goals. Everyone's goal should be to improve their recorded personal best.

For proper weapons handling and marksmanship coaching, seek out well respected firearms instructors and courses.

Train safe. Train hard. Train to win.

Afterwards:

Upon mastering all the drills in this book, continue to increase your skills by utilizing the entire Gunfighter training log book series.

Gunfighter Skill Books 2016 © - Gunfighter, LLC - All Rights Reserved
ISBN: 9781072792130 Revised 2019

Round Count Log

Weapon Make & Model: SN#:

Date	Ammo	Lot #	Fired	Total

Date	Ammo	Lot #	Fired	Total

Notes:

This Page	
Previous Page	
TOTAL	

www.GUNFIGHTERSERIES.com ©

Round Count Log

Weapon Make & Model: SN#:

Date	Ammo	Lot #	Fired	Total	Date	Ammo	Lot #	Fired	Total

Notes:

This Page	
Previous Page	
TOTAL	

Round Count Log

Weapon Make & Model: SN#:

Date	Ammo	Lot #	Fired	Total	Date	Ammo	Lot #	Fired	Total

Notes:

This Page	
Previous Page	
TOTAL	

Round Count Log

Weapon Make & Model: SN#:

Date	Ammo	Lot #	Fired	Total	Date	Ammo	Lot #	Fired	Total

Notes:

This Page	
Previous Page	
TOTAL	

Maintenance Log

Weapon Make & Model: SN#:

Date	Full Cleaning	Damage Inspection
	Y / N	Y / N
	Y / N	Y / N
	Y / N	Y / N
	Y / N	Y / N
	Y / N	Y / N
	Y / N	Y / N
	Y / N	Y / N
	Y / N	Y / N
	Y / N	Y / N
	Y / N	Y / N
	Y / N	Y / N
	Y / N	Y / N
	Y / N	Y / N
	Y / N	Y / N

Parts Replaced:

Date	Full Cleaning	Damage Inspection
	Y / N	Y / N
	Y / N	Y / N
	Y / N	Y / N
	Y / N	Y / N
	Y / N	Y / N
	Y / N	Y / N
	Y / N	Y / N
	Y / N	Y / N
	Y / N	Y / N
	Y / N	Y / N
	Y / N	Y / N
	Y / N	Y / N
	Y / N	Y / N
	Y / N	Y / N

Notes:

BY PASS

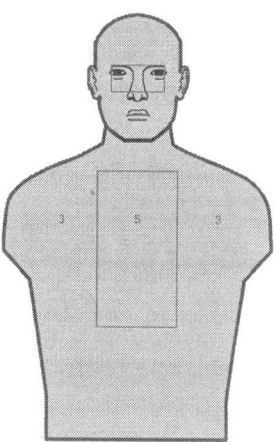

Purpose: Develop nervous system memory of an efficient retention draw position.

Distance: Arm's length from target.

Target: JD-QUAL1

Extra Equipment Needed: 10 DUMMY rounds.

Total Rounds Fired: 10 DUMMY rounds.

Repetitions: 10 Reps.

Starting Position & Condition: Standing – Surrender. Weapon Condition 1 using <u>dummy rounds for dry fire only</u>.

Description: At your own personal go, take your dominant firing hand/arm, bring your elbow straight back and clear your concealment garment (if you have one) with your firing hand and establish a good grip on the pistol. As your bring your firing to establish a good pistol grip, move your support hand to the side and just in front of your face with your palm facing to your dominant side, at the same time draw your pistol straight up just under your arm pit and rotate pistol towards target (5 point) A Zone body box. When you point your pistol at the target, lean the slide away from your body just enough so when fired from that position, it will not contact your clothing or chest causing a malfunction. Press trigger simulating a pistol shot. Reset and repeat drill 10 times.

Goal: The goals of this drill are to be smooth and deliberate while performing a dry fire retention draw.

BY PASS

Date	Location	Weapon	Holster Used	10 Reps	Notes
				Y / N	
				Y / N	
				Y / N	
				Y / N	
				Y / N	
				Y / N	
				Y / N	
				Y / N	
				Y / N	
				Y / N	
				Y / N	
				Y / N	
				Y / N	
				Y / N	
				Y / N	
				Y / N	
				Y / N	

Advanced Pistol ©

Warm Up Drill - 1

FRONT ONE

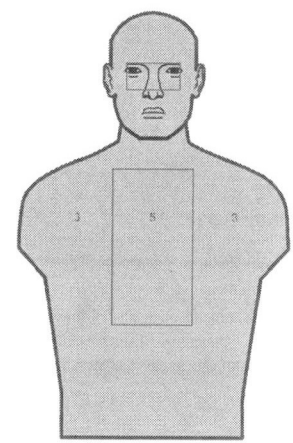

Purpose: Develop nervous system memory of an efficient one-handed draw.

Distance: 10 Yards.

Target: JD-QUAL1

Par Time: 2 Seconds.

Extra Equipment Needed: Shot timer, 10 DUMMY rounds.

Total Rounds Fired: 10 DUMMY rounds.

Repetitions: 10 Reps.

Starting Position & Condition: Standing – Hands to your side or surrender. Weapon Condition 1 using <u>dummy rounds for dry fire only</u>.

Description: At the timer beep, draw your pistol while pinning your support hand to your chest or to your support side, aim at target and press trigger simulating a pistol shot. Reset and repeat drill 10 times. Record if any reps were over par time.

Goal: The goals of this drill are to be smooth and deliberate while performing a dry fire one handed.

FRONT ONE

Date	Location	Weapon	Holster Used	10 Reps	All Under Par?	Notes
				Y / N	Y / N	
				Y / N	Y / N	
				Y / N	Y / N	
				Y / N	Y / N	
				Y / N	Y / N	
				Y / N	Y / N	
				Y / N	Y / N	
				Y / N	Y / N	
				Y / N	Y / N	
				Y / N	Y / N	
				Y / N	Y / N	
				Y / N	Y / N	
				Y / N	Y / N	
				Y / N	Y / N	
				Y / N	Y / N	
				Y / N	Y / N	
				Y / N	Y / N	

Advanced Pistol ©

Warm Up Drill - 2

OVER THE CENTER

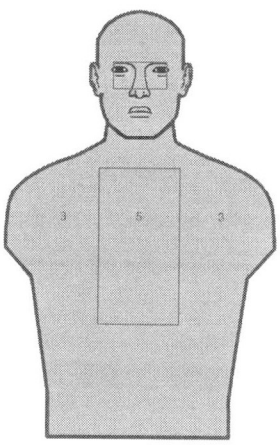

Purpose: Develop nervous system memory of an efficient support one handed draw.

Distance: 10 Yards.

Target: JD-QUAL1

Extra Equipment Needed: 10 DUMMY rounds.

Total Rounds Fired: 10 DUMMY rounds.

Repetitions: 10 Reps.

Starting Position & Condition: Standing – Hands to side or interview. Weapon Condition 1 using <u>dummy rounds for dry fire only</u>.

Description: At your own personal go, reach across your body and draw your pistol using only your support hand on the pistol grip. Keep all fingers and your thumb out of the trigger guard and off the trigger. Bring your pistol between your knees and trap the slide between your knees. Let go of the pistol grip and rotate your hand so you can secure a good grip hand position with your support hand. Bring the pistol up to aim at target, aim at target and press trigger simulating a pistol shot. While you are performing this first motion, let your dominant arm hang, then when bringing the pistol up on target, pin your dominant arm to your dominant side. Make sure you are aware of the muzzle direction at all times and make sure you never point your pistol at anything you do not intend to destroy. Make sure not to point your pistol at your feet. Practicing firearm safety is a major facet to this drill when you start performing this live fire. Reset and repeat drill 10 times.

Goal: The goal of this drill is to be safe, smooth and deliberate while performing a dry fire support one handed draw.

OVER THE CENTER

Date	Location	Weapon	Holster Used	10 Reps	Notes
				Y / N	
				Y / N	
				Y / N	
				Y / N	
				Y / N	
				Y / N	
				Y / N	
				Y / N	
				Y / N	
				Y / N	
				Y / N	
				Y / N	
				Y / N	
				Y / N	
				Y / N	
				Y / N	
				Y / N	

Warm Up Drill - 3

REORIENT

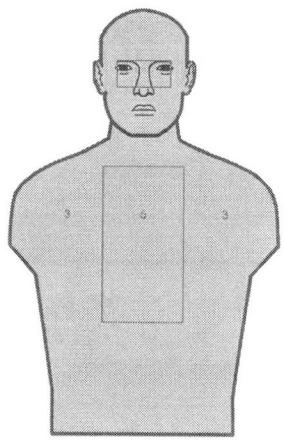

Purpose: Develop efficient nervous system memory of turning and shooting.

Distance: 7 Yards.

Target: JD-QUAL1

Par Time: 1.75 Seconds.

Extra Equipment Needed: Shot timer, 10 DUMMY rounds.

Total Rounds Fired: 10 DUMMY rounds.

Repetitions: 5 Reps each direction.

Starting Position & Condition: Standing – Hands to side or interview. Weapon Condition 1 using <u>dummy rounds for dry fire only</u>.

Description: At the timer beep, look in the direction you are going to turn, pivot on the ball of your foot and move until you are squared up facing the target. Once you have made your turn, draw your pistol, take aim at the (5 point) A Zone body box and press the trigger to the rear dry firing and simulating a shot. Repeat this drill in each direction, left and right, 5 times.

Goal: The goal of this drill is to be smooth and deliberate within a par time of 1.75 seconds.

Variations: Use each of the ready positions instead of a draw. Take care you do not break firearm safety rules and point your weapon at anyone or anything you do not wish to destroy. If your ready position is going to sweep a person or point in an unsafe direction, do not perform that ready position during the drill.

REORIENT

Date	Location	Weapon	10 Reps Left?	10 Reps Right?	All Under Par?	Starting Position
			Y / N	Y / N	Y / N	
			Y / N	Y / N	Y / N	
			Y / N	Y / N	Y / N	
			Y / N	Y / N	Y / N	
			Y / N	Y / N	Y / N	
			Y / N	Y / N	Y / N	
			Y / N	Y / N	Y / N	
			Y / N	Y / N	Y / N	
			Y / N	Y / N	Y / N	
			Y / N	Y / N	Y / N	
			Y / N	Y / N	Y / N	
			Y / N	Y / N	Y / N	
			Y / N	Y / N	Y / N	
			Y / N	Y / N	Y / N	
			Y / N	Y / N	Y / N	
			Y / N	Y / N	Y / N	
			Y / N	Y / N	Y / N	

Warm Up Drill - 4

AFTERMATH

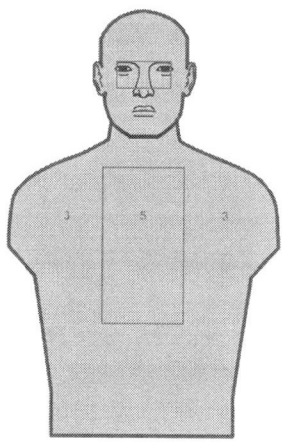

Purpose: Develop nervous system memory of getting off the X and performing a defensive scan after using a pistol in self-defense.

Distance: 5 Yards.

Target: JD-QUAL1

Extra Equipment Needed: 10 DUMMY rounds.

Total Rounds Fired: 10 DUMMY rounds.

Repetitions: 5 Reps each direction.

Starting Position & Condition: Standing – Pistol aimed at target. Weapon Condition 1 using <u>dummy rounds for dry fire only</u>.

Description: At your own personal go, press the trigger to the rear dry firing and simulating a shot at the (5 point) A Zone body box. Point your pistol down at the front of the target as if the threat had dropped, move quickly left or right to a new position at least 3 yards away, simulating the finding a piece of cover and do a defensive scan. Repeat this drill in each direction, left and right, 5 times

Goal: The goal of this drill is to get you use to moving off a static spot after you have been in a self-defense situation where you had to utilize your firearm.

Variations: Set up different situations, different barricade types, different distances in different locations. As an example, place the target by a car or cars while using an airsoft pistol shooting plastic bb's instead of dummy rounds.

AFTERMATH

Date	Location	Weapon	5 Reps Left?	5 Reps Right?	Types Of Cover Used	Notes
			Y / N	Y / N		
			Y / N	Y / N		
			Y / N	Y / N		
			Y / N	Y / N		
			Y / N	Y / N		
			Y / N	Y / N		
			Y / N	Y / N		
			Y / N	Y / N		
			Y / N	Y / N		
			Y / N	Y / N		
			Y / N	Y / N		
			Y / N	Y / N		
			Y / N	Y / N		
			Y / N	Y / N		
			Y / N	Y / N		
			Y / N	Y / N		
			Y / N	Y / N		

Warm Up Drill - 5

HAND LOADER

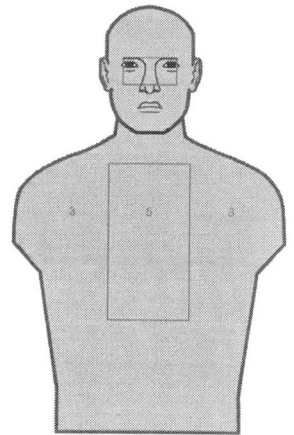

Purpose: Increase emergency reloading efficiency.

By: Adapted from a favorite of Billy Solares from Academi.

Distance: 8 Yards.

Target: JD-QUAL1

Par Time: 6 Seconds.

Extra Equipment Needed: Shot timer, 3 magazines downloaded with 1 round each.

Rounds Fired Per Rep: 3 Rounds.

Total Rounds Fired: 15 Rounds.

Point Penalty: Go / No Go.

Repetitions: 5 Reps.

Starting Position & Condition: Standing – Surrender/Interview. Weapon Condition 1.

Description: Load 3 magazines with 1 round each. At the timer beep, draw and fire 1 round into the A Zone (5 point) Body Box. Reload, fire 1 round into the A Zone (5 point) Body Box. Reload, fire 1 round into the A Zone (5 point) Body Box. Record your time and score. Repeat drill 5 times. All shots must be in the A Zone Body Box and under par or the repetition is a No / Go.

Note: This is a very hard drill to make the par time, so practice to find those efficiencies that will help you get the goal time. *Billy's base par time is 5 seconds.

Goal: All shots in A Zone body box under 6 second par time.   **Expert:** Under 5.5 second par time.   **Gunfighter:** Under 5 second par time.

Variations: Immediately before the start of the drill, run 50 yards or do 2X25 yard shuttle runs, do 10 push-ups or 10 jumping jacks to get your heart rate up. Increase distance. Aim for head box.

HAND LOADER

Date:	Location:	Weapon:	Holster:	Mag Placement:
Rep 1 Time:	Rep 2 Time:	Rep 3 Time:	Rep 4 Time:	Rep 5 Time:
Rep 1: Go / No Go	Rep 2: Go / No Go	Rep 3: Go / No Go	Rep 4: Go / No Go	Rep 5: Go / No Go
Heart Rate Stress: Y / N	Distance:	Notes:		**Total Score:**

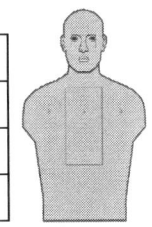

Date:	Location:	Weapon:	Holster:	Mag Placement:
Rep 1 Time:	Rep 2 Time:	Rep 3 Time:	Rep 4 Time:	Rep 5 Time:
Rep 1: Go / No Go	Rep 2: Go / No Go	Rep 3: Go / No Go	Rep 4: Go / No Go	Rep 5: Go / No Go
Heart Rate Stress: Y / N	Distance:	Notes:		**Total Score:**

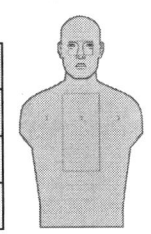

Date:	Location:	Weapon:	Holster:	Mag Placement:
Rep 1 Time:	Rep 2 Time:	Rep 3 Time:	Rep 4 Time:	Rep 5 Time:
Rep 1: Go / No Go	Rep 2: Go / No Go	Rep 3: Go / No Go	Rep 4: Go / No Go	Rep 5: Go / No Go
Heart Rate Stress: Y / N	Distance:	Notes:		**Total Score:**

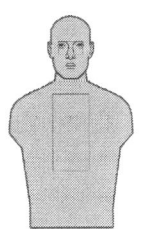

Date:	Location:	Weapon:	Holster:	Mag Placement:
Rep 1 Time:	Rep 2 Time:	Rep 3 Time:	Rep 4 Time:	Rep 5 Time:
Rep 1: Go / No Go	Rep 2: Go / No Go	Rep 3: Go / No Go	Rep 4: Go / No Go	Rep 5: Go / No Go
Heart Rate Stress: Y / N	Distance:	Notes:		**Total Score:**

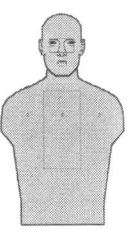

Advanced Pistol ©

Manipulation Drills - 1

www.GUNFIGHTERSERIES.com ©

HAND LOADER

Date:	Location:	Weapon:	Holster:	Mag Placement:
Rep 1 Time:	Rep 2 Time:	Rep 3 Time:	Rep 4 Time:	Rep 5 Time:
Rep 1: Go / No Go	Rep 2: Go / No Go	Rep 3: Go / No Go	Rep 4: Go / No Go	Rep 5: Go / No Go
Heart Rate Stress: Y / N	Distance:	Notes:		**Total Score:**

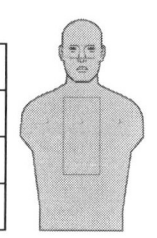

Date:	Location:	Weapon:	Holster:	Mag Placement:
Rep 1 Time:	Rep 2 Time:	Rep 3 Time:	Rep 4 Time:	Rep 5 Time:
Rep 1: Go / No Go	Rep 2: Go / No Go	Rep 3: Go / No Go	Rep 4: Go / No Go	Rep 5: Go / No Go
Heart Rate Stress: Y / N	Distance:	Notes:		**Total Score:**

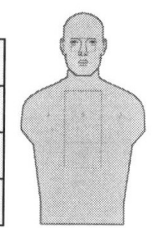

Date:	Location:	Weapon:	Holster:	Mag Placement:
Rep 1 Time:	Rep 2 Time:	Rep 3 Time:	Rep 4 Time:	Rep 5 Time:
Rep 1: Go / No Go	Rep 2: Go / No Go	Rep 3: Go / No Go	Rep 4: Go / No Go	Rep 5: Go / No Go
Heart Rate Stress: Y / N	Distance:	Notes:		**Total Score:**

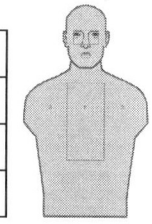

Date:	Location:	Weapon:	Holster:	Mag Placement:
Rep 1 Time:	Rep 2 Time:	Rep 3 Time:	Rep 4 Time:	Rep 5 Time:
Rep 1: Go / No Go	Rep 2: Go / No Go	Rep 3: Go / No Go	Rep 4: Go / No Go	Rep 5: Go / No Go
Heart Rate Stress: Y / N	Distance:	Notes:		**Total Score:**

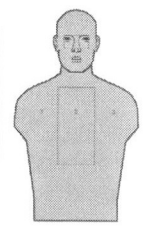

HAND LOADER

Date:	Location:	Weapon:	Holster:	Mag Placement:
Rep 1 Time:	Rep 2 Time:	Rep 3 Time:	Rep 4 Time:	Rep 5 Time:
Rep 1: Go / No Go	Rep 2: Go / No Go	Rep 3: Go / No Go	Rep 4: Go / No Go	Rep 5: Go / No Go
Heart Rate Stress: Y / N	Distance:	Notes:		Total Score:

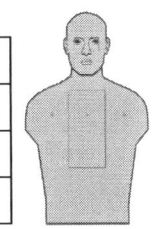

Date:	Location:	Weapon:	Holster:	Mag Placement:
Rep 1 Time:	Rep 2 Time:	Rep 3 Time:	Rep 4 Time:	Rep 5 Time:
Rep 1: Go / No Go	Rep 2: Go / No Go	Rep 3: Go / No Go	Rep 4: Go / No Go	Rep 5: Go / No Go
Heart Rate Stress: Y / N	Distance:	Notes:		Total Score:

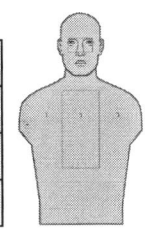

Date:	Location:	Weapon:	Holster:	Mag Placement:
Rep 1 Time:	Rep 2 Time:	Rep 3 Time:	Rep 4 Time:	Rep 5 Time:
Rep 1: Go / No Go	Rep 2: Go / No Go	Rep 3: Go / No Go	Rep 4: Go / No Go	Rep 5: Go / No Go
Heart Rate Stress: Y / N	Distance:	Notes:		Total Score:

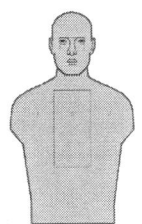

Date:	Location:	Weapon:	Holster:	Mag Placement:
Rep 1 Time:	Rep 2 Time:	Rep 3 Time:	Rep 4 Time:	Rep 5 Time:
Rep 1: Go / No Go	Rep 2: Go / No Go	Rep 3: Go / No Go	Rep 4: Go / No Go	Rep 5: Go / No Go
Heart Rate Stress: Y / N	Distance:	Notes:		Total Score:

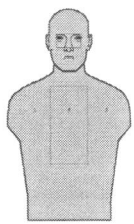

HAND LOADER

Date:	Location:	Weapon:	Holster:	Mag Placement:
Rep 1 Time:	Rep 2 Time:	Rep 3 Time:	Rep 4 Time:	Rep 5 Time:
Rep 1: Go / No Go	Rep 2: Go / No Go	Rep 3: Go / No Go	Rep 4: Go / No Go	Rep 5: Go / No Go
Heart Rate Stress: Y / N	Distance:	Notes:		**Total Score:**

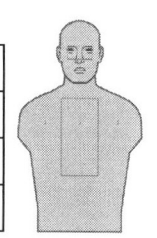

Date:	Location:	Weapon:	Holster:	Mag Placement:
Rep 1 Time:	Rep 2 Time:	Rep 3 Time:	Rep 4 Time:	Rep 5 Time:
Rep 1: Go / No Go	Rep 2: Go / No Go	Rep 3: Go / No Go	Rep 4: Go / No Go	Rep 5: Go / No Go
Heart Rate Stress: Y / N	Distance:	Notes:		**Total Score:**

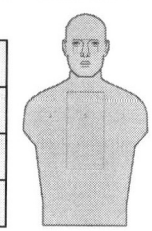

Date:	Location:	Weapon:	Holster:	Mag Placement:
Rep 1 Time:	Rep 2 Time:	Rep 3 Time:	Rep 4 Time:	Rep 5 Time:
Rep 1: Go / No Go	Rep 2: Go / No Go	Rep 3: Go / No Go	Rep 4: Go / No Go	Rep 5: Go / No Go
Heart Rate Stress: Y / N	Distance:	Notes:		**Total Score:**

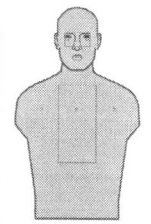

Date:	Location:	Weapon:	Holster:	Mag Placement:
Rep 1 Time:	Rep 2 Time:	Rep 3 Time:	Rep 4 Time:	Rep 5 Time:
Rep 1: Go / No Go	Rep 2: Go / No Go	Rep 3: Go / No Go	Rep 4: Go / No Go	Rep 5: Go / No Go
Heart Rate Stress: Y / N	Distance:	Notes:		**Total Score:**

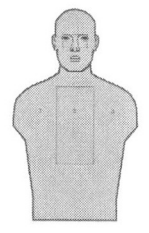

HAND LOADER

Date:	Location:	Weapon:	Holster:	Mag Placement:
Rep 1 Time:	Rep 2 Time:	Rep 3 Time:	Rep 4 Time:	Rep 5 Time:
Rep 1: Go / No Go	Rep 2: Go / No Go	Rep 3: Go / No Go	Rep 4: Go / No Go	Rep 5: Go / No Go
Heart Rate Stress: Y / N	Distance:	Notes:		Total Score:

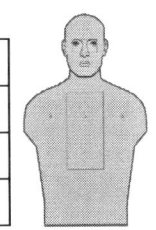

Date:	Location:	Weapon:	Holster:	Mag Placement:
Rep 1 Time:	Rep 2 Time:	Rep 3 Time:	Rep 4 Time:	Rep 5 Time:
Rep 1: Go / No Go	Rep 2: Go / No Go	Rep 3: Go / No Go	Rep 4: Go / No Go	Rep 5: Go / No Go
Heart Rate Stress: Y / N	Distance:	Notes:		Total Score:

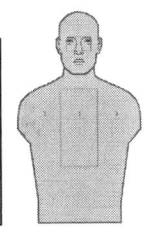

Date:	Location:	Weapon:	Holster:	Mag Placement:
Rep 1 Time:	Rep 2 Time:	Rep 3 Time:	Rep 4 Time:	Rep 5 Time:
Rep 1: Go / No Go	Rep 2: Go / No Go	Rep 3: Go / No Go	Rep 4: Go / No Go	Rep 5: Go / No Go
Heart Rate Stress: Y / N	Distance:	Notes:		Total Score:

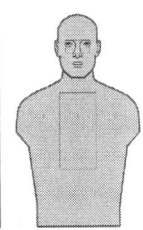

Date:	Location:	Weapon:	Holster:	Mag Placement:
Rep 1 Time:	Rep 2 Time:	Rep 3 Time:	Rep 4 Time:	Rep 5 Time:
Rep 1: Go / No Go	Rep 2: Go / No Go	Rep 3: Go / No Go	Rep 4: Go / No Go	Rep 5: Go / No Go
Heart Rate Stress: Y / N	Distance:	Notes:		Total Score:

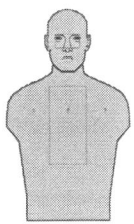

Advanced Pistol ©

Manipulation Drills - 1

RACK BABY RACK

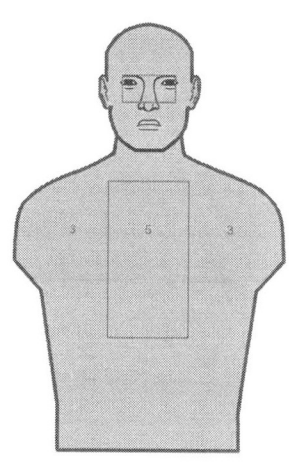

Purpose: Increase Type 1 malfunction clearing one-handed efficiency.

Distance: 7 Yards.

Target: JD-QUAL1

Rounds Fired Per Stage: 3 Rounds.

Total Rounds Fired: 6 Rounds.

Point Penalty: Go / No Go.

Repetitions: 1 Rep.

Starting Position & Condition: Standing – Low ready. Weapon Condition 3, hammer cocked.

Description: At your personal go, raise pistol and complete stage.

Stage 1 – Dominant hand firing. At your personal go, place your support hand on chest, raise pistol, take aim and press trigger to simulate firing a shot, getting a trigger click, tap the bottom of the magazine on your thigh, rack the slide using your rear sights on your belt or holster. To perform, place front of rear sight on belt, angle pistol outward, push down performing type 1 malfunction clearing. After clearing, fire one round into the (5 point) A Zone body box, repeat 3 times.

Stage 2 – Support hand firing. At your personal go, place your dominant hand on chest, raise pistol, take aim and press trigger to simulate firing a shot, getting a trigger click, tap the bottom of the magazine on your thigh, rack the slide using your rear sights on your belt. To perform place front of rear sight on belt, angle pistol outward, push down performing type 1 malfunction clearing. After clearing, fire one round into the (5 point) A Zone body box, repeat 3 times.

Goal: All shots in A Zone body box from 7 yards.   Expert: From 10 yards   Gunfighter: From 15 yards

Variations: Immediately before the start of the drill, run 50 yards or do 2X25 yard shuttle runs, do 10 push-ups or 10 jumping jacks to get your heart rate up.

RACK BABY RACK

Date:	Weapon:	Rack Technique?	
Distance:	Stage 1 All In: Y / N	Stage 2 All In: Y / N	Total Score:

Date:	Weapon:	Rack Technique?	
Distance:	Stage 1 All In: Y / N	Stage 2 All In: Y / N	Total Score:

Date:	Weapon:	Rack Technique?	
Distance:	Stage 1 All In: Y / N	Stage 2 All In: Y / N	Total Score:

Date:	Weapon:	Rack Technique?	
Distance:	Stage 1 All In: Y / N	Stage 2 All In: Y / N	Total Score:

Date:	Weapon:	Rack Technique?	
Distance:	Stage 1 All In: Y / N	Stage 2 All In: Y / N	Total Score:

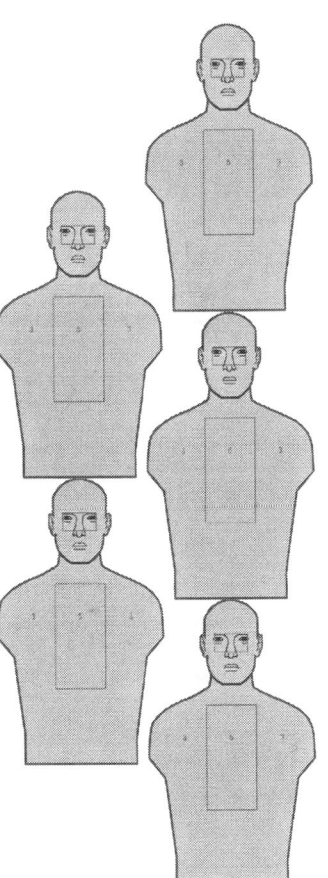

Advanced Pistol ©

RACK BABY RACK

Date:	Weapon:	Rack Technique?	
Distance:	Stage 1 All In: Y / N	Stage 2 All In: Y / N	Total Score:

Date:	Weapon:	Rack Technique?	
Distance:	Stage 1 All In: Y / N	Stage 2 All In: Y / N	Total Score:

Date:	Weapon:	Rack Technique?	
Distance:	Stage 1 All In: Y / N	Stage 2 All In: Y / N	Total Score:

Date:	Weapon:	Rack Technique?	
Distance:	Stage 1 All In: Y / N	Stage 2 All In: Y / N	Total Score:

Date:	Weapon:	Rack Technique?	
Distance:	Stage 1 All In: Y / N	Stage 2 All In: Y / N	Total Score:

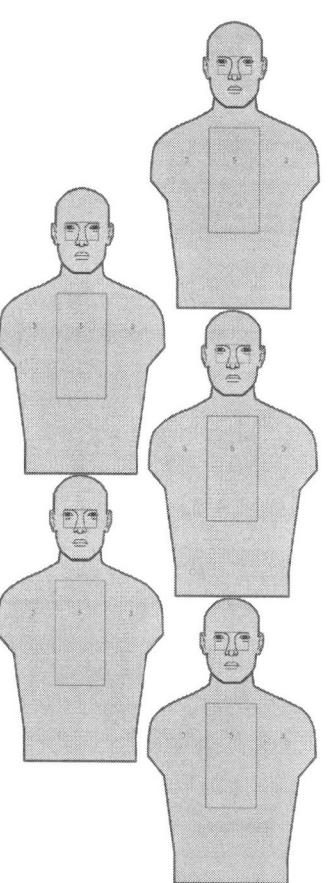

RACK BABY RACK

Date:	Weapon:	Rack Technique?	
Distance:	Stage 1 All In: Y / N	Stage 2 All In: Y / N	Total Score:

Date:	Weapon:	Rack Technique?	
Distance:	Stage 1 All In: Y / N	Stage 2 All In: Y / N	Total Score:

Date:	Weapon:	Rack Technique?	
Distance:	Stage 1 All In: Y / N	Stage 2 All In: Y / N	Total Score:

Date:	Weapon:	Rack Technique?	
Distance:	Stage 1 All In: Y / N	Stage 2 All In: Y / N	Total Score:

Date:	Weapon:	Rack Technique?	
Distance:	Stage 1 All In: Y / N	Stage 2 All In: Y / N	Total Score:

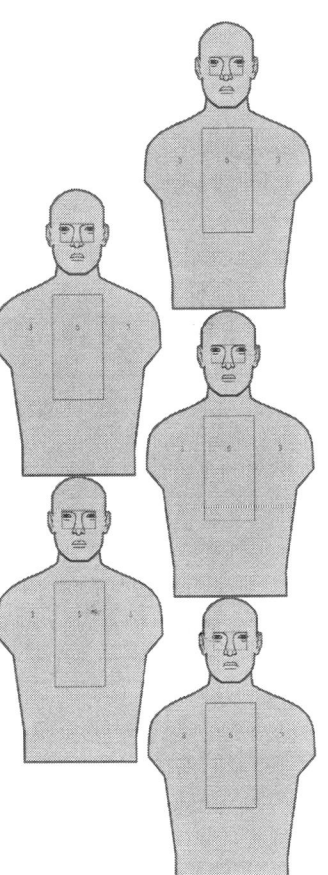

Advanced Pistol ©

Manipulation Drills - 2

RACK BABY RACK

Date:	Weapon:	Rack Technique?	
Distance:	Stage 1 All In: Y / N	Stage 2 All In: Y / N	Total Score:

Date:	Weapon:	Rack Technique?	
Distance:	Stage 1 All In: Y / N	Stage 2 All In: Y / N	Total Score:

Date:	Weapon:	Rack Technique?	
Distance:	Stage 1 All In: Y / N	Stage 2 All In: Y / N	Total Score:

Date:	Weapon:	Rack Technique?	
Distance:	Stage 1 All In: Y / N	Stage 2 All In: Y / N	Total Score:

Date:	Weapon:	Rack Technique?	
Distance:	Stage 1 All In: Y / N	Stage 2 All In: Y / N	Total Score:

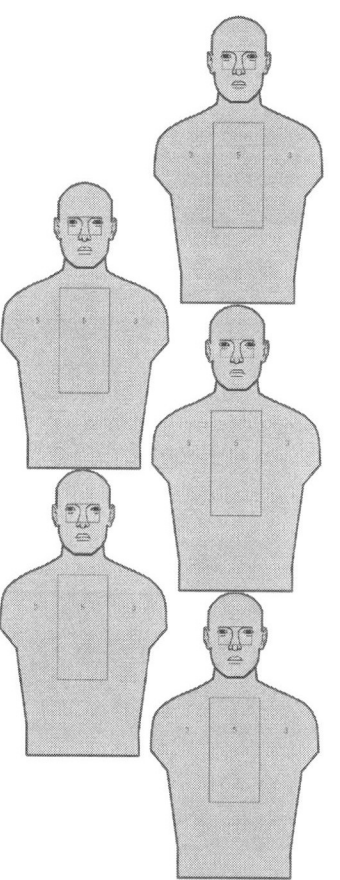

RACK BABY RACK

Date:	Weapon:	Rack Technique?	
Distance:	Stage 1 All In: Y / N	Stage 2 All In: Y / N	Total Score:

Date:	Weapon:	Rack Technique?	
Distance:	Stage 1 All In: Y / N	Stage 2 All In: Y / N	Total Score:

Date:	Weapon:	Rack Technique?	
Distance:	Stage 1 All In: Y / N	Stage 2 All In: Y / N	Total Score:

Date:	Weapon:	Rack Technique?	
Distance:	Stage 1 All In: Y / N	Stage 2 All In: Y / N	Total Score:

Date:	Weapon:	Rack Technique?	
Distance:	Stage 1 All In: Y / N	Stage 2 All In: Y / N	Total Score:

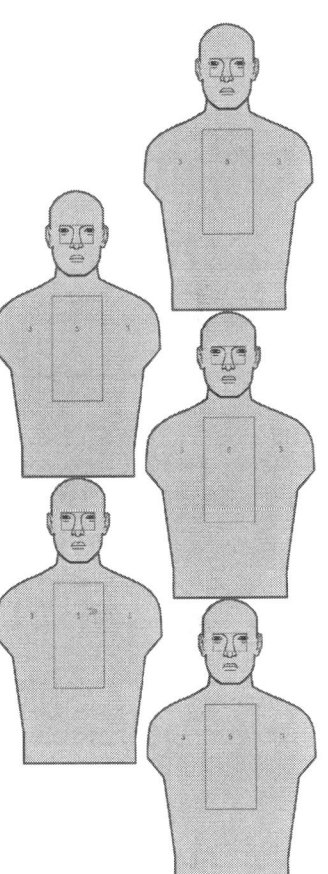

Advanced Pistol ©

EVERYBODY GETS A RACK

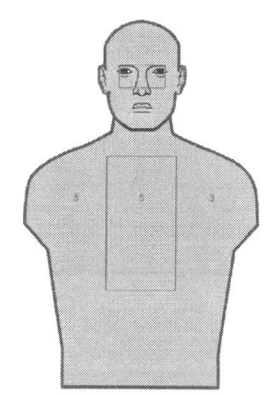

Purpose: Increase Type 1 malfunction clearing one-handed efficiency.

Distance: 25 Yards.   **Target:** JD-QUAL1

Extra Equipment Required: 3 Magazines, 15 dummy rounds, holster, 2 magazine pouches.

Rounds Fired Per Stage: 5 Rounds.   **Total Rounds Fired:** 15 Rounds.

Point Penalty: Go / No Go.   **Repetitions:** 1 Rep.

Starting Position & Condition: Standing – Surrender / Interview. Weapon Condition 3, hammer cocked.

Description: Set up each of your magazines with 5 dummy rounds and 5 live rounds staggered differently in each magazine. At your personal go, draw pistol and complete stage.

Stage 1 – Two handed firing. At your personal go, draw your pistol, take aim and press trigger to fire a shot into the (5 point) A Zone Body Box, if you get a click instead of a shot, perform a type 1 malfunction clearing, after clearing, fire one round into the (5 point) A Zone Body Box, keep firing until you get slide lock, perform an emergency reload, then reholster.

Stage 2 – Dominant hand firing. At your personal go, place your support hand on chest, draw your pistol, take aim and press trigger to fire a shot into the (5 point) A Zone Body Box, if you get a click instead of a shot, tap the magazine on your thigh, kneel down and rack the slide on the heel of your shoe performing type 1 malfunction clearing, after clearing, stand back up and fire one round into the (5 point) A Zone Body Box, keep firing until you get slide lock, perform a one handed emergency reload then reholster.

Stage 3 – Support hand firing. At your personal go, place your dominant hand on chest, from low ready or draw your pistol, take aim and press trigger to fire a shot into the (5 point) A Zone Body Box, if you get a click instead of a shot, tap the magazine on your thigh, kneel down and rack the slide on the heel of your shoe performing type 1 malfunction clearing, after clearing, stand back up and fire one round into the (5 point) A Zone Body Box, keep firing until you get slide lock, perform a one handed emergency reload, then reholster.

Goal: All shots in JD-QUAL1 silhouette.   Expert: 10 shots in the (5 point) A Zone body box and rest in Silhouette.   Gunfighter: All shots in the (5 point) A Zone body box.

Variations: Immediately before the start of the drill, run 50 yards or do 2X25 yard shuttle runs, do 10 push-ups or 10 jumping jacks to get your heart rate up.   Time each stage.

EVERYBODY GETS A RACK

Date:	Weapon:	Heart Rate Stress: Y / N	Rack Technique?
Stage 1 Time:	Stage 2 Time:	Stage 3 Time:	
Stage 1 Score:	Stage 2 Score:	Stage 3 Score:	**Total Score:**

Date:	Weapon:	Heart Rate Stress: Y / N	Rack Technique?
Stage 1 Time:	Stage 2 Time:	Stage 3 Time:	
Stage 1 Score:	Stage 2 Score:	Stage 3 Score:	**Total Score:**

Date:	Weapon:	Heart Rate Stress: Y / N	Rack Technique?
Stage 1 Time:	Stage 2 Time:	Stage 3 Time:	
Stage 1 Score:	Stage 2 Score:	Stage 3 Score:	**Total Score:**

Date:	Weapon:	Heart Rate Stress: Y / N	Rack Technique?
Stage 1 Time:	Stage 2 Time:	Stage 3 Time:	
Stage 1 Score:	Stage 2 Score:	Stage 3 Score:	**Total Score:**

Date:	Weapon:	Heart Rate Stress: Y / N	Rack Technique?
Stage 1 Time:	Stage 2 Time:	Stage 3 Time:	
Stage 1 Score:	Stage 2 Score:	Stage 3 Score:	**Total Score:**

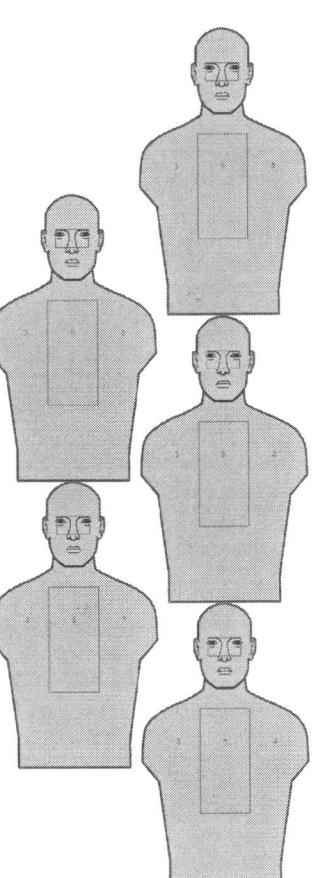

EVERYBODY GETS A RACK

Date:	Weapon:	Heart Rate Stress: Y / N	Rack Technique?
Stage 1 Time:	Stage 2 Time:	Stage 3 Time:	
Stage 1 Score:	Stage 2 Score:	Stage 3 Score:	**Total Score:**

Date:	Weapon:	Heart Rate Stress: Y / N	Rack Technique?
Stage 1 Time:	Stage 2 Time:	Stage 3 Time:	
Stage 1 Score:	Stage 2 Score:	Stage 3 Score:	**Total Score:**

Date:	Weapon:	Heart Rate Stress: Y / N	Rack Technique?
Stage 1 Time:	Stage 2 Time:	Stage 3 Time:	
Stage 1 Score:	Stage 2 Score:	Stage 3 Score:	**Total Score:**

Date:	Weapon:	Heart Rate Stress: Y / N	Rack Technique?
Stage 1 Time:	Stage 2 Time:	Stage 3 Time:	
Stage 1 Score:	Stage 2 Score:	Stage 3 Score:	**Total Score:**

Date:	Weapon:	Heart Rate Stress: Y / N	Rack Technique?
Stage 1 Time:	Stage 2 Time:	Stage 3 Time:	
Stage 1 Score:	Stage 2 Score:	Stage 3 Score:	**Total Score:**

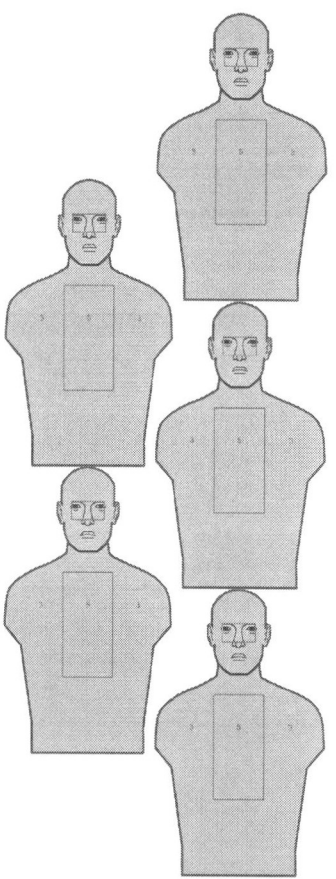

EVERYBODY GETS A RACK

Date:	Weapon:	Heart Rate Stress: Y / N	Rack Technique?
Stage 1 Time:	Stage 2 Time:	Stage 3 Time:	
Stage 1 Score:	Stage 2 Score:	Stage 3 Score:	**Total Score:**

Date:	Weapon:	Heart Rate Stress: Y / N	Rack Technique?
Stage 1 Time:	Stage 2 Time:	Stage 3 Time:	
Stage 1 Score:	Stage 2 Score:	Stage 3 Score:	**Total Score:**

Date:	Weapon:	Heart Rate Stress: Y / N	Rack Technique?
Stage 1 Time:	Stage 2 Time:	Stage 3 Time:	
Stage 1 Score:	Stage 2 Score:	Stage 3 Score:	**Total Score:**

Date:	Weapon:	Heart Rate Stress: Y / N	Rack Technique?
Stage 1 Time:	Stage 2 Time:	Stage 3 Time:	
Stage 1 Score:	Stage 2 Score:	Stage 3 Score:	**Total Score:**

Date:	Weapon:	Heart Rate Stress: Y / N	Rack Technique?
Stage 1 Time:	Stage 2 Time:	Stage 3 Time:	
Stage 1 Score:	Stage 2 Score:	Stage 3 Score:	**Total Score:**

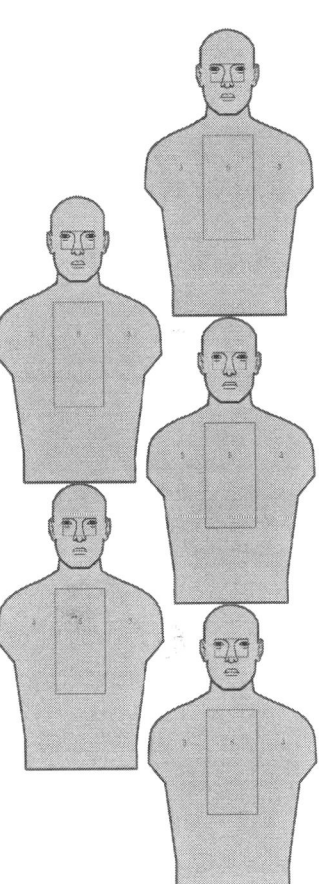

EVERYBODY GETS A RACK

Date:	Weapon:	Heart Rate Stress: Y / N	Rack Technique?
Stage 1 Time:	Stage 2 Time:	Stage 3 Time:	
Stage 1 Score:	Stage 2 Score:	Stage 3 Score:	**Total Score:**

Date:	Weapon:	Heart Rate Stress: Y / N	Rack Technique?
Stage 1 Time:	Stage 2 Time:	Stage 3 Time:	
Stage 1 Score:	Stage 2 Score:	Stage 3 Score:	**Total Score:**

Date:	Weapon:	Heart Rate Stress: Y / N	Rack Technique?
Stage 1 Time:	Stage 2 Time:	Stage 3 Time:	
Stage 1 Score:	Stage 2 Score:	Stage 3 Score:	**Total Score:**

Date:	Weapon:	Heart Rate Stress: Y / N	Rack Technique?
Stage 1 Time:	Stage 2 Time:	Stage 3 Time:	
Stage 1 Score:	Stage 2 Score:	Stage 3 Score:	**Total Score:**

Date:	Weapon:	Heart Rate Stress: Y / N	Rack Technique?
Stage 1 Time:	Stage 2 Time:	Stage 3 Time:	
Stage 1 Score:	Stage 2 Score:	Stage 3 Score:	**Total Score:**

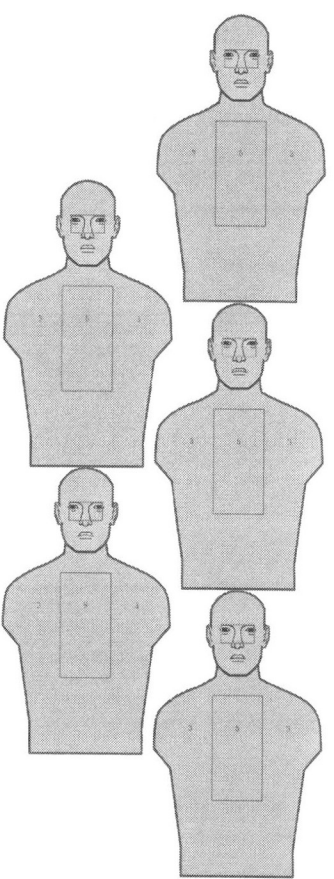

EVERYBODY GETS A RACK

Date:	Weapon:	Heart Rate Stress: Y / N	Rack Technique?
Stage 1 Time:	Stage 2 Time:	Stage 3 Time:	
Stage 1 Score:	Stage 2 Score:	Stage 3 Score:	**Total Score:**

Date:	Weapon:	Heart Rate Stress: Y / N	Rack Technique?
Stage 1 Time:	Stage 2 Time:	Stage 3 Time:	
Stage 1 Score:	Stage 2 Score:	Stage 3 Score:	**Total Score:**

Date:	Weapon:	Heart Rate Stress: Y / N	Rack Technique?
Stage 1 Time:	Stage 2 Time:	Stage 3 Time:	
Stage 1 Score:	Stage 2 Score:	Stage 3 Score:	**Total Score:**

Date:	Weapon:	Heart Rate Stress: Y / N	Rack Technique?
Stage 1 Time:	Stage 2 Time:	Stage 3 Time:	
Stage 1 Score:	Stage 2 Score:	Stage 3 Score:	**Total Score:**

Date:	Weapon:	Heart Rate Stress: Y / N	Rack Technique?
Stage 1 Time:	Stage 2 Time:	Stage 3 Time:	
Stage 1 Score:	Stage 2 Score:	Stage 3 Score:	**Total Score:**

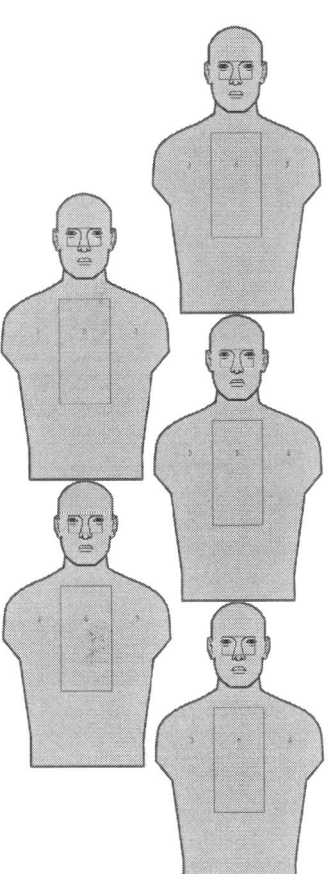

Advanced Pistol ©

www.gunfighterseries.com ©

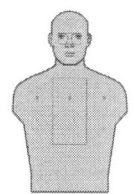

SO YOU HAD A BAD DAY

Purpose: Develop nervous system memory of moving to cover when confronted with a double feed malfunction.

Distance: 15 Yards.

Target: JD-QUAL1

Extra Equipment Required: Shot timer, 2 dummy rounds, 2 magazines, 1 magazine pouch, barricades/barriers for cover.

Rounds Fired Per Rep: 3 Rounds.   **Total Rounds Fired:** 18 Rounds.

Point Penalty: As per target score.

Repetitions: 6 Reps.

Starting Position & Condition: Standing – Aimed at target. Weapon Condition 4 with staged Type 2 malfunction.

Description: Standing - pistol pointed at target with pistol put in a Type 2 (double feed) malfunction condition using 2 dummy rounds. At the timer beep, press the trigger and attempt to fire. Hearing no round go off; tilt the pistol up and observe the chamber. Upon seeing the double feed, move quickly to cover, left or right, your choice. Clear the double feed behind cover, use cover properly, aim and fire 3 rounds into the (5 point) A Zone body.

Record the time to track speed progress. Repeat 5 more times firing a total of 3 reps from the left side of cover and 3 reps from the right side of cover.

Goal: 70 Points.   Expert: 80 Points.   Gunfighter: 90 Points.

Variations: Add number of targets, add round count. Shoot A Zone head box.

SO YOU HAD A BAD DAY

Date:	Location:	Weapon:	Sights:	
Rep 1 1st Shot Time:	Rep 2 1st Shot Time:	Rep 3 1st Shot Time:	Cover Used: Y / N	
Rep 1 Time:	Rep 2 Time:	Rep 3 Time:	Notes:	
Rep 4 1st Shot Time:	Rep 5 1st Shot Time:	Rep 6 1st Shot Time:		
Rep 4 Time:	Rep 5 Time:	Rep 6 Time:	**Total Score:**	

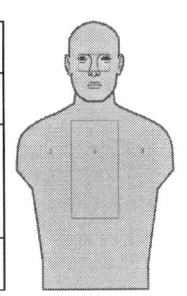

Date:	Location:	Weapon:	Sights:
Rep 1 1st Shot Time:	Rep 2 1st Shot Time:	Rep 3 1st Shot Time:	Cover Used: Y / N
Rep 1 Time:	Rep 2 Time:	Rep 3 Time:	Notes:
Rep 4 1st Shot Time:	Rep 5 1st Shot Time:	Rep 6 1st Shot Time:	
Rep 4 Time:	Rep 5 Time:	Rep 6 Time:	**Total Score:**

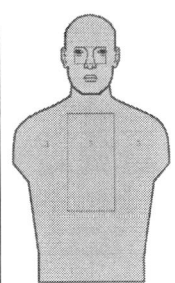

Date:	Location:	Weapon:	Sights:
Rep 1 1st Shot Time:	Rep 2 1st Shot Time:	Rep 3 1st Shot Time:	Cover Used: Y / N
Rep 1 Time:	Rep 2 Time:	Rep 3 Time:	Notes:
Rep 4 1st Shot Time:	Rep 5 1st Shot Time:	Rep 6 1st Shot Time:	
Rep 4 Time:	Rep 5 Time:	Rep 6 Time:	**Total Score:**

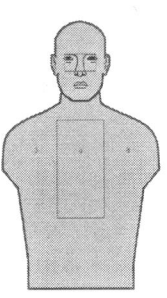

SO YOU HAD A BAD DAY

Date:	Location:	Weapon:	Sights:
Rep 1 1st Shot Time:	Rep 2 1st Shot Time:	Rep 3 1st Shot Time:	Cover Used: Y / N
Rep 1 Time:	Rep 2 Time:	Rep 3 Time:	Notes:
Rep 4 1st Shot Time:	Rep 5 1st Shot Time:	Rep 6 1st Shot Time:	
Rep 4 Time:	Rep 5 Time:	Rep 6 Time:	**Total Score:**

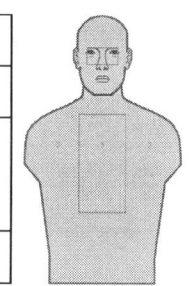

Date:	Location:	Weapon:	Sights:
Rep 1 1st Shot Time:	Rep 2 1st Shot Time:	Rep 3 1st Shot Time:	Cover Used: Y / N
Rep 1 Time:	Rep 2 Time:	Rep 3 Time:	Notes:
Rep 4 1st Shot Time:	Rep 5 1st Shot Time:	Rep 6 1st Shot Time:	
Rep 4 Time:	Rep 5 Time:	Rep 6 Time:	**Total Score:**

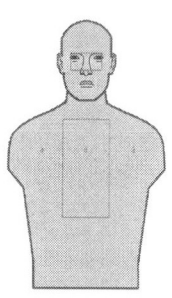

Date:	Location:	Weapon:	Sights:
Rep 1 1st Shot Time:	Rep 2 1st Shot Time:	Rep 3 1st Shot Time:	Cover Used: Y / N
Rep 1 Time:	Rep 2 Time:	Rep 3 Time:	Notes:
Rep 4 1st Shot Time:	Rep 5 1st Shot Time:	Rep 6 1st Shot Time:	
Rep 4 Time:	Rep 5 Time:	Rep 6 Time:	**Total Score:**

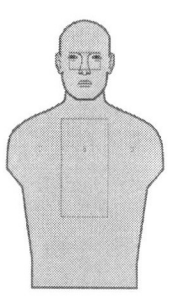

SO YOU HAD A BAD DAY

Date:	Location:	Weapon:	Sights:
Rep 1 1st Shot Time:	Rep 2 1st Shot Time:	Rep 3 1st Shot Time:	Cover Used: Y / N
Rep 1 Time:	Rep 2 Time:	Rep 3 Time:	Notes:
Rep 4 1st Shot Time:	Rep 5 1st Shot Time:	Rep 6 1st Shot Time:	
Rep 4 Time:	Rep 5 Time:	Rep 6 Time:	Total Score:

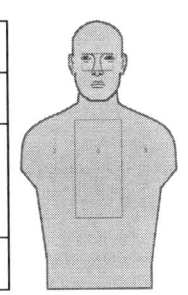

Date:	Location:	Weapon:	Sights:
Rep 1 1st Shot Time:	Rep 2 1st Shot Time:	Rep 3 1st Shot Time:	Cover Used: Y / N
Rep 1 Time:	Rep 2 Time:	Rep 3 Time:	Notes:
Rep 4 1st Shot Time:	Rep 5 1st Shot Time:	Rep 6 1st Shot Time:	
Rep 4 Time:	Rep 5 Time:	Rep 6 Time:	Total Score:

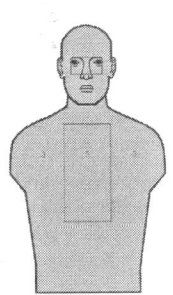

Date:	Location:	Weapon:	Sights:
Rep 1 1st Shot Time:	Rep 2 1st Shot Time:	Rep 3 1st Shot Time:	Cover Used: Y / N
Rep 1 Time:	Rep 2 Time:	Rep 3 Time:	Notes:
Rep 4 1st Shot Time:	Rep 5 1st Shot Time:	Rep 6 1st Shot Time:	
Rep 4 Time:	Rep 5 Time:	Rep 6 Time:	Total Score:

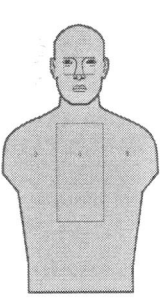

Advanced Pistol ©

Manipulation Drills - 1

SO YOU HAD A BAD DAY

Date:	Location:	Weapon:	Sights:
Rep 1 1st Shot Time:	Rep 2 1st Shot Time:	Rep 3 1st Shot Time:	Cover Used: Y / N
Rep 1 Time:	Rep 2 Time:	Rep 3 Time:	Notes:
Rep 4 1st Shot Time:	Rep 5 1st Shot Time:	Rep 6 1st Shot Time:	
Rep 4 Time:	Rep 5 Time:	Rep 6 Time:	**Total Score:**

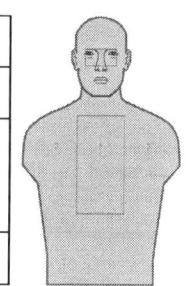

Date:	Location:	Weapon:	Sights:
Rep 1 1st Shot Time:	Rep 2 1st Shot Time:	Rep 3 1st Shot Time:	Cover Used: Y / N
Rep 1 Time:	Rep 2 Time:	Rep 3 Time:	Notes:
Rep 4 1st Shot Time:	Rep 5 1st Shot Time:	Rep 6 1st Shot Time:	
Rep 4 Time:	Rep 5 Time:	Rep 6 Time:	**Total Score:**

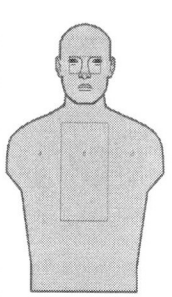

Date:	Location:	Weapon:	Sights:
Rep 1 1st Shot Time:	Rep 2 1st Shot Time:	Rep 3 1st Shot Time:	Cover Used: Y / N
Rep 1 Time:	Rep 2 Time:	Rep 3 Time:	Notes:
Rep 4 1st Shot Time:	Rep 5 1st Shot Time:	Rep 6 1st Shot Time:	
Rep 4 Time:	Rep 5 Time:	Rep 6 Time:	**Total Score:**

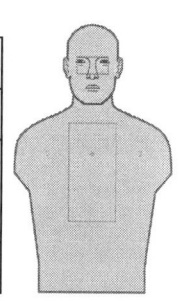

SO YOU HAD A BAD DAY

Date:	Location:	Weapon:	Sights:
Rep 1 1st Shot Time:	Rep 2 1st Shot Time:	Rep 3 1st Shot Time:	Cover Used: Y / N
Rep 1 Time:	Rep 2 Time:	Rep 3 Time:	Notes:
Rep 4 1st Shot Time:	Rep 5 1st Shot Time:	Rep 6 1st Shot Time:	
Rep 4 Time:	Rep 5 Time:	Rep 6 Time:	Total Score:

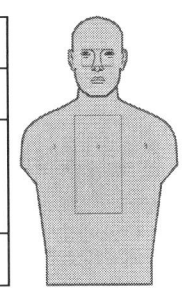

Date:	Location:	Weapon:	Sights:
Rep 1 1st Shot Time:	Rep 2 1st Shot Time:	Rep 3 1st Shot Time:	Cover Used: Y / N
Rep 1 Time:	Rep 2 Time:	Rep 3 Time:	Notes:
Rep 4 1st Shot Time:	Rep 5 1st Shot Time:	Rep 6 1st Shot Time:	
Rep 4 Time:	Rep 5 Time:	Rep 6 Time:	Total Score:

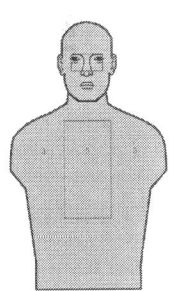

Date:	Location:	Weapon:	Sights:
Rep 1 1st Shot Time:	Rep 2 1st Shot Time:	Rep 3 1st Shot Time:	Cover Used: Y / N
Rep 1 Time:	Rep 2 Time:	Rep 3 Time:	Notes:
Rep 4 1st Shot Time:	Rep 5 1st Shot Time:	Rep 6 1st Shot Time:	
Rep 4 Time:	Rep 5 Time:	Rep 6 Time:	Total Score:

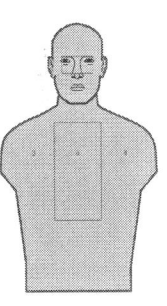

Advanced Pistol ©

Manipulation Drills - 1

JAMMIN

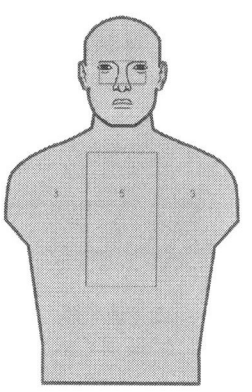

Purpose: Increase efficiency and develop nervous system memory of one-handed emergency loading a pistol.

Distance: 15 Yards.   **Target:** JD-QUAL1

Extra Equipment Required: 1 magazine pouch, 2 mag.

Rounds Fired Per Rep: 5 Rounds (Load 1 mag of 2 rounds &1 mag of 3 rounds)   **Total Rounds Fired:** 30 Rounds.

Point Penalty: As per target score.   **Repetitions:** 6 Reps.

Starting Position & Condition: Standing – Pistol aimed at target using only dominant hand. Weapon condition 1 with a mag loaded with 2 or 3 rounds.

Description: At your own personal go, aim and fire at the (5 point) A Zone body box until pistol is empty, tilt pistol, observe empty pistol, as you bring your pistol back towards you, press magazine release dropping the empty magazine to the ground, rotate and bring your pistol down between your knees trapping the slide between your knees. Secure a full magazine and insert it into the magazine well pushing it in until you hear a click or feel it seat. Secure a good grip hand position with your dominant hand. Rack the slide using your rear sights on your belt or holster or press the slide release. Bring the pistol up to aim at target, aim, fire all remaining rounds into the (5 point) A Zone body box.

While you are performing the first reloading motion using your dominant hand, let your support arm hang, then when bringing the pistol up on target, pin your support arm to your support side. Perform 3 reps on with dominant hand and 3 reps with support hand. Make sure you are aware of the muzzle direction at all times and make sure you never point your pistol at anything you do not intend to destroy. Practicing firearm safety is a major facet to this drill during live fire. Record your times and score for personal progress tracking.

Goal of this drill is to be smooth and deliberate.

JAMMIN

Date:	Location:	Weapon:	Sights:
Rep 1 Reload Time:	Rep 2 Reload Time:	Rep 3 Reload Time:	**Dominant Side Score:**
Rep 1 Time:	Rep 2 Time:	Rep 3 Time:	Rack Technique?
Rep 4 Reload Time:	Rep 5 Reload Time:	Rep 6 Reload Time:	
Rep 4 Time:	Rep 5 Time:	Rep 6 Time:	**Support Side Score:**

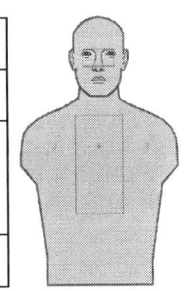

Date:	Location:	Weapon:	Sights:
Rep 1 Reload Time:	Rep 2 Reload Time:	Rep 3 Reload Time:	**Dominant Side Score:**
Rep 1 Time:	Rep 2 Time:	Rep 3 Time:	Rack Technique?
Rep 4 Reload Time:	Rep 5 Reload Time:	Rep 6 Reload Time:	
Rep 4 Time:	Rep 5 Time:	Rep 6 Time:	**Support Side Score:**

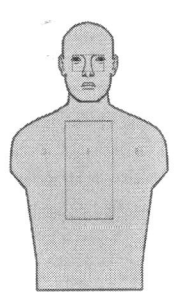

Date:	Location:	Weapon:	Sights:
Rep 1 Reload Time:	Rep 2 Reload Time:	Rep 3 Reload Time:	**Dominant Side Score:**
Rep 1 Time:	Rep 2 Time:	Rep 3 Time:	Rack Technique?
Rep 4 Reload Time:	Rep 5 Reload Time:	Rep 6 Reload Time:	
Rep 4 Time:	Rep 5 Time:	Rep 6 Time:	**Support Side Score:**

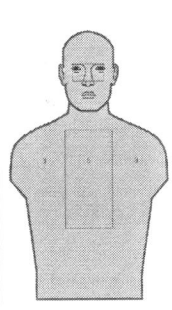

JAMMIN

Date:	Location:	Weapon:	Sights:
Rep 1 Reload Time:	Rep 2 Reload Time:	Rep 3 Reload Time:	**Dominant Side Score:**
Rep 1 Time:	Rep 2 Time:	Rep 3 Time:	Rack Technique?
Rep 4 Reload Time:	Rep 5 Reload Time:	Rep 6 Reload Time:	
Rep 4 Time:	Rep 5 Time:	Rep 6 Time:	**Support Side Score:**

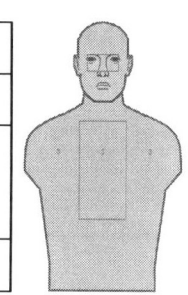

Date:	Location:	Weapon:	Sights:
Rep 1 Reload Time:	Rep 2 Reload Time:	Rep 3 Reload Time:	**Dominant Side Score:**
Rep 1 Time:	Rep 2 Time:	Rep 3 Time:	Rack Technique?
Rep 4 Reload Time:	Rep 5 Reload Time:	Rep 6 Reload Time:	
Rep 4 Time:	Rep 5 Time:	Rep 6 Time:	**Support Side Score:**

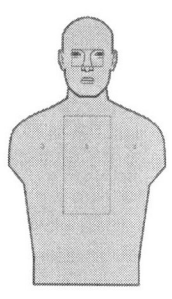

Date:	Location:	Weapon:	Sights:
Rep 1 Reload Time:	Rep 2 Reload Time:	Rep 3 Reload Time:	**Dominant Side Score:**
Rep 1 Time:	Rep 2 Time:	Rep 3 Time:	Rack Technique?
Rep 4 Reload Time:	Rep 5 Reload Time:	Rep 6 Reload Time:	
Rep 4 Time:	Rep 5 Time:	Rep 6 Time:	**Support Side Score:**

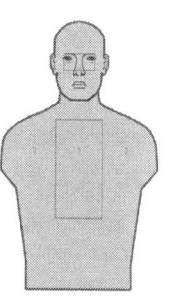

JAMMIN

Date:	Location:	Weapon:	Sights:
Rep 1 Reload Time:	Rep 2 Reload Time:	Rep 3 Reload Time:	**Dominant Side Score:**
Rep 1 Time:	Rep 2 Time:	Rep 3 Time:	Rack Technique?
Rep 4 Reload Time:	Rep 5 Reload Time:	Rep 6 Reload Time:	
Rep 4 Time:	Rep 5 Time:	Rep 6 Time:	**Support Side Score:**

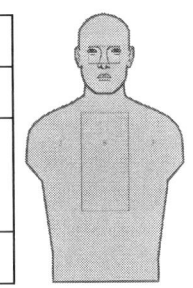

Date:	Location:	Weapon:	Sights:
Rep 1 Reload Time:	Rep 2 Reload Time:	Rep 3 Reload Time:	**Dominant Side Score:**
Rep 1 Time:	Rep 2 Time:	Rep 3 Time:	Rack Technique?
Rep 4 Reload Time:	Rep 5 Reload Time:	Rep 6 Reload Time:	
Rep 4 Time:	Rep 5 Time:	Rep 6 Time:	**Support Side Score:**

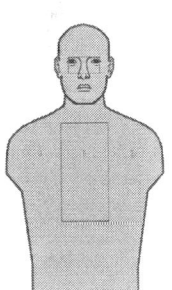

Date:	Location:	Weapon:	Sights:
Rep 1 Reload Time:	Rep 2 Reload Time:	Rep 3 Reload Time:	**Dominant Side Score:**
Rep 1 Time:	Rep 2 Time:	Rep 3 Time:	Rack Technique?
Rep 4 Reload Time:	Rep 5 Reload Time:	Rep 6 Reload Time:	
Rep 4 Time:	Rep 5 Time:	Rep 6 Time:	**Support Side Score:**

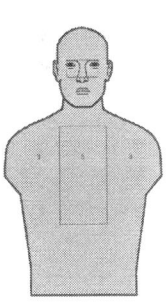

JAMMIN

Date:	Location:	Weapon:	Sights:	
Rep 1 Reload Time:	Rep 2 Reload Time:	Rep 3 Reload Time:	**Dominant Side Score:**	
Rep 1 Time:	Rep 2 Time:	Rep 3 Time:	Rack Technique?	
Rep 4 Reload Time:	Rep 5 Reload Time:	Rep 6 Reload Time:		
Rep 4 Time:	Rep 5 Time:	Rep 6 Time:	**Support Side Score:**	

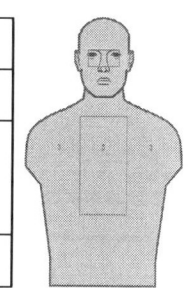

Date:	Location:	Weapon:	Sights:	
Rep 1 Reload Time:	Rep 2 Reload Time:	Rep 3 Reload Time:	**Dominant Side Score:**	
Rep 1 Time:	Rep 2 Time:	Rep 3 Time:	Rack Technique?	
Rep 4 Reload Time:	Rep 5 Reload Time:	Rep 6 Reload Time:		
Rep 4 Time:	Rep 5 Time:	Rep 6 Time:	**Support Side Score:**	

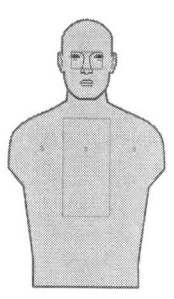

Date:	Location:	Weapon:	Sights:	
Rep 1 Reload Time:	Rep 2 Reload Time:	Rep 3 Reload Time:	**Dominant Side Score:**	
Rep 1 Time:	Rep 2 Time:	Rep 3 Time:	Rack Technique?	
Rep 4 Reload Time:	Rep 5 Reload Time:	Rep 6 Reload Time:		
Rep 4 Time:	Rep 5 Time:	Rep 6 Time:	**Support Side Score:**	

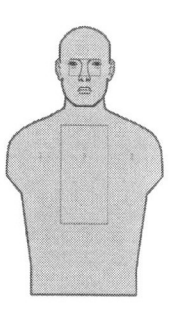

JAMMIN

Date:	Location:	Weapon:	Sights:
Rep 1 Reload Time:	Rep 2 Reload Time:	Rep 3 Reload Time:	**Dominant Side Score:**
Rep 1 Time:	Rep 2 Time:	Rep 3 Time:	Rack Technique?
Rep 4 Reload Time:	Rep 5 Reload Time:	Rep 6 Reload Time:	
Rep 4 Time:	Rep 5 Time:	Rep 6 Time:	**Support Side Score:**

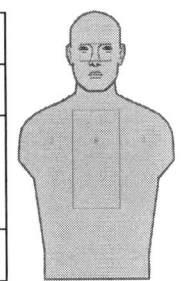

Date:	Location:	Weapon:	Sights:
Rep 1 Reload Time:	Rep 2 Reload Time:	Rep 3 Reload Time:	**Dominant Side Score:**
Rep 1 Time:	Rep 2 Time:	Rep 3 Time:	Rack Technique?
Rep 4 Reload Time:	Rep 5 Reload Time:	Rep 6 Reload Time:	
Rep 4 Time:	Rep 5 Time:	Rep 6 Time:	**Support Side Score:**

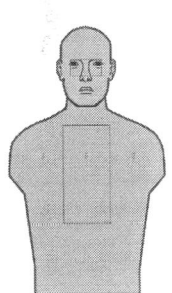

Date:	Location:	Weapon:	Sights:
Rep 1 Reload Time:	Rep 2 Reload Time:	Rep 3 Reload Time:	**Dominant Side Score:**
Rep 1 Time:	Rep 2 Time:	Rep 3 Time:	Rack Technique?
Rep 4 Reload Time:	Rep 5 Reload Time:	Rep 6 Reload Time:	
Rep 4 Time:	Rep 5 Time:	Rep 6 Time:	**Support Side Score:**

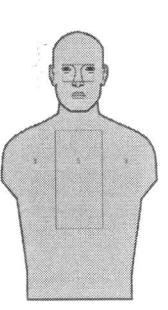

WARM BRASS

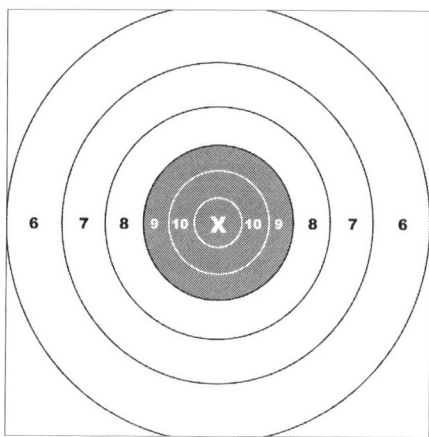

Purpose: Increase efficiency of an accurate sight picture, trigger control and focus.

Distance: 3, 5, and 7 Yards.

Target: GF-2

Rounds Fired Per Distance: 3 Rounds.   **Total Rounds Fired:** 9 Rounds.

Point Penalty: As per target score.

Repetitions: 1 Rep.

Starting Position & Condition: Standing – Surrender / Interview. Weapon Condition 1.

Description: At your own personal go, draw your pistol and fire three rounds into the GF-2 target at 3 yards. Put pistol on safe if applicable and holster it safely. Move back to 5 yards. Repeat drill at 5 yards. Put pistol on safe if applicable and holster it safely. Move back to 7 yards. Repeat drill at 7 yards. This drill has no time limit, so take your time and make good shots. Good hand placement during the draw and trigger control is essential to master this drill.

Goal: 81 points with all rounds in or touching the 9 ring.   Expert: 90 points   Gunfighter: 90 points with 9X's

Variation: Move distances to 5, 7, 10 yards when Gunfighter goal level is consistently achieved and/or add timer and record how quickly you can perform goal at your ability distance.

WARM BRASS

Date:	Weapon:	Sights	Positive Trigger Reset? Y / N
# of 6's:	# of 7's:	# of 8's:	Notes:
# of 9's:	# of 10's:	TOTAL SCORE: X's	

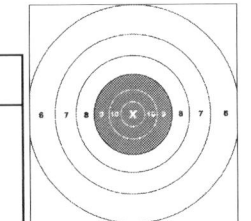

Date:	Weapon:	Sights	Positive Trigger Reset? Y / N
# of 6's:	# of 7's:	# of 8's:	Notes:
# of 9's:	# of 10's:	TOTAL SCORE: X's	

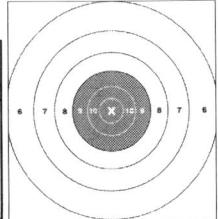

Date:	Weapon:	Sights	Positive Trigger Reset? Y / N
# of 6's:	# of 7's:	# of 8's:	Notes:
# of 9's:	# of 10's:	TOTAL SCORE: X's	

Date:	Weapon:	Sights	Positive Trigger Reset? Y / N
# of 6's:	# of 7's:	# of 8's:	Notes:
# of 9's:	# of 10's:	TOTAL SCORE: X's	

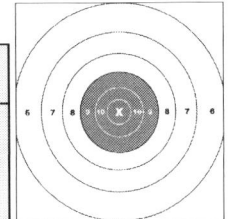

Accuracy Drills - 1

WARM BRASS

Date:	Weapon:	Sights	Positive Trigger Reset? Y / N
# of 6's:	# of 7's:	# of 8's:	Notes:
# of 9's:	# of 10's:	TOTAL SCORE: X's	

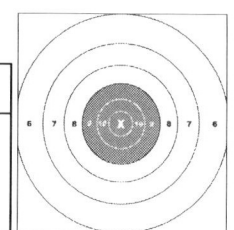

Date:	Weapon:	Sights	Positive Trigger Reset? Y / N
# of 6's:	# of 7's:	# of 8's:	Notes:
# of 9's:	# of 10's:	TOTAL SCORE: X's	

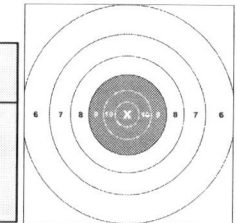

Date:	Weapon:	Sights	Positive Trigger Reset? Y / N
# of 6's:	# of 7's:	# of 8's:	Notes:
# of 9's:	# of 10's:	TOTAL SCORE: X's	

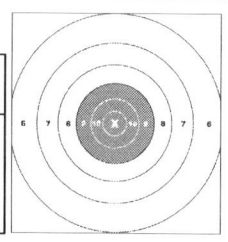

Date:	Weapon:	Sights	Positive Trigger Reset? Y / N
# of 6's:	# of 7's:	# of 8's:	Notes:
# of 9's:	# of 10's:	TOTAL SCORE: X's	

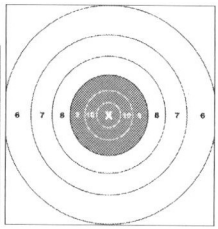

WARM BRASS

Date:	Weapon:	Sights	Positive Trigger Reset? Y / N
# of 6's:	# of 7's:	# of 8's:	Notes:
# of 9's:	# of 10's:	TOTAL SCORE: X's	

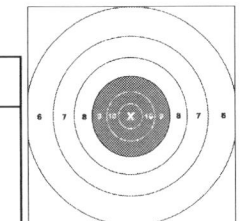

Date:	Weapon:	Sights	Positive Trigger Reset? Y / N
# of 6's:	# of 7's:	# of 8's:	Notes:
# of 9's:	# of 10's:	TOTAL SCORE: X's	

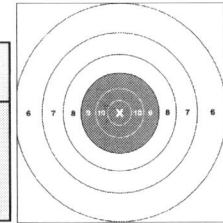

Date:	Weapon:	Sights	Positive Trigger Reset? Y / N
# of 6's:	# of 7's:	# of 8's:	Notes:
# of 9's:	# of 10's:	TOTAL SCORE: X's	

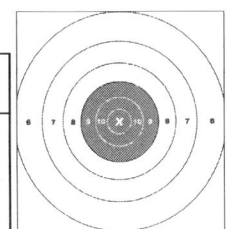

Date:	Weapon:	Sights	Positive Trigger Reset? Y / N
# of 6's:	# of 7's:	# of 8's:	Notes:
# of 9's:	# of 10's:	TOTAL SCORE: X's	

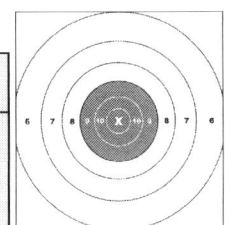

Advanced Pistol ©

WARM BRASS

Date:	Weapon:	Sights:	Positive Trigger Reset? Y / N
# of 6's:	# of 7's:	# of 8's:	Notes:
# of 9's:	# of 10's:	TOTAL SCORE: X's	

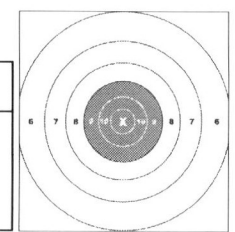

Date:	Weapon:	Sights:	Positive Trigger Reset? Y / N
# of 6's:	# of 7's:	# of 8's:	Notes:
# of 9's:	# of 10's:	TOTAL SCORE: X's	

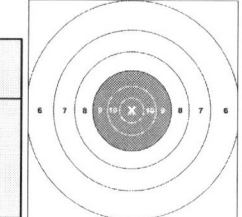

Date:	Weapon:	Sights:	Positive Trigger Reset? Y / N
# of 6's:	# of 7's:	# of 8's:	Notes:
# of 9's:	# of 10's:	TOTAL SCORE: X's	

Date:	Weapon:	Sights:	Positive Trigger Reset? Y / N
# of 6's:	# of 7's:	# of 8's:	Notes:
# of 9's:	# of 10's:	TOTAL SCORE: X's	

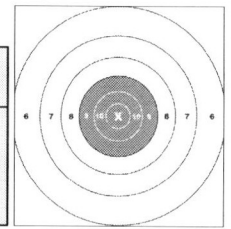

WARM BRASS

Date:	Weapon:	Sights	Positive Trigger Reset? Y / N
# of 6's:	# of 7's:	# of 8's:	Notes:
# of 9's:	# of 10's:	TOTAL SCORE: X's	

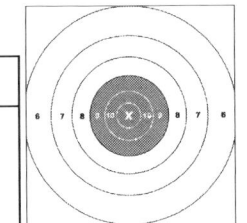

Date:	Weapon:	Sights	Positive Trigger Reset? Y / N
# of 6's:	# of 7's:	# of 8's:	Notes:
# of 9's:	# of 10's:	TOTAL SCORE: X's	

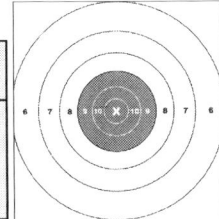

Date:	Weapon:	Sights	Positive Trigger Reset? Y / N
# of 6's:	# of 7's:	# of 8's:	Notes:
# of 9's:	# of 10's:	TOTAL SCORE: X's	

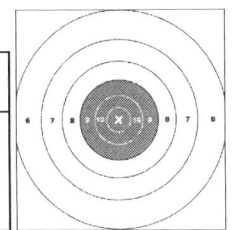

Date:	Weapon:	Sights	Positive Trigger Reset? Y / N
# of 6's:	# of 7's:	# of 8's:	Notes:
# of 9's:	# of 10's:	TOTAL SCORE: X's	

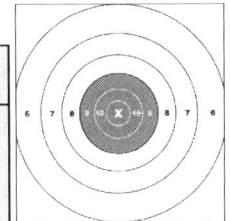

Advanced Pistol ©

Accuracy Drills - 1

WOW

1 Inch Square

Purpose: Develop consistent trigger control and focus.

Distance: 3, 5 or 7 Yards.

Target: 1 Inch square

Extra Equipment Required: Shot timer (optional).

Total Rounds Fired: 10 Rounds.

Point Penalty: Go / No Go.

Starting Position & Condition: Standing – Surrender / Interview. Weapon Condition 1.

Description: At your own personal go, draw your pistol and fire ten rounds into the 1 inch square target at 3 yards. Once you can consistently fire all 10 rounds into or touching the 1 inch square target, use the 5 yard distance as your shooting distance. Once you can make shots consistently at 5 yards, use the 7 yard distance. This drill has no time limit, so take your time and make good shots. Good hand placement during the draw and trigger control is essential to master this drill.

Goals: 3 Yards, all in or touching.   Expert: 5 Yards, all in or touching.   Gunfighter: 7 Yards, all in or touching.

Variations: Add timer and record how quickly you can perform goal at your ability distance.

WOW

Date:	Weapon:	Sights:	Notes:		
Drill Time:	Distance: 3Y / 5Y / 7Y		# Out:	Go / No Go	

Date:	Weapon:	Sights:	Notes:		
Drill Time:	Distance: 3Y / 5Y / 7Y		# Out:	Go / No Go	

Date:	Weapon:	Sights:	Notes:		
Drill Time:	Distance: 3Y / 5Y / 7Y		# Out:	Go / No Go	

Date:	Weapon:	Sights:	Notes:		
Drill Time:	Distance: 3Y / 5Y / 7Y		# Out:	Go / No Go	

Date:	Weapon:	Sights:	Notes:		
Drill Time:	Distance: 3Y / 5Y / 7Y		# Out:	Go / No Go	

Accuracy Drills - 2

www.GUNFIGHTERSERIES.com ©

WOW

Date:	Weapon:	Sights:	Notes:	
Drill Time:	Distance: 3Y / 5Y / 7Y		# Out:	Go / No Go

Date:	Weapon:	Sights:	Notes:	
Drill Time:	Distance: 3Y / 5Y / 7Y		# Out:	Go / No Go

Date:	Weapon:	Sights:	Notes:	
Drill Time:	Distance: 3Y / 5Y / 7Y		# Out:	Go / No Go

Date:	Weapon:	Sights:	Notes:	
Drill Time:	Distance: 3Y / 5Y / 7Y		# Out:	Go / No Go

Date:	Weapon:	Sights:	Notes:	
Drill Time:	Distance: 3Y / 5Y / 7Y		# Out:	Go / No Go

WOW

Date:	Weapon:	Sights:	Notes:	
Drill Time:	Distance: 3Y / 5Y / 7Y		# Out:	Go / No Go

Date:	Weapon:	Sights:	Notes:	
Drill Time:	Distance: 3Y / 5Y / 7Y		# Out:	Go / No Go

Date:	Weapon:	Sights:	Notes:	
Drill Time:	Distance: 3Y / 5Y / 7Y		# Out:	Go / No Go

Date:	Weapon:	Sights:	Notes:	
Drill Time:	Distance: 3Y / 5Y / 7Y		# Out:	Go / No Go

Date:	Weapon:	Sights:	Notes:	
Drill Time:	Distance: 3Y / 5Y / 7Y		# Out:	Go / No Go

Accuracy Drills - 2

www.GUNFIGHTERSERIES.com ©

WOW

Date:	Weapon:	Sights:	Notes:	
Drill Time:	Distance: 3Y / 5Y / 7Y		# Out:	Go / No Go

Date:	Weapon:	Sights:	Notes:	
Drill Time:	Distance: 3Y / 5Y / 7Y		# Out:	Go / No Go

Date:	Weapon:	Sights:	Notes:	
Drill Time:	Distance: 3Y / 5Y / 7Y		# Out:	Go / No Go

Date:	Weapon:	Sights:	Notes:	
Drill Time:	Distance: 3Y / 5Y / 7Y		# Out:	Go / No Go

Date:	Weapon:	Sights:	Notes:	
Drill Time:	Distance: 3Y / 5Y / 7Y		# Out:	Go / No Go

WOW

Date:	Weapon:	Sights:	Notes:		
Drill Time:	Distance: 3Y / 5Y / 7Y		# Out:	Go / No Go	

Date:	Weapon:	Sights:	Notes:		
Drill Time:	Distance: 3Y / 5Y / 7Y		# Out:	Go / No Go	

Date:	Weapon:	Sights:	Notes:		
Drill Time:	Distance: 3Y / 5Y / 7Y		# Out:	Go / No Go	

Date:	Weapon:	Sights:	Notes:		
Drill Time:	Distance: 3Y / 5Y / 7Y		# Out:	Go / No Go	

Date:	Weapon:	Sights:	Notes:		
Drill Time:	Distance: 3Y / 5Y / 7Y		# Out:	Go / No Go	

Advanced Pistol ©

Accuracy Drills - 2

TRIGGERED

Purpose: Develop consistent trigger control and focus.

Distance: 3, 4, 5, 6, 7 Yards.   **Target:** KYRL

Rounds Fired Per String: 5 Rounds.   **Total Rounds Fired:** 15 Rounds.

Point Penalty: As per target score. <u>A miss does not zero out your score.</u>

Repetitions: 1 Rep of 3 strings.

Starting Position & Condition: Standing – Surrender / Interview. Weapon Condition 1.

Description: At your own personal go, draw your pistol and fire one round into the top large left side black circle target from 3 yards. Put pistol on safe if applicable and holster it safely. Move back 1 yard to 4 yards. Repeat drill from 4 yards, but move down one circle to the next smallest circle target. Repeat sequence of moving back, drawing and shooting the next smallest circle target. By the time you have reached 7 yards, you should be shooting at the smallest ¼" circle target. This first string of fire is for practice and has no score, as no numbers are in the target circles. Once you have shot the whole practice string of fire, move back up to 3 yards and repeat this string of fire the same way two more times on the other target circles for score. Each black circle should only receive one shot. This drill has no time limit and if you feel you made a bad draw or are not going to make a decent shot, stop, take a break and start the drawing sequence and firing over. Good hand placement during the draw and trigger control is essential to master this drill.

Goals: 18 Points   Expert: 30 Points   Gunfighter: 45 Points

Variations: Try different shooting positions. Dominant or support hand only.

TRIGGERED

Date:	Location:	Weapon:	Sights:
String 1 Best Dot: 2" / 1.5" / 1" / .75" / .5"		Position:	2 Hand / Dominant / Support
String 2 Best Dot: 2" / 1.5" / 1" / .75" / .5"		String 2 Score:	**Total Score:**
String 3 Best Dot: 2" / 1.5" / 1" / .75" / .5"		String 3 Score:	
Notes:			

Date:	Location:	Weapon:	Sights:
String 1 Best Dot: 2" / 1.5" / 1" / .75" / .5"		Position:	2 Hand / Dominant / Support
String 2 Best Dot: 2" / 1.5" / 1" / .75" / .5"		String 2 Score:	**Total Score:**
String 3 Best Dot: 2" / 1.5" / 1" / .75" / .5"		String 3 Score:	
Notes:			

Date:	Location:	Weapon:	Sights:
String 1 Best Dot: 2" / 1.5" / 1" / .75" / .5"		Position:	2 Hand / Dominant / Support
String 2 Best Dot: 2" / 1.5" / 1" / .75" / .5"		String 2 Score:	**Total Score:**
String 3 Best Dot: 2" / 1.5" / 1" / .75" / .5"		String 3 Score:	
Notes:			

Advanced Pistol ©

Accuracy Drills - 3

www.GUNFIGHTERSERIES.com ©

TRIGGERED

Date:	Location:	Weapon:	Sights:
String 1 Best Dot: 2" / 1.5" / 1" / .75" / .5"		Position:	2 Hand / Dominant / Support
String 2 Best Dot: 2" / 1.5" / 1" / .75" / .5"		String 2 Score:	**Total Score:**
String 3 Best Dot: 2" / 1.5" / 1" / .75" / .5"		String 3 Score:	
Notes:			

Date:	Location:	Weapon:	Sights:
String 1 Best Dot: 2" / 1.5" / 1" / .75" / .5"		Position:	2 Hand / Dominant / Support
String 2 Best Dot: 2" / 1.5" / 1" / .75" / .5"		String 2 Score:	**Total Score:**
String 3 Best Dot: 2" / 1.5" / 1" / .75" / .5"		String 3 Score:	
Notes:			

Date:	Location:	Weapon:	Sights:
String 1 Best Dot: 2" / 1.5" / 1" / .75" / .5"		Position:	2 Hand / Dominant / Support
String 2 Best Dot: 2" / 1.5" / 1" / .75" / .5"		String 2 Score:	**Total Score:**
String 3 Best Dot: 2" / 1.5" / 1" / .75" / .5"		String 3 Score:	
Notes:			

TRIGGERED

Date:	Location:	Weapon:	Sights:
String 1 Best Dot: 2" / 1.5" / 1" / .75" / .5"		Position:	2 Hand / Dominant / Support
String 2 Best Dot: 2" / 1.5" / 1" / .75" / .5"		String 2 Score:	**Total Score:**
String 3 Best Dot: 2" / 1.5" / 1" / .75" / .5"		String 3 Score:	
Notes:			

Date:	Location:	Weapon:	Sights:
String 1 Best Dot: 2" / 1.5" / 1" / .75" / .5"		Position:	2 Hand / Dominant / Support
String 2 Best Dot: 2" / 1.5" / 1" / .75" / .5"		String 2 Score:	**Total Score:**
String 3 Best Dot: 2" / 1.5" / 1" / .75" / .5"		String 3 Score:	
Notes:			

Date:	Location:	Weapon:	Sights:
String 1 Best Dot: 2" / 1.5" / 1" / .75" / .5"		Position:	2 Hand / Dominant / Support
String 2 Best Dot: 2" / 1.5" / 1" / .75" / .5"		String 2 Score:	**Total Score:**
String 3 Best Dot: 2" / 1.5" / 1" / .75" / .5"		String 3 Score:	
Notes:			

Accuracy Drills - 3

TRIGGERED

Date:	Location:	Weapon:	Sights:
String 1 Best Dot: 2" / 1.5" / 1" / .75" / .5"		Position:	2 Hand / Dominant / Support
String 2 Best Dot: 2" / 1.5" / 1" / .75" / .5"		String 2 Score:	**Total Score:**
String 3 Best Dot: 2" / 1.5" / 1" / .75" / .5"		String 3 Score:	
Notes:			

Date:	Location:	Weapon:	Sights:
String 1 Best Dot: 2" / 1.5" / 1" / .75" / .5"		Position:	2 Hand / Dominant / Support
String 2 Best Dot: 2" / 1.5" / 1" / .75" / .5"		String 2 Score:	**Total Score:**
String 3 Best Dot: 2" / 1.5" / 1" / .75" / .5"		String 3 Score:	
Notes:			

Date:	Location:	Weapon:	Sights:
String 1 Best Dot: 2" / 1.5" / 1" / .75" / .5"		Position:	2 Hand / Dominant / Support
String 2 Best Dot: 2" / 1.5" / 1" / .75" / .5"		String 2 Score:	**Total Score:**
String 3 Best Dot: 2" / 1.5" / 1" / .75" / .5"		String 3 Score:	
Notes:			

TRIGGERED

Date:	Location:	Weapon:	Sights:
String 1 Best Dot: 2" / 1.5" / 1" / .75" / .5"		Position:	2 Hand / Dominant / Support
String 2 Best Dot: 2" / 1.5" / 1" / .75" / .5"		String 2 Score:	**Total Score:**
String 3 Best Dot: 2" / 1.5" / 1" / .75" / .5"		String 3 Score:	
Notes:			

Date:	Location:	Weapon:	Sights:
String 1 Best Dot: 2" / 1.5" / 1" / .75" / .5"		Position:	2 Hand / Dominant / Support
String 2 Best Dot: 2" / 1.5" / 1" / .75" / .5"		String 2 Score:	**Total Score:**
String 3 Best Dot: 2" / 1.5" / 1" / .75" / .5"		String 3 Score:	
Notes:			

Date:	Location:	Weapon:	Sights:
String 1 Best Dot: 2" / 1.5" / 1" / .75" / .5"		Position:	2 Hand / Dominant / Support
String 2 Best Dot: 2" / 1.5" / 1" / .75" / .5"		String 2 Score:	**Total Score:**
String 3 Best Dot: 2" / 1.5" / 1" / .75" / .5"		String 3 Score:	
Notes:			

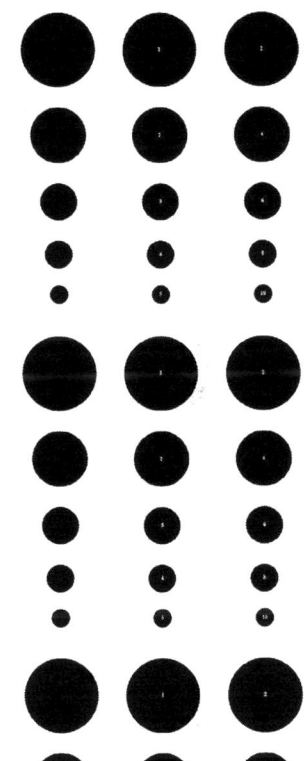

Advanced Pistol ©

Accuracy Drills - 3

GUT CHECK

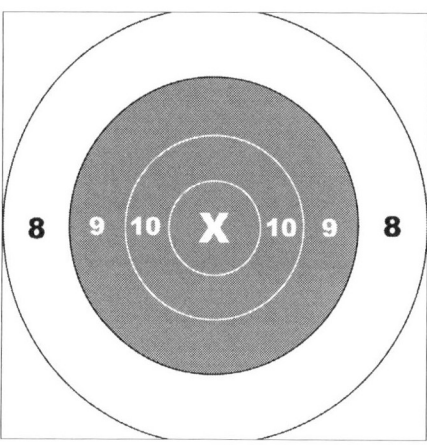

Purpose: Develop consistent draw and trigger control with one-handed shooting.

Distance: 3, 4, 5, 6, 7 Yards.

Target: GF-1

Rounds Fired Per Distance: 3 Rounds.

Total Rounds Fired: 15 Rounds.

Point Penalty: As per target score.

Repetitions: 1 Rep.

Starting Position & Condition: Standing – Surrender / Interview. Weapon Condition 1.

Description: At your own personal go, draw your pistol and fire one round into the target with a two-handed grip from 3 yards. Put pistol on safe if applicable and holster it safely. Repeat the 3 yard shot, but only use dominant hand. Place support hand on chest while performing draw and shot. Put pistol on safe if applicable and holster it safely. Repeat the 3 yard shot, but only use support hand for the draw and shot. Support hand draw should only be done if you have been taught the correct use of support hand holster draw application by a knowledgeable instructor. Otherwise safely switch hands from dominate to support. Place dominant hand on chest while performing support hand draw and shot. Put pistol on safe if applicable and holster it. Move back 1 yard to 4 yards. Repeat drill from 4 yards, 5 yards, 6 yards and 7 yards. Once you have shot all distances, score your target. This drill has no time limit and if you feel you made a bad draw or are not going to make a decent shot, stop, take a break and start the drawing sequence and firing over. Good hand placement during the draw and trigger control is essential to master this drill.

Goals: All shots in or touching black portion of the target.   Expert: 150 points   Gunfighter: 150 points with 10X's

Variations: Double the distance. Try different shooting positions.

GUT CHECK

Date:	Location:	Weapon:	Sights:
# of 8's:	# of 9's:	# of 10's:	Notes:
Distance Multiplier: X1 / X2	Standing / Kneeling / Prone	Total Score: X's	
Date:	Location:	Weapon:	Sights:
# of 8's:	# of 9's:	# of 10's:	Notes:
Distance Multiplier: X1 / X2	Standing / Kneeling / Prone	Total Score:	
Date:	Location:	Weapon:	Sights:
# of 8's:	# of 9's:	# of 10's:	Notes:
Distance Multiplier: X1 / X2	Standing / Kneeling / Prone	Total Score:	
Date:	Location:	Weapon:	Sights:
# of 8's:	# of 9's:	# of 10's:	Notes:
Distance Multiplier: X1 / X2	Standing / Kneeling / Prone	Total Score:	
Date:	Location:	Weapon:	Sights:
# of 8's:	# of 9's:	# of 10's:	Notes:
Distance Multiplier: X1 / X2	Standing / Kneeling / Prone	Total Score:	

Advanced Pistol ©

Accuracy Drills - 4

GUT CHECK

Date:	Location:	Weapon:	Sights:	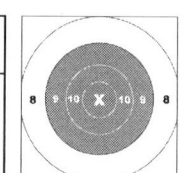
# of 8's:	# of 9's:	# of 10's:	Notes:	
Distance Multiplier: X1 / X2	Standing / Kneeling / Prone	Total Score: X's		

Date:	Location:	Weapon:	Sights:	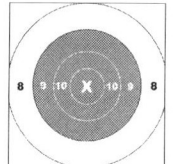
# of 8's:	# of 9's:	# of 10's:	Notes:	
Distance Multiplier: X1 / X2	Standing / Kneeling / Prone	Total Score:		

Date:	Location:	Weapon:	Sights:	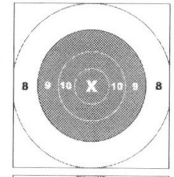
# of 8's:	# of 9's:	# of 10's:	Notes:	
Distance Multiplier: X1 / X2	Standing / Kneeling / Prone	Total Score:		

Date:	Location:	Weapon:	Sights:	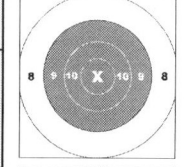
# of 8's:	# of 9's:	# of 10's:	Notes:	
Distance Multiplier: X1 / X2	Standing / Kneeling / Prone	Total Score:		

Date:	Location:	Weapon:	Sights:	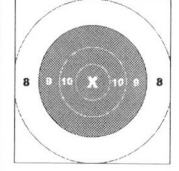
# of 8's:	# of 9's:	# of 10's:	Notes:	
Distance Multiplier: X1 / X2	Standing / Kneeling / Prone	Total Score:		

GUT CHECK

Date:	Location:	Weapon:	Sights:
# of 8's:	# of 9's:	# of 10's:	Notes:
Distance Multiplier: X1 / X2	Standing / Kneeling / Prone	Total Score: X's	
Date:	Location:	Weapon:	Sights:
# of 8's:	# of 9's:	# of 10's:	Notes:
Distance Multiplier: X1 / X2	Standing / Kneeling / Prone	Total Score:	
Date:	Location:	Weapon:	Sights:
# of 8's:	# of 9's:	# of 10's:	Notes:
Distance Multiplier: X1 / X2	Standing / Kneeling / Prone	Total Score:	
Date:	Location:	Weapon:	Sights:
# of 8's:	# of 9's:	# of 10's:	Notes:
Distance Multiplier: X1 / X2	Standing / Kneeling / Prone	Total Score:	
Date:	Location:	Weapon:	Sights:
# of 8's:	# of 9's:	# of 10's:	Notes:
Distance Multiplier: X1 / X2	Standing / Kneeling / Prone	Total Score:	

www.gunfighterseries.com ©

GUT CHECK

Date:	Location:	Weapon:	Sights:	
# of 8's:	# of 9's:	# of 10's:	Notes:	
Distance Multiplier: X1 / X2	Standing / Kneeling / Prone	Total Score: X's		
Date:	Location:	Weapon:	Sights:	
# of 8's:	# of 9's:	# of 10's:	Notes:	
Distance Multiplier: X1 / X2	Standing / Kneeling / Prone	Total Score:		
Date:	Location:	Weapon:	Sights:	
# of 8's:	# of 9's:	# of 10's:	Notes:	
Distance Multiplier: X1 / X2	Standing / Kneeling / Prone	Total Score:		
Date:	Location:	Weapon:	Sights:	
# of 8's:	# of 9's:	# of 10's:	Notes:	
Distance Multiplier: X1 / X2	Standing / Kneeling / Prone	Total Score:		
Date:	Location:	Weapon:	Sights:	
# of 8's:	# of 9's:	# of 10's:	Notes:	
Distance Multiplier: X1 / X2	Standing / Kneeling / Prone	Total Score:		

GUT CHECK

Date:	Location:	Weapon:	Sights:
# of 8's:	# of 9's:	# of 10's:	Notes:
Distance Multiplier: X1 / X2	Standing / Kneeling / Prone	Total Score: X's	
Date:	Location:	Weapon:	Sights:
# of 8's:	# of 9's:	# of 10's:	Notes:
Distance Multiplier: X1 / X2	Standing / Kneeling / Prone	Total Score:	
Date:	Location:	Weapon:	Sights:
# of 8's:	# of 9's:	# of 10's:	Notes:
Distance Multiplier: X1 / X2	Standing / Kneeling / Prone	Total Score:	
Date:	Location:	Weapon:	Sights:
# of 8's:	# of 9's:	# of 10's:	Notes:
Distance Multiplier: X1 / X2	Standing / Kneeling / Prone	Total Score:	
Date:	Location:	Weapon:	Sights:
# of 8's:	# of 9's:	# of 10's:	Notes:
Distance Multiplier: X1 / X2	Standing / Kneeling / Prone	Total Score:	

Advanced Pistol ©

Accuracy Drills - 4

LONG ARM

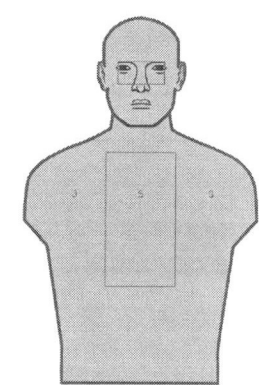

Purpose: Ambidextrous one-handed accuracy.

Distance: 5, 7, 10, 15, 25 Yards.

Target: JD-QUAL1

Rounds Fired Per Rep: 5 Rounds.

Total Rounds Fired: 20 Rounds.

Point Penalty: As per target score.

Repetitions: 4 Reps.

Starting Position & Condition: Standing – Surrender / Interview. Weapon Condition 1.

Description: At your own personal go, draw your pistol and fire one round while only using your dominant hand into the (5 point) A zone body box from each distance. Put pistol on safe if applicable and holster it safely when you move back in yardage. Repeat the drill sequence only using your support hand. Support hand draw should only be done if you have been taught the correct use of support hand holster draw application by a knowledgeable instructor. Otherwise safely switch hands from dominant to support and use a low ready starting position. Repeat the dominant and support sequence 1 more time each for a total of 2 dominant hand reps and 2 support hand reps. This drill has no time limit, so take your time and make good shots. Good hand placement during the draw, locking arm solid and trigger control is essential to master this drill. Any hits outside the silhouette and the drill is a No Go.

Goal: 84 Points.   Expert: 92 Points.   Gunfighter: 100 Points.

LONG ARM

Date:	Location:	Weapon:	Sights:	Notes:
Rep 1: Go / No Go	Rep 2: Go / No Go	Rep 3: Go / No Go	Rep 4: Go / No Go	
Rep 1 Score:	Rep 2 Score:	Rep 3 Score:	Rep 4 Score:	**Total Score:**

Date:	Location:	Weapon:	Sights:	Notes:
Rep 1: Go / No Go	Rep 2: Go / No Go	Rep 3: Go / No Go	Rep 4: Go / No Go	
Rep 1 Score:	Rep 2 Score:	Rep 3 Score:	Rep 4 Score:	**Total Score:**

Date:	Location:	Weapon:	Sights:	Notes:
Rep 1: Go / No Go	Rep 2: Go / No Go	Rep 3: Go / No Go	Rep 4: Go / No Go	
Rep 1 Score:	Rep 2 Score:	Rep 3 Score:	Rep 4 Score:	**Total Score:**

Date:	Location:	Weapon:	Sights:	Notes:
Rep 1: Go / No Go	Rep 2: Go / No Go	Rep 3: Go / No Go	Rep 4: Go / No Go	
Rep 1 Score:	Rep 2 Score:	Rep 3 Score:	Rep 4 Score:	**Total Score:**

Date:	Location:	Weapon:	Sights:	Notes:
Rep 1: Go / No Go	Rep 2: Go / No Go	Rep 3: Go / No Go	Rep 4: Go / No Go	
Rep 1 Score:	Rep 2 Score:	Rep 3 Score:	Rep 4 Score:	**Total Score:**

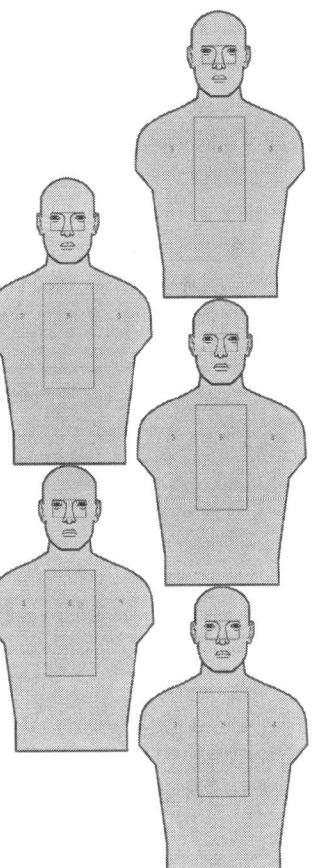

Advanced Pistol ©

LONG ARM

Date:	Location:	Weapon:	Sights:	Notes:
Rep 1: Go / No Go	Rep 2: Go / No Go	Rep 3: Go / No Go	Rep 4: Go / No Go	
Rep 1 Score:	Rep 2 Score:	Rep 3 Score:	Rep 4 Score:	**Total Score:**

Date:	Location:	Weapon:	Sights:	Notes:
Rep 1: Go / No Go	Rep 2: Go / No Go	Rep 3: Go / No Go	Rep 4: Go / No Go	
Rep 1 Score:	Rep 2 Score:	Rep 3 Score:	Rep 4 Score:	**Total Score:**

Date:	Location:	Weapon:	Sights:	Notes:
Rep 1: Go / No Go	Rep 2: Go / No Go	Rep 3: Go / No Go	Rep 4: Go / No Go	
Rep 1 Score:	Rep 2 Score:	Rep 3 Score:	Rep 4 Score:	**Total Score:**

Date:	Location:	Weapon:	Sights:	Notes:
Rep 1: Go / No Go	Rep 2: Go / No Go	Rep 3: Go / No Go	Rep 4: Go / No Go	
Rep 1 Score:	Rep 2 Score:	Rep 3 Score:	Rep 4 Score:	**Total Score:**

Date:	Location:	Weapon:	Sights:	Notes:
Rep 1: Go / No Go	Rep 2: Go / No Go	Rep 3: Go / No Go	Rep 4: Go / No Go	
Rep 1 Score:	Rep 2 Score:	Rep 3 Score:	Rep 4 Score:	**Total Score:**

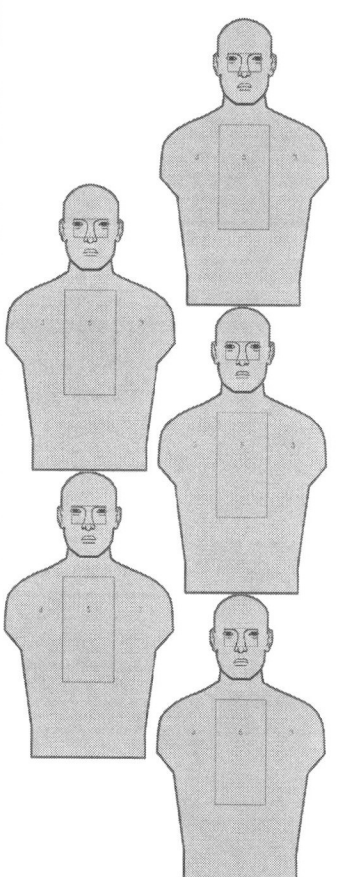

LONG ARM

Date:	Location:	Weapon:	Sights:	Notes:
Rep 1: Go / No Go	Rep 2: Go / No Go	Rep 3: Go / No Go	Rep 4: Go / No Go	
Rep 1 Score:	Rep 2 Score:	Rep 3 Score:	Rep 4 Score:	**Total Score:**

Date:	Location:	Weapon:	Sights:	Notes:
Rep 1: Go / No Go	Rep 2: Go / No Go	Rep 3: Go / No Go	Rep 4: Go / No Go	
Rep 1 Score:	Rep 2 Score:	Rep 3 Score:	Rep 4 Score:	**Total Score:**

Date:	Location:	Weapon:	Sights:	Notes:
Rep 1: Go / No Go	Rep 2: Go / No Go	Rep 3: Go / No Go	Rep 4: Go / No Go	
Rep 1 Score:	Rep 2 Score:	Rep 3 Score:	Rep 4 Score:	**Total Score:**

Date:	Location:	Weapon:	Sights:	Notes:
Rep 1: Go / No Go	Rep 2: Go / No Go	Rep 3: Go / No Go	Rep 4: Go / No Go	
Rep 1 Score:	Rep 2 Score:	Rep 3 Score:	Rep 4 Score:	**Total Score:**

Date:	Location:	Weapon:	Sights:	Notes:
Rep 1: Go / No Go	Rep 2: Go / No Go	Rep 3: Go / No Go	Rep 4: Go / No Go	
Rep 1 Score:	Rep 2 Score:	Rep 3 Score:	Rep 4 Score:	**Total Score:**

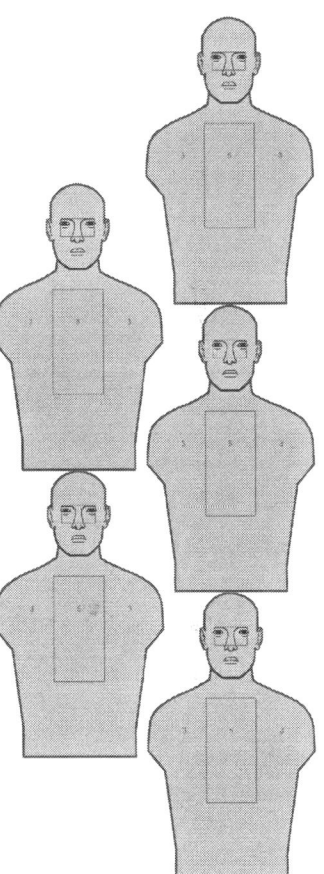

Advanced Pistol ©

LONG ARM

Date:	Location:	Weapon:	Sights:	Notes:
Rep 1: Go / No Go	Rep 2: Go / No Go	Rep 3: Go / No Go	Rep 4: Go / No Go	
Rep 1 Score:	Rep 2 Score:	Rep 3 Score:	Rep 4 Score:	**Total Score:**

Date:	Location:	Weapon:	Sights:	Notes:
Rep 1: Go / No Go	Rep 2: Go / No Go	Rep 3: Go / No Go	Rep 4: Go / No Go	
Rep 1 Score:	Rep 2 Score:	Rep 3 Score:	Rep 4 Score:	**Total Score:**

Date:	Location:	Weapon:	Sights:	Notes:
Rep 1: Go / No Go	Rep 2: Go / No Go	Rep 3: Go / No Go	Rep 4: Go / No Go	
Rep 1 Score:	Rep 2 Score:	Rep 3 Score:	Rep 4 Score:	**Total Score:**

Date:	Location:	Weapon:	Sights:	Notes:
Rep 1: Go / No Go	Rep 2: Go / No Go	Rep 3: Go / No Go	Rep 4: Go / No Go	
Rep 1 Score:	Rep 2 Score:	Rep 3 Score:	Rep 4 Score:	**Total Score:**

Date:	Location:	Weapon:	Sights:	Notes:
Rep 1: Go / No Go	Rep 2: Go / No Go	Rep 3: Go / No Go	Rep 4: Go / No Go	
Rep 1 Score:	Rep 2 Score:	Rep 3 Score:	Rep 4 Score:	**Total Score:**

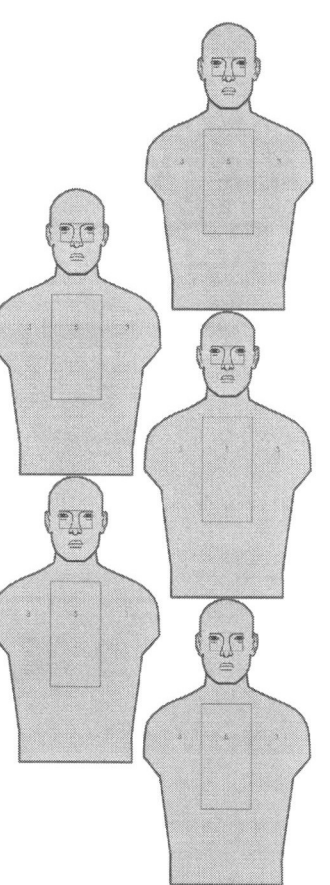

LONG ARM

Date:	Location:	Weapon:	Sights:	Notes:
Rep 1: Go / No Go	Rep 2: Go / No Go	Rep 3: Go / No Go	Rep 4: Go / No Go	
Rep 1 Score:	Rep 2 Score:	Rep 3 Score:	Rep 4 Score:	Total Score:

Date:	Location:	Weapon:	Sights:	Notes:
Rep 1: Go / No Go	Rep 2: Go / No Go	Rep 3: Go / No Go	Rep 4: Go / No Go	
Rep 1 Score:	Rep 2 Score:	Rep 3 Score:	Rep 4 Score:	Total Score:

Date:	Location:	Weapon:	Sights:	Notes:
Rep 1: Go / No Go	Rep 2: Go / No Go	Rep 3: Go / No Go	Rep 4: Go / No Go	
Rep 1 Score:	Rep 2 Score:	Rep 3 Score:	Rep 4 Score:	Total Score:

Date:	Location:	Weapon:	Sights:	Notes:
Rep 1: Go / No Go	Rep 2: Go / No Go	Rep 3: Go / No Go	Rep 4: Go / No Go	
Rep 1 Score:	Rep 2 Score:	Rep 3 Score:	Rep 4 Score:	Total Score:

Date:	Location:	Weapon:	Sights:	Notes:
Rep 1: Go / No Go	Rep 2: Go / No Go	Rep 3: Go / No Go	Rep 4: Go / No Go	
Rep 1 Score:	Rep 2 Score:	Rep 3 Score:	Rep 4 Score:	Total Score:

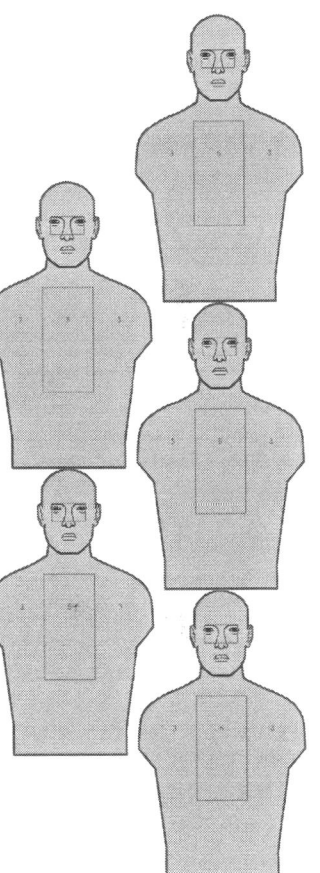

Advanced Pistol ©

BREAKING BAD

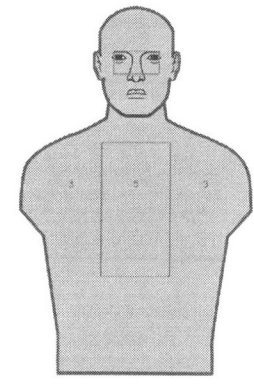

Purpose: Increase flash sight efficiency and focus.

Distance: 5, 7, and 10 Yards.

Target: JD-QUAL1

Par Time: 2.75 Seconds.

Extra Equipment Required: Shot timer.

Rounds Fired Per Distance: 3 Rounds.   **Total Rounds Fired:** 9 Rounds.

Point Penalty: As per target score.

Repetitions: 1 Rep each distance.

Starting Position & Condition: Standing – Surrender / Interview. Weapon Condition 1.

Description: At the timer beep, draw your pistol and fire 3 rounds into the (5 point) A Zone Body Box from 5 yards. Put pistol on safe if applicable, holster it safely, then record time and score. Repeat drill from 7 yards and 10 yards. A fast draw time, excellent recoil management and the use of body positioning is key to mastering this skill.

Goal: 37 points within par.   Expert: 41 points within a 2.4 second par.   Gunfighter: 45 points within a 2 second par.

BREAKING BAD

Date:	Location:	Weapon:	Sights:	Holster:
5 Yard Time:	7 Yard Time:	10 Yard Time:	**Total Score:**	Notes:
5 Yard Score:	7 Yard Score:	10 Yard Score:		

Date:	Location:	Weapon:	Sights:	Holster:
5 Yard Time:	7 Yard Time:	10 Yard Time:	**Total Score:**	Notes:
5 Yard Score:	7 Yard Score:	10 Yard Score:		

Date:	Location:	Weapon:	Sights:	Holster:
5 Yard Time:	7 Yard Time:	10 Yard Time:	**Total Score:**	Notes:
5 Yard Score:	7 Yard Score:	10 Yard Score:		

Date:	Location:	Weapon:	Sights:	Holster:
5 Yard Time:	7 Yard Time:	10 Yard Time:	**Total Score:**	Notes:
5 Yard Score:	7 Yard Score:	10 Yard Score:		

Date:	Location:	Weapon:	Sights:	Holster:
5 Yard Time:	7 Yard Time:	10 Yard Time:	**Total Score:**	Notes:
5 Yard Score:	7 Yard Score:	10 Yard Score:		

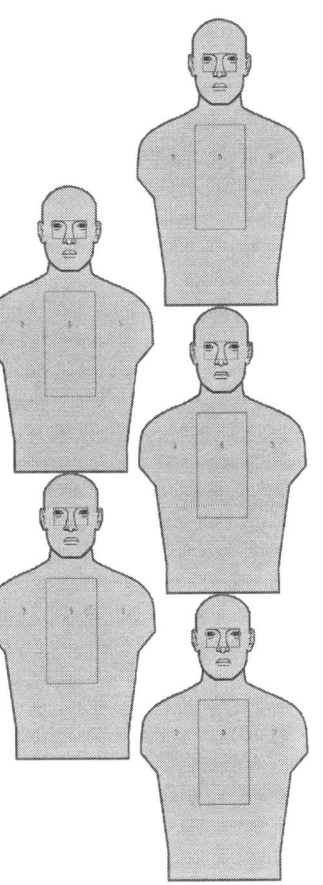

BREAKING BAD

Date:	Location:	Weapon:	Sights:	Holster:
5 Yard Time:	7 Yard Time:	10 Yard Time:	**Total Score:**	Notes:
5 Yard Score:	7 Yard Score:	10 Yard Score:		

Date:	Location:	Weapon:	Sights:	Holster:
5 Yard Time:	7 Yard Time:	10 Yard Time:	**Total Score:**	Notes:
5 Yard Score:	7 Yard Score:	10 Yard Score:		

Date:	Location:	Weapon:	Sights:	Holster:
5 Yard Time:	7 Yard Time:	10 Yard Time:	**Total Score:**	Notes:
5 Yard Score:	7 Yard Score:	10 Yard Score:		

Date:	Location:	Weapon:	Sights:	Holster:
5 Yard Time:	7 Yard Time:	10 Yard Time:	**Total Score:**	Notes:
5 Yard Score:	7 Yard Score:	10 Yard Score:		

Date:	Location:	Weapon:	Sights:	Holster:
5 Yard Time:	7 Yard Time:	10 Yard Time:	**Total Score:**	Notes:
5 Yard Score:	7 Yard Score:	10 Yard Score:		

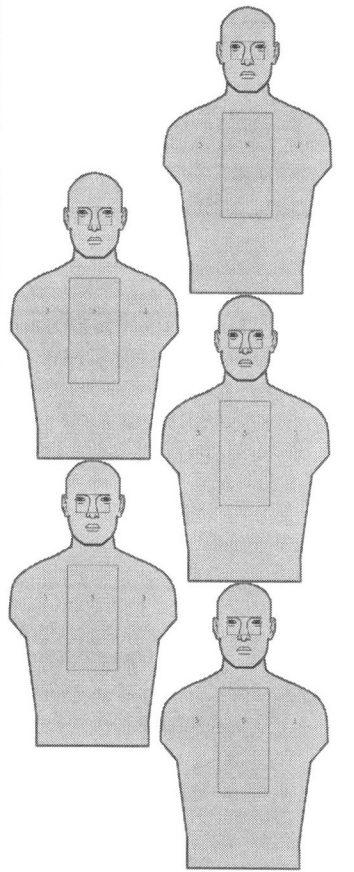

BREAKING BAD

Date:	Location:	Weapon:	Sights:	Holster:
5 Yard Time:	7 Yard Time:	10 Yard Time:	**Total Score:**	Notes:
5 Yard Score:	7 Yard Score:	10 Yard Score:		

Date:	Location:	Weapon:	Sights:	Holster:
5 Yard Time:	7 Yard Time:	10 Yard Time:	**Total Score:**	Notes:
5 Yard Score:	7 Yard Score:	10 Yard Score:		

Date:	Location:	Weapon:	Sights:	Holster:
5 Yard Time:	7 Yard Time:	10 Yard Time:	**Total Score:**	Notes:
5 Yard Score:	7 Yard Score:	10 Yard Score:		

Date:	Location:	Weapon:	Sights:	Holster:
5 Yard Time:	7 Yard Time:	10 Yard Time:	**Total Score:**	Notes:
5 Yard Score:	7 Yard Score:	10 Yard Score:		

Date:	Location:	Weapon:	Sights:	Holster:
5 Yard Time:	7 Yard Time:	10 Yard Time:	**Total Score:**	Notes:
5 Yard Score:	7 Yard Score:	10 Yard Score:		

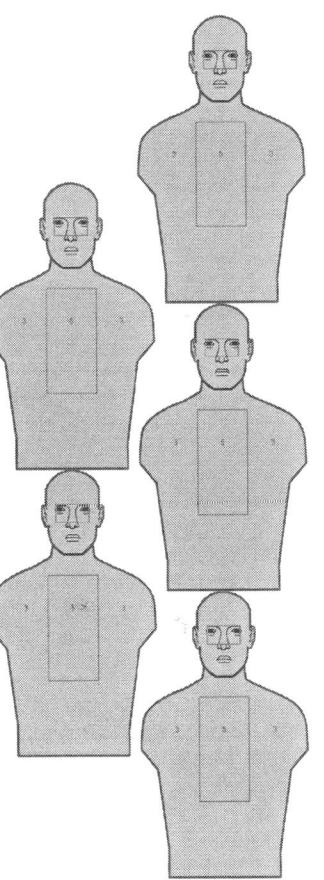

Advanced Pistol ©

BREAKING BAD

Date:	Location:	Weapon:	Sights:	Holster:
5 Yard Time:	7 Yard Time:	10 Yard Time:	**Total Score:**	Notes:
5 Yard Score:	7 Yard Score:	10 Yard Score:		

Date:	Location:	Weapon:	Sights:	Holster:
5 Yard Time:	7 Yard Time:	10 Yard Time:	**Total Score:**	Notes:
5 Yard Score:	7 Yard Score:	10 Yard Score:		

Date:	Location:	Weapon:	Sights:	Holster:
5 Yard Time:	7 Yard Time:	10 Yard Time:	**Total Score:**	Notes:
5 Yard Score:	7 Yard Score:	10 Yard Score:		

Date:	Location:	Weapon:	Sights:	Holster:
5 Yard Time:	7 Yard Time:	10 Yard Time:	**Total Score:**	Notes:
5 Yard Score:	7 Yard Score:	10 Yard Score:		

Date:	Location:	Weapon:	Sights:	Holster:
5 Yard Time:	7 Yard Time:	10 Yard Time:	**Total Score:**	Notes:
5 Yard Score:	7 Yard Score:	10 Yard Score:		

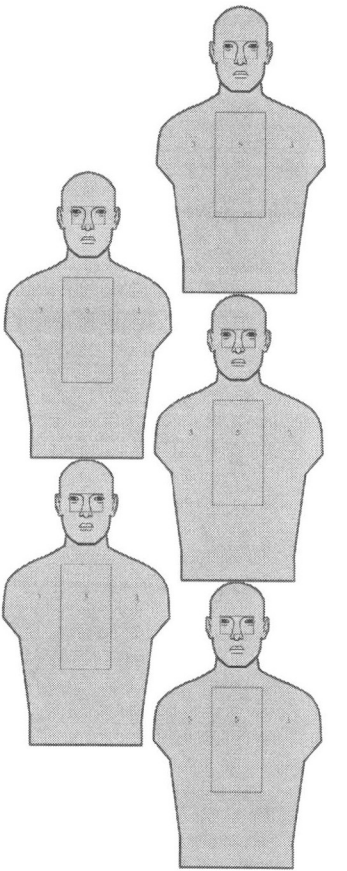

BREAKING BAD

Date:	Location:	Weapon:	Sights:	Holster:
5 Yard Time:	7 Yard Time:	10 Yard Time:	**Total Score:**	Notes:
5 Yard Score:	7 Yard Score:	10 Yard Score:		

Date:	Location:	Weapon:	Sights:	Holster:
5 Yard Time:	7 Yard Time:	10 Yard Time:	**Total Score:**	Notes:
5 Yard Score:	7 Yard Score:	10 Yard Score:		

Date:	Location:	Weapon:	Sights:	Holster:
5 Yard Time:	7 Yard Time:	10 Yard Time:	**Total Score:**	Notes:
5 Yard Score:	7 Yard Score:	10 Yard Score:		

Date:	Location:	Weapon:	Sights:	Holster:
5 Yard Time:	7 Yard Time:	10 Yard Time:	**Total Score:**	Notes:
5 Yard Score:	7 Yard Score:	10 Yard Score:		

Date:	Location:	Weapon:	Sights:	Holster:
5 Yard Time:	7 Yard Time:	10 Yard Time:	**Total Score:**	Notes:
5 Yard Score:	7 Yard Score:	10 Yard Score:		

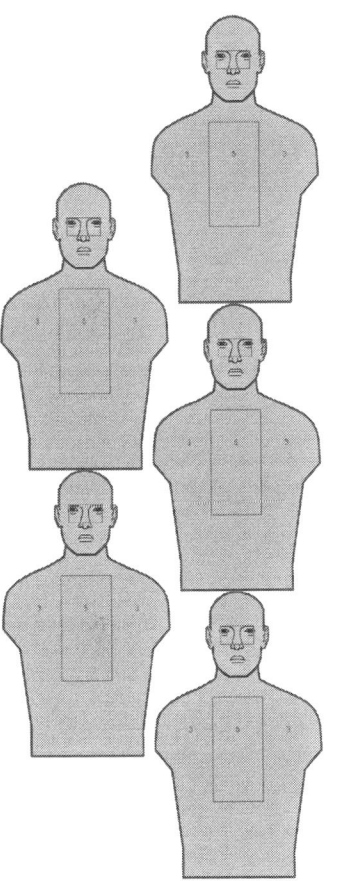

Advanced Pistol ©

Accuracy Drills - 6

CLOSE ENCOUNTER

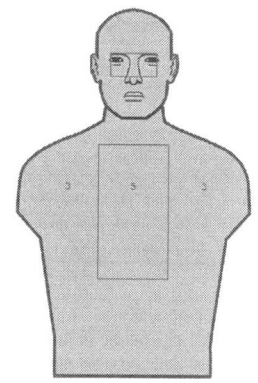

Purpose: Increase speed and accuracy with retention shooting.

Distance: Arms length from target.

Target: JD-QUAL1

Par Time: 1.25 Seconds.

Extra Equipment Required: Shot timer.

Rounds Fired Per Rep: 1 Round.

Total Rounds Fired: 5 Rounds.

Point Penalty: Go / No Go.

Repetitions: 5 Reps.

Starting Position & Condition: Standing – Surrender / Interview. Weapon Condition 1.

Description: At the timer beep, take your dominant firing hand/arm, bring your elbow straight back and clear your concealment garment (if you have one) with your dominant hand and establish a good grip on the pistol. As you bring your firing hand to establish a good pistol grip, move your support hand to the side and just in front of your face with your palm facing to your dominant side, at the same time draw your pistol straight up just under your arm pit and rotate pistol towards target (5 point) A Zone body box. When you point your pistol at the target, lean the slide away from your body just enough so when fired from that position, it will not contact your clothing or chest causing a malfunction. Make sure you are not pointing your pistol at your support arm or any other body part when you are firing. If any rounds are over par time or are out of the A Zone body box, the drill is a No Go. Record time. Reset drill and repeat 5 times.

Goal: 1.25 Seconds.   **Expert:** 1.10 Seconds.   **Gunfighter:** 1 Second.

Variations: Immediately before the start of the drill, run 50 yards or do 2X25 yard shuttle runs, do 10 push-ups or 10 jumping jacks to get your heart rate up. Add shots to drill, with adding time for each shot at (base goal) .5 seconds (expert) .35 seconds (Gunfighter) .25 seconds. Wear a concealment over garment.

CLOSE ENCOUNTER

Date:	Location:	Weapon:	Holster:	Cover Garment: Y / N
Rep 1 Time:	Rep 2 Time:	Rep 3 Time:	Rep 4 Time:	Rep 5 Time:
Rep 1: Go / No Go	Rep 2: Go / No Go	Rep 3: Go / No Go	Rep 4: Go / No Go	Rep 5: Go / No Go
Heart Rate Stress: Y / N	Rounds Per Rep:	Notes:		**Total Score:**

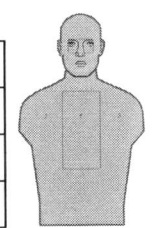

Date:	Location:	Weapon:	Holster:	Cover Garment: Y / N
Rep 1 Time:	Rep 2 Time:	Rep 3 Time:	Rep 4 Time:	Rep 5 Time:
Rep 1: Go / No Go	Rep 2: Go / No Go	Rep 3: Go / No Go	Rep 4: Go / No Go	Rep 5: Go / No Go
Heart Rate Stress: Y / N	Rounds Per Rep:	Notes:		**Total Score:**

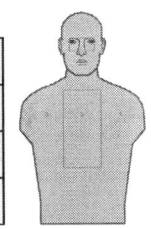

Date:	Location:	Weapon:	Holster:	Cover Garment: Y / N
Rep 1 Time:	Rep 2 Time:	Rep 3 Time:	Rep 4 Time:	Rep 5 Time:
Rep 1: Go / No Go	Rep 2: Go / No Go	Rep 3: Go / No Go	Rep 4: Go / No Go	Rep 5: Go / No Go
Heart Rate Stress: Y / N	Rounds Per Rep:	Notes:		**Total Score:**

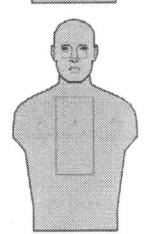

Date:	Location:	Weapon:	Holster:	Cover Garment: Y / N
Rep 1 Time:	Rep 2 Time:	Rep 3 Time:	Rep 4 Time:	Rep 5 Time:
Rep 1: Go / No Go	Rep 2: Go / No Go	Rep 3: Go / No Go	Rep 4: Go / No Go	Rep 5: Go / No Go
Heart Rate Stress: Y / N	Rounds Per Rep:	Notes:		**Total Score:**

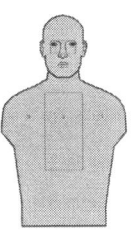

Advanced Pistol ©

CLOSE ENCOUNTER

Date:	Location:	Weapon:	Holster:	Cover Garment: Y / N
Rep 1 Time:	Rep 2 Time:	Rep 3 Time:	Rep 4 Time:	Rep 5 Time:
Rep 1: Go / No Go	Rep 2: Go / No Go	Rep 3: Go / No Go	Rep 4: Go / No Go	Rep 5: Go / No Go
Heart Rate Stress: Y / N	Rounds Per Rep:	Notes:		**Total Score:**

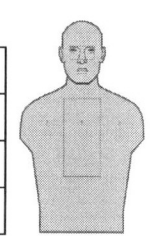

Date:	Location:	Weapon:	Holster:	Cover Garment: Y / N
Rep 1 Time:	Rep 2 Time:	Rep 3 Time:	Rep 4 Time:	Rep 5 Time:
Rep 1: Go / No Go	Rep 2: Go / No Go	Rep 3: Go / No Go	Rep 4: Go / No Go	Rep 5: Go / No Go
Heart Rate Stress: Y / N	Rounds Per Rep:	Notes:		**Total Score:**

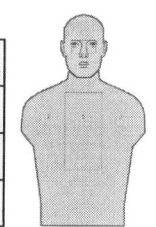

Date:	Location:	Weapon:	Holster:	Cover Garment: Y / N
Rep 1 Time:	Rep 2 Time:	Rep 3 Time:	Rep 4 Time:	Rep 5 Time:
Rep 1: Go / No Go	Rep 2: Go / No Go	Rep 3: Go / No Go	Rep 4: Go / No Go	Rep 5: Go / No Go
Heart Rate Stress: Y / N	Rounds Per Rep:	Notes:		**Total Score:**

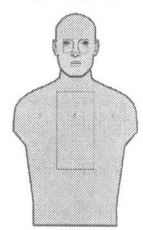

Date:	Location:	Weapon:	Holster:	Cover Garment: Y / N
Rep 1 Time:	Rep 2 Time:	Rep 3 Time:	Rep 4 Time:	Rep 5 Time:
Rep 1: Go / No Go	Rep 2: Go / No Go	Rep 3: Go / No Go	Rep 4: Go / No Go	Rep 5: Go / No Go
Heart Rate Stress: Y / N	Rounds Per Rep:	Notes:		**Total Score:**

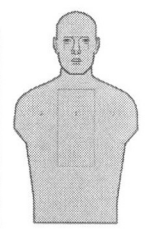

CLOSE ENCOUNTER

Date:	Location:	Weapon:	Holster:	Cover Garment: Y / N
Rep 1 Time:	Rep 2 Time:	Rep 3 Time:	Rep 4 Time:	Rep 5 Time:
Rep 1: Go / No Go	Rep 2: Go / No Go	Rep 3: Go / No Go	Rep 4: Go / No Go	Rep 5: Go / No Go
Heart Rate Stress: Y / N	Rounds Per Rep:	Notes:		Total Score:

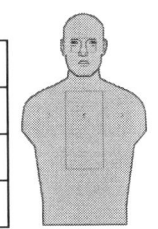

Date:	Location:	Weapon:	Holster:	Cover Garment: Y / N
Rep 1 Time:	Rep 2 Time:	Rep 3 Time:	Rep 4 Time:	Rep 5 Time:
Rep 1: Go / No Go	Rep 2: Go / No Go	Rep 3: Go / No Go	Rep 4: Go / No Go	Rep 5: Go / No Go
Heart Rate Stress: Y / N	Rounds Per Rep:	Notes:		Total Score:

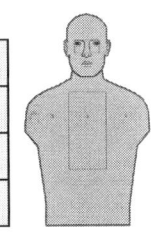

Date:	Location:	Weapon:	Holster:	Cover Garment: Y / N
Rep 1 Time:	Rep 2 Time:	Rep 3 Time:	Rep 4 Time:	Rep 5 Time:
Rep 1: Go / No Go	Rep 2: Go / No Go	Rep 3: Go / No Go	Rep 4: Go / No Go	Rep 5: Go / No Go
Heart Rate Stress: Y / N	Rounds Per Rep:	Notes:		Total Score:

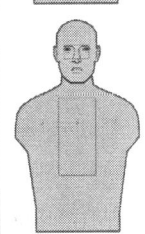

Date:	Location:	Weapon:	Holster:	Cover Garment: Y / N
Rep 1 Time:	Rep 2 Time:	Rep 3 Time:	Rep 4 Time:	Rep 5 Time:
Rep 1: Go / No Go	Rep 2: Go / No Go	Rep 3: Go / No Go	Rep 4: Go / No Go	Rep 5: Go / No Go
Heart Rate Stress: Y / N	Rounds Per Rep:	Notes:		Total Score:

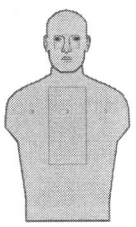

Advanced Pistol ©

CLOSE ENCOUNTER

Date:	Location:	Weapon:	Holster:	Cover Garment: Y / N
Rep 1 Time:	Rep 2 Time:	Rep 3 Time:	Rep 4 Time:	Rep 5 Time:
Rep 1: Go / No Go	Rep 2: Go / No Go	Rep 3: Go / No Go	Rep 4: Go / No Go	Rep 5: Go / No Go
Heart Rate Stress: Y / N	Rounds Per Rep:	Notes:		**Total Score:**

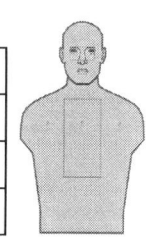

Date:	Location:	Weapon:	Holster:	Cover Garment: Y / N
Rep 1 Time:	Rep 2 Time:	Rep 3 Time:	Rep 4 Time:	Rep 5 Time:
Rep 1: Go / No Go	Rep 2: Go / No Go	Rep 3: Go / No Go	Rep 4: Go / No Go	Rep 5: Go / No Go
Heart Rate Stress: Y / N	Rounds Per Rep:	Notes:		**Total Score:**

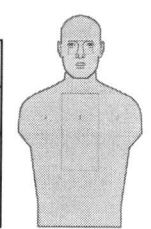

Date:	Location:	Weapon:	Holster:	Cover Garment: Y / N
Rep 1 Time:	Rep 2 Time:	Rep 3 Time:	Rep 4 Time:	Rep 5 Time:
Rep 1: Go / No Go	Rep 2: Go / No Go	Rep 3: Go / No Go	Rep 4: Go / No Go	Rep 5: Go / No Go
Heart Rate Stress: Y / N	Rounds Per Rep:	Notes:		**Total Score:**

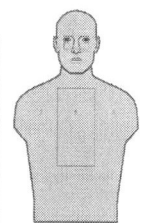

Date:	Location:	Weapon:	Holster:	Cover Garment: Y / N
Rep 1 Time:	Rep 2 Time:	Rep 3 Time:	Rep 4 Time:	Rep 5 Time:
Rep 1: Go / No Go	Rep 2: Go / No Go	Rep 3: Go / No Go	Rep 4: Go / No Go	Rep 5: Go / No Go
Heart Rate Stress: Y / N	Rounds Per Rep:	Notes:		**Total Score:**

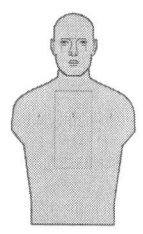

CLOSE ENCOUNTER

Date:	Location:	Weapon:	Holster:	Cover Garment: Y / N
Rep 1 Time:	Rep 2 Time:	Rep 3 Time:	Rep 4 Time:	Rep 5 Time:
Rep 1: Go / No Go	Rep 2: Go / No Go	Rep 3: Go / No Go	Rep 4: Go / No Go	Rep 5: Go / No Go
Heart Rate Stress: Y / N	Rounds Per Rep:	Notes:		**Total Score:**

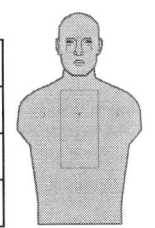

Date:	Location:	Weapon:	Holster:	Cover Garment: Y / N
Rep 1 Time:	Rep 2 Time:	Rep 3 Time:	Rep 4 Time:	Rep 5 Time:
Rep 1: Go / No Go	Rep 2: Go / No Go	Rep 3: Go / No Go	Rep 4: Go / No Go	Rep 5: Go / No Go
Heart Rate Stress: Y / N	Rounds Per Rep:	Notes:		**Total Score:**

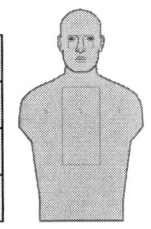

Date:	Location:	Weapon:	Holster:	Cover Garment: Y / N
Rep 1 Time:	Rep 2 Time:	Rep 3 Time:	Rep 4 Time:	Rep 5 Time:
Rep 1: Go / No Go	Rep 2: Go / No Go	Rep 3: Go / No Go	Rep 4: Go / No Go	Rep 5: Go / No Go
Heart Rate Stress: Y / N	Rounds Per Rep:	Notes:		**Total Score:**

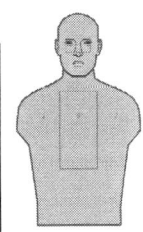

Date:	Location:	Weapon:	Holster:	Cover Garment: Y / N
Rep 1 Time:	Rep 2 Time:	Rep 3 Time:	Rep 4 Time:	Rep 5 Time:
Rep 1: Go / No Go	Rep 2: Go / No Go	Rep 3: Go / No Go	Rep 4: Go / No Go	Rep 5: Go / No Go
Heart Rate Stress: Y / N	Rounds Per Rep:	Notes:		**Total Score:**

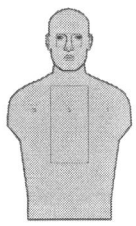

FRONTAL

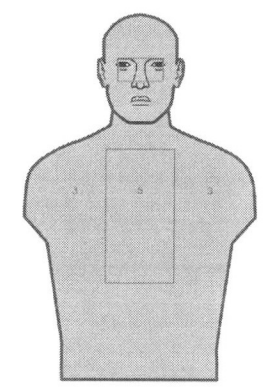

Purpose: Increase speed and accuracy with one-handed draw and shooting.

Distance: 10 Yards.

Target: JD-QUAL1

Par Time: Per goal standards.

Extra Equipment Required: Shot timer.

Rounds Fired Per Rep: 1 Round. **Total Rounds Fired:** 10 Rounds.

Point Penalty: As per target score.

Repetitions: 10 Reps.

Starting Position & Condition: Standing – Hands to side or interview. Weapon Condition 1.

Description: At the beep of the timer, draw your pistol while pinning your support hand to your chest or to your support side, aim and fire 1 round into the (5 point) A Zone body box. Reset and repeat drill 10 times.

Goal: 2 Seconds with 40 points.   Expert: 1.8 Seconds with 42 points.   Gunfighter: 1.6 Seconds with 45 points.

Variations: Immediately before the start of the drill, run 50 yards or do 2X25 yard shuttle runs, do 10 push-ups or 10 jumping jacks to get your heart rate up. Add shots to drill, with adding time for each shot at (base goal) .5 seconds (expert) .35 seconds (Gunfighter) .25 seconds. Wear a concealment over garment.

FRONTAL

Date:	Location:	Weapon:	Holster:	Cover Garment: Y / N
Rep 1 Time:	Rep 2 Time:	Rep 3 Time:	Rep 4 Time:	Rep 5 Time:
Rep 6 Time:	Rep 7 Time:	Rep 8 Time:	Rep 9 Time:	Rep 10 Time:
Heart Rate Stress: Y / N	Rounds Per Rep:	Notes:		**All Rounds In: Y / N**

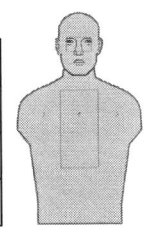

Date:	Location:	Weapon:	Holster:	Cover Garment: Y / N
Rep 1 Time:	Rep 2 Time:	Rep 3 Time:	Rep 4 Time:	Rep 5 Time:
Rep 6 Time:	Rep 7 Time:	Rep 8 Time:	Rep 9 Time:	Rep 10 Time:
Heart Rate Stress: Y / N	Rounds Per Rep:	Notes:		**All Rounds In: Y / N**

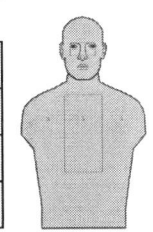

Date:	Location:	Weapon:	Holster:	Cover Garment: Y / N
Rep 1 Time:	Rep 2 Time:	Rep 3 Time:	Rep 4 Time:	Rep 5 Time:
Rep 6 Time:	Rep 7 Time:	Rep 8 Time:	Rep 9 Time:	Rep 10 Time:
Heart Rate Stress: Y / N	Rounds Per Rep:	Notes:		**All Rounds In: Y / N**

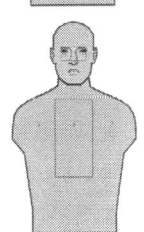

Date:	Location:	Weapon:	Holster:	Cover Garment: Y / N
Rep 1 Time:	Rep 2 Time:	Rep 3 Time:	Rep 4 Time:	Rep 5 Time:
Rep 6 Time:	Rep 7 Time:	Rep 8 Time:	Rep 9 Time:	Rep 10 Time:
Heart Rate Stress: Y / N	Rounds Per Rep:	Notes:		**All Rounds In: Y / N**

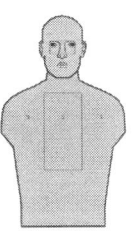

Advanced Pistol ©

Draw Drills - 2

FRONTAL

Date:	Location:	Weapon:	Holster:	Cover Garment: Y / N
Rep 1 Time:	Rep 2 Time:	Rep 3 Time:	Rep 4 Time:	Rep 5 Time:
Rep 6 Time:	Rep 7 Time:	Rep 8 Time:	Rep 9 Time:	Rep 10 Time:
Heart Rate Stress: Y / N	Rounds Per Rep:	Notes:		All Rounds In: Y / N

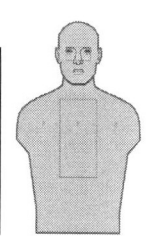

Date:	Location:	Weapon:	Holster:	Cover Garment: Y / N
Rep 1 Time:	Rep 2 Time:	Rep 3 Time:	Rep 4 Time:	Rep 5 Time:
Rep 6 Time:	Rep 7 Time:	Rep 8 Time:	Rep 9 Time:	Rep 10 Time:
Heart Rate Stress: Y / N	Rounds Per Rep:	Notes:		All Rounds In: Y / N

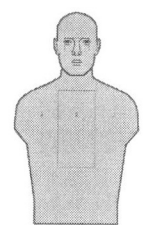

Date:	Location:	Weapon:	Holster:	Cover Garment: Y / N
Rep 1 Time:	Rep 2 Time:	Rep 3 Time:	Rep 4 Time:	Rep 5 Time:
Rep 6 Time:	Rep 7 Time:	Rep 8 Time:	Rep 9 Time:	Rep 10 Time:
Heart Rate Stress: Y / N	Rounds Per Rep:	Notes:		All Rounds In: Y / N

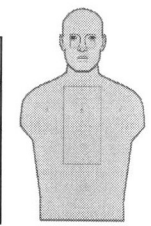

Date:	Location:	Weapon:	Holster:	Cover Garment: Y / N
Rep 1 Time:	Rep 2 Time:	Rep 3 Time:	Rep 4 Time:	Rep 5 Time:
Rep 6 Time:	Rep 7 Time:	Rep 8 Time:	Rep 9 Time:	Rep 10 Time:
Heart Rate Stress: Y / N	Rounds Per Rep:	Notes:		All Rounds In: Y / N

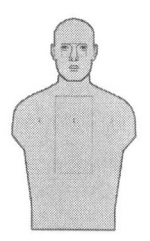

FRONTAL

Date:	Location:	Weapon:	Holster:	Cover Garment: Y / N
Rep 1 Time:	Rep 2 Time:	Rep 3 Time:	Rep 4 Time:	Rep 5 Time:
Rep 6 Time:	Rep 7 Time:	Rep 8 Time:	Rep 9 Time:	Rep 10 Time:
Heart Rate Stress: Y / N	Rounds Per Rep:	Notes:		**All Rounds In: Y / N**

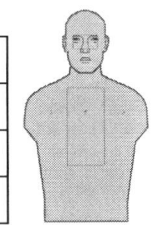

Date:	Location:	Weapon:	Holster:	Cover Garment: Y / N
Rep 1 Time:	Rep 2 Time:	Rep 3 Time:	Rep 4 Time:	Rep 5 Time:
Rep 6 Time:	Rep 7 Time:	Rep 8 Time:	Rep 9 Time:	Rep 10 Time:
Heart Rate Stress: Y / N	Rounds Per Rep:	Notes:		**All Rounds In: Y / N**

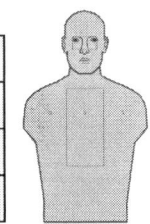

Date:	Location:	Weapon:	Holster:	Cover Garment: Y / N
Rep 1 Time:	Rep 2 Time:	Rep 3 Time:	Rep 4 Time:	Rep 5 Time:
Rep 6 Time:	Rep 7 Time:	Rep 8 Time:	Rep 9 Time:	Rep 10 Time:
Heart Rate Stress: Y / N	Rounds Per Rep:	Notes:		**All Rounds In: Y / N**

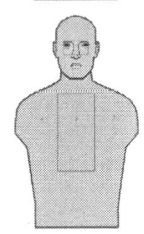

Date:	Location:	Weapon:	Holster:	Cover Garment: Y / N
Rep 1 Time:	Rep 2 Time:	Rep 3 Time:	Rep 4 Time:	Rep 5 Time:
Rep 6 Time:	Rep 7 Time:	Rep 8 Time:	Rep 9 Time:	Rep 10 Time:
Heart Rate Stress: Y / N	Rounds Per Rep:	Notes:		**All Rounds In: Y / N**

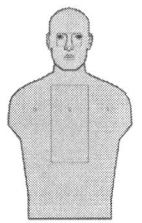

FRONTAL

Date:	Location:	Weapon:	Holster:	Cover Garment: Y / N
Rep 1 Time:	Rep 2 Time:	Rep 3 Time:	Rep 4 Time:	Rep 5 Time:
Rep 6 Time:	Rep 7 Time:	Rep 8 Time:	Rep 9 Time:	Rep 10 Time:
Heart Rate Stress: Y / N	Rounds Per Rep:	Notes:		**All Rounds In: Y / N**

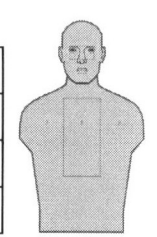

Date:	Location:	Weapon:	Holster:	Cover Garment: Y / N
Rep 1 Time:	Rep 2 Time:	Rep 3 Time:	Rep 4 Time:	Rep 5 Time:
Rep 6 Time:	Rep 7 Time:	Rep 8 Time:	Rep 9 Time:	Rep 10 Time:
Heart Rate Stress: Y / N	Rounds Per Rep:	Notes:		**All Rounds In: Y / N**

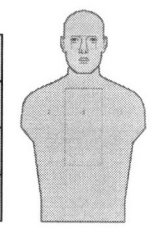

Date:	Location:	Weapon:	Holster:	Cover Garment: Y / N
Rep 1 Time:	Rep 2 Time:	Rep 3 Time:	Rep 4 Time:	Rep 5 Time:
Rep 6 Time:	Rep 7 Time:	Rep 8 Time:	Rep 9 Time:	Rep 10 Time:
Heart Rate Stress: Y / N	Rounds Per Rep:	Notes:		**All Rounds In: Y / N**

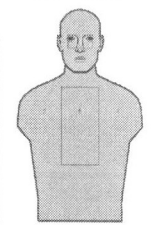

Date:	Location:	Weapon:	Holster:	Cover Garment: Y / N
Rep 1 Time:	Rep 2 Time:	Rep 3 Time:	Rep 4 Time:	Rep 5 Time:
Rep 6 Time:	Rep 7 Time:	Rep 8 Time:	Rep 9 Time:	Rep 10 Time:
Heart Rate Stress: Y / N	Rounds Per Rep:	Notes:		**All Rounds In: Y / N**

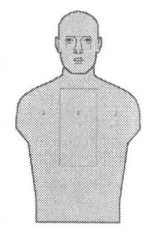

FRONTAL

Date:	Location:	Weapon:	Holster:	Cover Garment: Y / N
Rep 1 Time:	Rep 2 Time:	Rep 3 Time:	Rep 4 Time:	Rep 5 Time:
Rep 6 Time:	Rep 7 Time:	Rep 8 Time:	Rep 9 Time:	Rep 10 Time:
Heart Rate Stress: Y / N	Rounds Per Rep:	Notes:		**All Rounds In: Y / N**

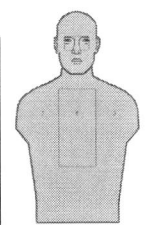

Date:	Location:	Weapon:	Holster:	Cover Garment: Y / N
Rep 1 Time:	Rep 2 Time:	Rep 3 Time:	Rep 4 Time:	Rep 5 Time:
Rep 6 Time:	Rep 7 Time:	Rep 8 Time:	Rep 9 Time:	Rep 10 Time:
Heart Rate Stress: Y / N	Rounds Per Rep:	Notes:		**All Rounds In: Y / N**

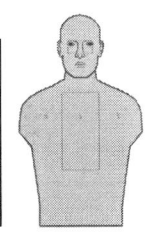

Date:	Location:	Weapon:	Holster:	Cover Garment: Y / N
Rep 1 Time:	Rep 2 Time:	Rep 3 Time:	Rep 4 Time:	Rep 5 Time:
Rep 6 Time:	Rep 7 Time:	Rep 8 Time:	Rep 9 Time:	Rep 10 Time:
Heart Rate Stress: Y / N	Rounds Per Rep:	Notes:		**All Rounds In: Y / N**

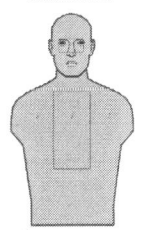

Date:	Location:	Weapon:	Holster:	Cover Garment: Y / N
Rep 1 Time:	Rep 2 Time:	Rep 3 Time:	Rep 4 Time:	Rep 5 Time:
Rep 6 Time:	Rep 7 Time:	Rep 8 Time:	Rep 9 Time:	Rep 10 Time:
Heart Rate Stress: Y / N	Rounds Per Rep:	Notes:		**All Rounds In: Y / N**

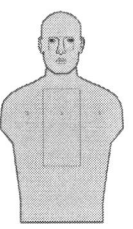

Draw Drills - 2

SIDE SHOT

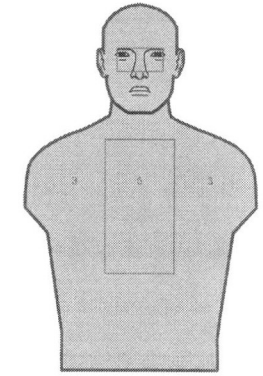

Purpose: Increase speed and accuracy with one-handed draw and shooting to the side.

Distance: 3 and 5 yards.

Target: JD-QUAL1

Par Time: 1.5 Seconds (3 yards) and 1.75 seconds (5 yards).

Extra Equipment Required: Shot timer.

Rounds Fired Per Rep: 1 Round.

Total Rounds Fired: 20 Rounds.

Point Penalty: Go / No Go.

Repetitions: 20 Reps.

Starting Position & Condition: Standing – Hands to side or interview. Weapon Condition 1.

Description: From 3 yards, face 90 degrees to your target with your left or right shoulder towards the target. At the timer beep, draw your pistol and fire 1 round into the (5 point) A Zone body box without moving your feet. Reset and repeat drill 5 times. Change your position 180 degrees so your other shoulder is facing the target, repeat drill 5 times. Move back to 5 yards and repeat sequence. If any rounds are over par time or are out of the (5 point) A Zone body box, the drill is a No Go.

Goal: 1.5 Seconds (3 yards) and 1.75 seconds (5 yards) with all rounds in body box.

Expert: 1.30 Seconds (3 yards) and 1.55 seconds (5 yards) with all rounds in body box.

Gunfighter: 1.1 Seconds (3 yards) and 1.40 seconds (5 yards) with all rounds in body box.

Variations: Immediately before the start of the drill, run 50 yards or do 2X25 yard shuttle runs, do 10 push-ups or 10 jumping jacks to get your heart rate up. Add shots to drill, with adding time for each shot at (base goal) .5 seconds (expert) .35 seconds (Gunfighter) .25 seconds. Wear a concealment over garment.

SIDE SHOT

Date:	Location:	Weapon:	Sights:	Holster:
Heart Rate Stress: Y / N	Rounds Per Rep:	Cover Garment: Y / N	Notes:	
3Y Left # Under Par:	3Y Right # Under Par:	5Y Left # Under Par:	5Y Right # Under Par:	Total # Under Par:
3Y Left: Go / No Go	3Y Right: Go / No Go	5Y Left: Go / No Go	5Y Right: Go / No Go	Total # in A Box:

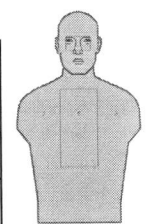

Date:	Location:	Weapon:	Sights:	Holster:
Heart Rate Stress: Y / N	Rounds Per Rep:	Cover Garment: Y / N	Notes:	
3Y Left # Under Par:	3Y Right # Under Par:	5Y Left # Under Par:	5Y Right # Under Par:	Total # Under Par:
3Y Left: Go / No Go	3Y Right: Go / No Go	5Y Left: Go / No Go	5Y Right: Go / No Go	Total # in A Box:

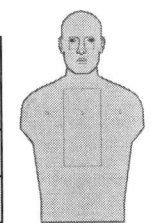

Date:	Location:	Weapon:	Sights:	Holster:
Heart Rate Stress: Y / N	Rounds Per Rep:	Cover Garment: Y / N	Notes:	
3Y Left # Under Par:	3Y Right # Under Par:	5Y Left # Under Par:	5Y Right # Under Par:	Total # Under Par:
3Y Left: Go / No Go	3Y Right: Go / No Go	5Y Left: Go / No Go	5Y Right: Go / No Go	Total # in A Box:

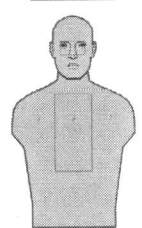

Date:	Location:	Weapon:	Sights:	Holster:
Heart Rate Stress: Y / N	Rounds Per Rep:	Cover Garment: Y / N	Notes:	
3Y Left # Under Par:	3Y Right # Under Par:	5Y Left # Under Par:	5Y Right # Under Par:	Total # Under Par:
3Y Left: Go / No Go	3Y Right: Go / No Go	5Y Left: Go / No Go	5Y Right: Go / No Go	Total # in A Box:

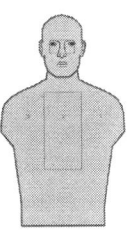

Advanced Pistol ©

SIDE SHOT

Date:	Location:	Weapon:	Sights:	Holster:
Heart Rate Stress: Y / N	Rounds Per Rep:	Cover Garment: Y / N	Notes:	
3Y Left # Under Par:	3Y Right # Under Par:	5Y Left # Under Par:	5Y Right # Under Par:	**Total # Under Par:**
3Y Left: Go / No Go	3Y Right: Go / No Go	5Y Left: Go / No Go	5Y Right: Go / No Go	**Total # in A Box:**

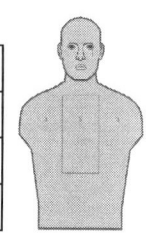

Date:	Location:	Weapon:	Sights:	Holster:
Heart Rate Stress: Y / N	Rounds Per Rep:	Cover Garment: Y / N	Notes:	
3Y Left # Under Par:	3Y Right # Under Par:	5Y Left # Under Par:	5Y Right # Under Par:	**Total # Under Par:**
3Y Left: Go / No Go	3Y Right: Go / No Go	5Y Left: Go / No Go	5Y Right: Go / No Go	**Total # in A Box:**

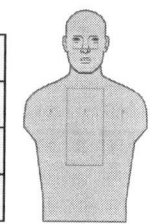

Date:	Location:	Weapon:	Sights:	Holster:
Heart Rate Stress: Y / N	Rounds Per Rep:	Cover Garment: Y / N	Notes:	
3Y Left # Under Par:	3Y Right # Under Par:	5Y Left # Under Par:	5Y Right # Under Par:	**Total # Under Par:**
3Y Left: Go / No Go	3Y Right: Go / No Go	5Y Left: Go / No Go	5Y Right: Go / No Go	**Total # in A Box:**

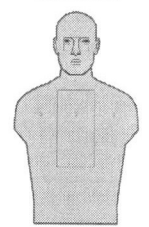

Date:	Location:	Weapon:	Sights:	Holster:
Heart Rate Stress: Y / N	Rounds Per Rep:	Cover Garment: Y / N	Notes:	
3Y Left # Under Par:	3Y Right # Under Par:	5Y Left # Under Par:	5Y Right # Under Par:	**Total # Under Par:**
3Y Left: Go / No Go	3Y Right: Go / No Go	5Y Left: Go / No Go	5Y Right: Go / No Go	**Total # in A Box:**

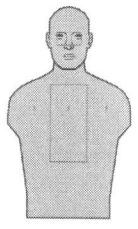

SIDE SHOT

Date:	Location:	Weapon:	Sights:	Holster:
Heart Rate Stress: Y / N	Rounds Per Rep:	Cover Garment: Y / N	Notes:	
3Y Left # Under Par:	3Y Right # Under Par:	5Y Left # Under Par:	5Y Right # Under Par:	**Total # Under Par:**
3Y Left: Go / No Go	3Y Right: Go / No Go	5Y Left: Go / No Go	5Y Right: Go / No Go	**Total # in A Box:**

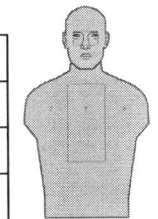

Date:	Location:	Weapon:	Sights:	Holster:
Heart Rate Stress: Y / N	Rounds Per Rep:	Cover Garment: Y / N	Notes:	
3Y Left # Under Par:	3Y Right # Under Par:	5Y Left # Under Par:	5Y Right # Under Par:	**Total # Under Par:**
3Y Left: Go / No Go	3Y Right: Go / No Go	5Y Left: Go / No Go	5Y Right: Go / No Go	**Total # in A Box:**

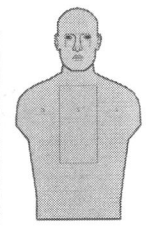

Date:	Location:	Weapon:	Sights:	Holster:
Heart Rate Stress: Y / N	Rounds Per Rep:	Cover Garment: Y / N	Notes:	
3Y Left # Under Par:	3Y Right # Under Par:	5Y Left # Under Par:	5Y Right # Under Par:	**Total # Under Par:**
3Y Left: Go / No Go	3Y Right: Go / No Go	5Y Left: Go / No Go	5Y Right: Go / No Go	**Total # in A Box:**

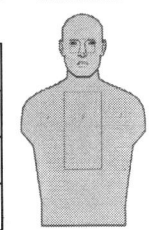

Date:	Location:	Weapon:	Sights:	Holster:
Heart Rate Stress: Y / N	Rounds Per Rep:	Cover Garment: Y / N	Notes:	
3Y Left # Under Par:	3Y Right # Under Par:	5Y Left # Under Par:	5Y Right # Under Par:	**Total # Under Par:**
3Y Left: Go / No Go	3Y Right: Go / No Go	5Y Left: Go / No Go	5Y Right: Go / No Go	**Total # in A Box:**

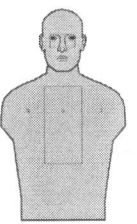

Advanced Pistol ©

SIDE SHOT

www.GUNFIGHTERSERIES.com ©

Date:	Location:	Weapon:	Sights:	Holster:	
Heart Rate Stress: Y / N	Rounds Per Rep:	Cover Garment: Y / N	Notes:		
3Y Left # Under Par:	3Y Right # Under Par:	5Y Left # Under Par:	5Y Right # Under Par:	**Total # Under Par:**	
3Y Left: Go / No Go	3Y Right: Go / No Go	5Y Left: Go / No Go	5Y Right: Go / No Go	**Total # in A Box:**	

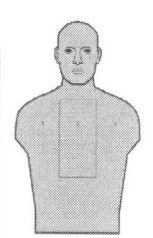

Date:	Location:	Weapon:	Sights:	Holster:
Heart Rate Stress: Y / N	Rounds Per Rep:	Cover Garment: Y / N	Notes:	
3Y Left # Under Par:	3Y Right # Under Par:	5Y Left # Under Par:	5Y Right # Under Par:	**Total # Under Par:**
3Y Left: Go / No Go	3Y Right: Go / No Go	5Y Left: Go / No Go	5Y Right: Go / No Go	**Total # in A Box:**

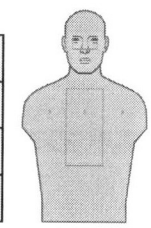

Date:	Location:	Weapon:	Sights:	Holster:
Heart Rate Stress: Y / N	Rounds Per Rep:	Cover Garment: Y / N	Notes:	
3Y Left # Under Par:	3Y Right # Under Par:	5Y Left # Under Par:	5Y Right # Under Par:	**Total # Under Par:**
3Y Left: Go / No Go	3Y Right: Go / No Go	5Y Left: Go / No Go	5Y Right: Go / No Go	**Total # in A Box:**

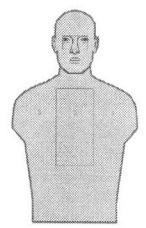

Date:	Location:	Weapon:	Sights:	Holster:
Heart Rate Stress: Y / N	Rounds Per Rep:	Cover Garment: Y / N	Notes:	
3Y Left # Under Par:	3Y Right # Under Par:	5Y Left # Under Par:	5Y Right # Under Par:	**Total # Under Par:**
3Y Left: Go / No Go	3Y Right: Go / No Go	5Y Left: Go / No Go	5Y Right: Go / No Go	**Total # in A Box:**

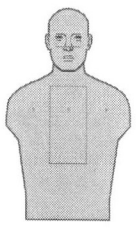

SIDE SHOT

Date:	Location:	Weapon:	Sights:	Holster:
Heart Rate Stress: Y / N	Rounds Per Rep:	Cover Garment: Y / N	Notes:	
3Y Left # Under Par:	3Y Right # Under Par:	5Y Left # Under Par:	5Y Right # Under Par:	**Total # Under Par:**
3Y Left: Go / No Go	3Y Right: Go / No Go	5Y Left: Go / No Go	5Y Right: Go / No Go	**Total # in A Box:**

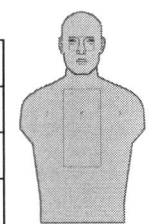

Date:	Location:	Weapon:	Sights:	Holster:
Heart Rate Stress: Y / N	Rounds Per Rep:	Cover Garment: Y / N	Notes:	
3Y Left # Under Par:	3Y Right # Under Par:	5Y Left # Under Par:	5Y Right # Under Par:	**Total # Under Par:**
3Y Left: Go / No Go	3Y Right: Go / No Go	5Y Left: Go / No Go	5Y Right: Go / No Go	**Total # in A Box:**

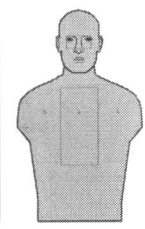

Date:	Location:	Weapon:	Sights:	Holster:
Heart Rate Stress: Y / N	Rounds Per Rep:	Cover Garment: Y / N	Notes:	
3Y Left # Under Par:	3Y Right # Under Par:	5Y Left # Under Par:	5Y Right # Under Par:	**Total # Under Par:**
3Y Left: Go / No Go	3Y Right: Go / No Go	5Y Left: Go / No Go	5Y Right: Go / No Go	**Total # in A Box:**

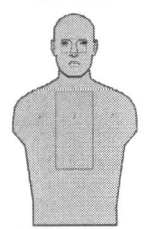

Date:	Location:	Weapon:	Sights:	Holster:
Heart Rate Stress: Y / N	Rounds Per Rep:	Cover Garment: Y / N	Notes:	
3Y Left # Under Par:	3Y Right # Under Par:	5Y Left # Under Par:	5Y Right # Under Par:	**Total # Under Par:**
3Y Left: Go / No Go	3Y Right: Go / No Go	5Y Left: Go / No Go	5Y Right: Go / No Go	**Total # in A Box:**

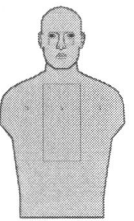

TURN LEFT - TURN RIGHT

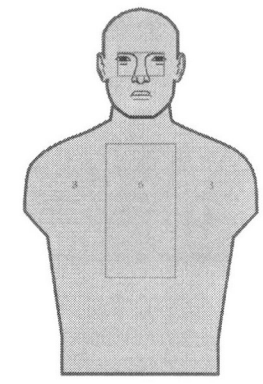

Purpose: Increase speed and accuracy with turning and shooting.

Distance: 7 Yards.

Target: JD-QUAL1

Par Time: 1.75 Seconds.

Extra Equipment Required: Shot timer.

Rounds Fired Per Rep: 1 Round.

Total Rounds Fired: 10 Rounds.

Point Penalty: Go / No Go.

Repetitions: 10 Reps (5 Each direction).

Starting Position & Condition: Standing – Hands to side or interview. Weapon Condition 1.

Description: Face 90 degrees to your target with your left or right shoulder towards the target. At the timer beep, look in the direction you are going to turn, pivot on the ball of your foot and move until you are squared up facing the target. Once you have made your turn, draw your pistol, fire 1 round into the (5 point) A Zone body box. Repeat this drill in each direction 5 times.

Goal: The goal of this drill is to be smooth and deliberate within a par time of 1.75 seconds with all rounds in the body box.

Variations: Use each of the ready positions instead of a draw. Take care you do not break firearm safety rules and point your weapon at anyone or anything you do not wish to destroy. If your ready position is going to sweep a person or point in an unsafe direction, do not perform that ready position during the drill. Immediately before the start of the drill, run 50 yards or do 2X25 yard shuttle runs, do 10 push-ups or 10 jumping jacks to get your heart rate up. Add shots to drill, with adding time for each shot at (base goal) .5 seconds (expert) .35 seconds (Gunfighter) .25 seconds.

TURN LEFT - TURN RIGHT

Date:	Weapon:	Holster:	Starting Position:	
Heart Rate Stress: Y / N	Rounds Per Rep:	Turning Left	# Under Par:	# In A Box:
Notes:		Turning Right	# Under Par:	# In A Box:

Date:	Weapon:	Holster:	Starting Position:	
Heart Rate Stress: Y / N	Rounds Per Rep:	Turning Left	# Under Par:	# In A Box:
Notes:		Turning Right	# Under Par:	# In A Box:

Date:	Weapon:	Holster:	Starting Position:	
Heart Rate Stress: Y / N	Rounds Per Rep:	Turning Left	# Under Par:	# In A Box:
Notes:		Turning Right	# Under Par:	# In A Box:

Date:	Weapon:	Holster:	Starting Position:	
Heart Rate Stress: Y / N	Rounds Per Rep:	Turning Left	# Under Par:	# In A Box:
Notes:		Turning Right	# Under Par:	# In A Box:

Date:	Weapon:	Holster:	Starting Position:	
Heart Rate Stress: Y / N	Rounds Per Rep:	Turning Left	# Under Par:	# In A Box:
Notes:		Turning Right	# Under Par:	# In A Box:

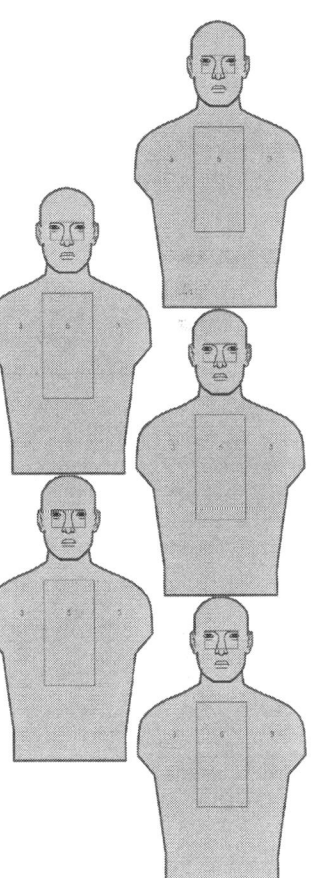

Advanced Pistol ©

TURN LEFT - TURN RIGHT

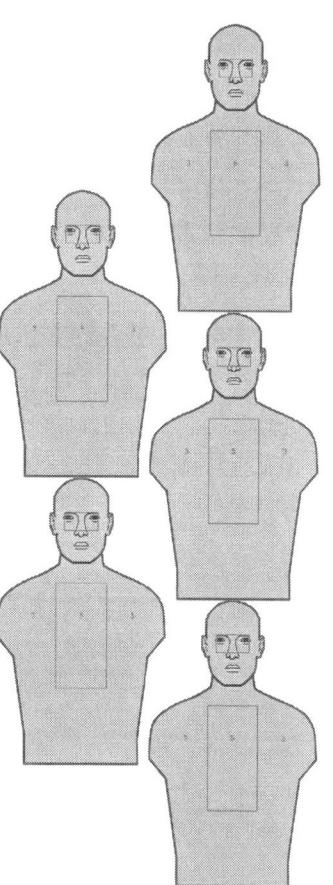

Date:		Weapon:		Holster:		Starting Position:		
Heart Rate Stress: Y / N		Rounds Per Rep:		Turning Left		# Under Par:		# In A Box:
Notes:				Turning Right		# Under Par:		# In A Box:

Date:		Weapon:		Holster:		Starting Position:		
Heart Rate Stress: Y / N		Rounds Per Rep:		Turning Left		# Under Par:		# In A Box:
Notes:				Turning Right		# Under Par:		# In A Box:

Date:		Weapon:		Holster:		Starting Position:		
Heart Rate Stress: Y / N		Rounds Per Rep:		Turning Left		# Under Par:		# In A Box:
Notes:				Turning Right		# Under Par:		# In A Box:

Date:		Weapon:		Holster:		Starting Position:		
Heart Rate Stress: Y / N		Rounds Per Rep:		Turning Left		# Under Par:		# In A Box:
Notes:				Turning Right		# Under Par:		# In A Box:

Date:		Weapon:		Holster:		Starting Position:		
Heart Rate Stress: Y / N		Rounds Per Rep:		Turning Left		# Under Par:		# In A Box:
Notes:				Turning Right		# Under Par:		# In A Box:

TURN LEFT - TURN RIGHT

Date:	Weapon:	Holster:	Starting Position:		
Heart Rate Stress: Y / N	Rounds Per Rep:	Turning Left	# Under Par:	# In A Box:	
Notes:		Turning Right	# Under Par:	# In A Box:	

Date:	Weapon:	Holster:	Starting Position:		
Heart Rate Stress: Y / N	Rounds Per Rep:	Turning Left	# Under Par:	# In A Box:	
Notes:		Turning Right	# Under Par:	# In A Box:	

Date:	Weapon:	Holster:	Starting Position:		
Heart Rate Stress: Y / N	Rounds Per Rep:	Turning Left	# Under Par:	# In A Box:	
Notes:		Turning Right	# Under Par:	# In A Box:	

Date:	Weapon:	Holster:	Starting Position:		
Heart Rate Stress: Y / N	Rounds Per Rep:	Turning Left	# Under Par:	# In A Box:	
Notes:		Turning Right	# Under Par:	# In A Box:	

Date:	Weapon:	Holster:	Starting Position:		
Heart Rate Stress: Y / N	Rounds Per Rep:	Turning Left	# Under Par:	# In A Box:	
Notes:		Turning Right	# Under Par:	# In A Box:	

Advanced Pistol ©

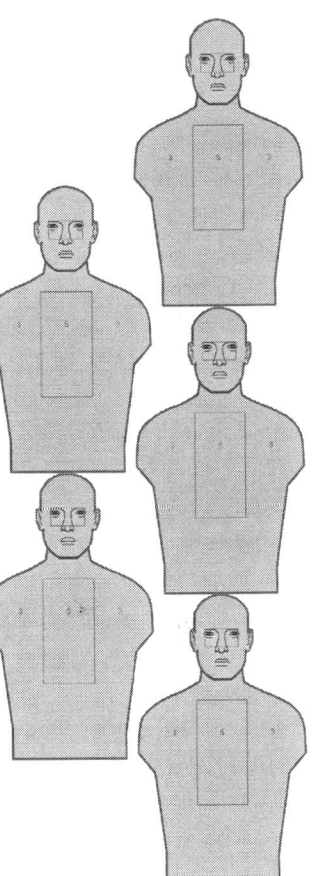

TURN LEFT - TURN RIGHT

Date:		Weapon:		Holster:		Starting Position:		
Heart Rate Stress: Y / N		Rounds Per Rep:		Turning Left		# Under Par:		# In A Box:
Notes:				Turning Right		# Under Par:		# In A Box:

Date:		Weapon:		Holster:		Starting Position:		
Heart Rate Stress: Y / N		Rounds Per Rep:		Turning Left		# Under Par:		# In A Box:
Notes:				Turning Right		# Under Par:		# In A Box:

Date:		Weapon:		Holster:		Starting Position:		
Heart Rate Stress: Y / N		Rounds Per Rep:		Turning Left		# Under Par:		# In A Box:
Notes:				Turning Right		# Under Par:		# In A Box:

Date:		Weapon:		Holster:		Starting Position:		
Heart Rate Stress: Y / N		Rounds Per Rep:		Turning Left		# Under Par:		# In A Box:
Notes:				Turning Right		# Under Par:		# In A Box:

Date:		Weapon:		Holster:		Starting Position:		
Heart Rate Stress: Y / N		Rounds Per Rep:		Turning Left		# Under Par:		# In A Box:
Notes:				Turning Right		# Under Par:		# In A Box:

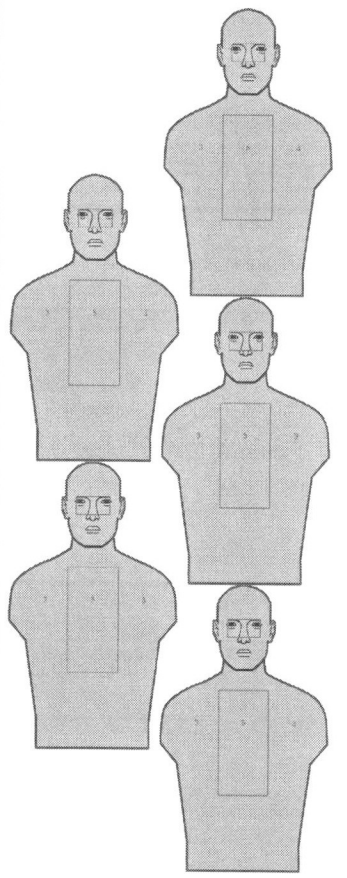

TURN LEFT - TURN RIGHT

Date:	Weapon:	Holster:	Starting Position:	
Heart Rate Stress: Y / N	Rounds Per Rep:	Turning Left	# Under Par:	# In A Box:
Notes:		Turning Right	# Under Par:	# In A Box:

Date:	Weapon:	Holster:	Starting Position:	
Heart Rate Stress: Y / N	Rounds Per Rep:	Turning Left	# Under Par:	# In A Box:
Notes:		Turning Right	# Under Par:	# In A Box:

Date:	Weapon:	Holster:	Starting Position:	
Heart Rate Stress: Y / N	Rounds Per Rep:	Turning Left	# Under Par:	# In A Box:
Notes:		Turning Right	# Under Par:	# In A Box:

Date:	Weapon:	Holster:	Starting Position:	
Heart Rate Stress: Y / N	Rounds Per Rep:	Turning Left	# Under Par:	# In A Box:
Notes:		Turning Right	# Under Par:	# In A Box:

Date:	Weapon:	Holster:	Starting Position:	
Heart Rate Stress: Y / N	Rounds Per Rep:	Turning Left	# Under Par:	# In A Box:
Notes:		Turning Right	# Under Par:	# In A Box:

Advanced Pistol ©

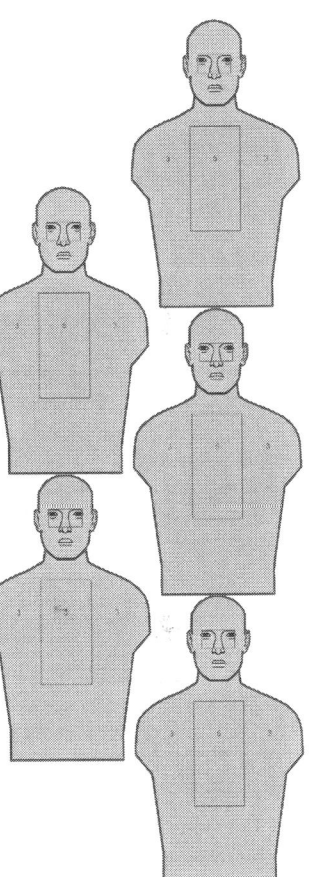

IN A WORLD OF HURT

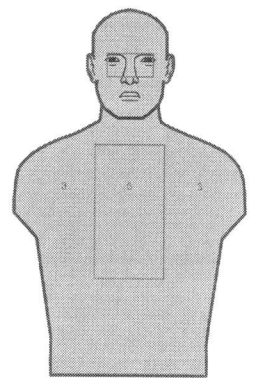

Purpose: Increase nervous system memory ability of an efficient support one-handed draw.

Distance: 10 Yards.

Target: JD-QUAL1

Extra Equipment Required: Shot timer.

Rounds Fired Per Rep: 2 Rounds.

Total Rounds Fired: 10 Rounds.

Point Penalty: Go / No Go.

Repetitions: 5 Reps.

Starting Position & Condition: Standing – Hands to side or interview. Weapon Condition 1.

Description: At the timer beep, reach across your body and draw your pistol using only your support hand on the pistol grip. Keep all fingers and your thumb out of the trigger guard and off the trigger. Bring your pistol between your knees and trap the slide between your knees. Let go of the pistol grip and rotate your hand so you can secure a good grip hand position with your support hand. Bring the pistol up to aim at target, aim, fire 2 rounds into the (5 point) A Zone body box. While you are performing this first motion, let your dominant arm hang, then when bringing the pistol up on target, pin your dominant arm to your dominant side. Make sure you are aware of the muzzle direction at all times and make sure you never point your pistol at anything you do not intend to destroy. Make sure not to point your pistol at your feet. Practicing firearm safety is a major facet to this drill during live fire. Record your time and score. Reset and repeat drill 5 times. Any rounds out of the body box makes the drill a No Go.

Goal: To be safe, smooth and deliberate with a support one-handed draw and all rounds within the (5 point) A Zone body box.

Variations: Set up a barrier at least 3 yards away and move to cover before drawing your pistol when the timer beep goes off. Add rounds and keep that same round count per rep.

IN A WORLD OF HURT

Date:	Location:	Weapon:	Holster:	Move To Cover: Y / N
Rep 1 Time:	Rep 2 Time:	Rep 3 Time:	Rep 4 Time:	Rep 5 Time:
Rep 1: Go / No Go	Rep 2: Go / No Go	Rep 3: Go / No Go	Rep 4: Go / No Go	Rep 5: Go / No Go
Rounds Per Rep:	Notes:			**All Rounds In: Y / N**

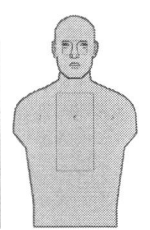

Date:	Location:	Weapon:	Holster:	Move To Cover: Y / N
Rep 1 Time:	Rep 2 Time:	Rep 3 Time:	Rep 4 Time:	Rep 5 Time:
Rep 1: Go / No Go	Rep 2: Go / No Go	Rep 3: Go / No Go	Rep 4: Go / No Go	Rep 5: Go / No Go
Rounds Per Rep:	Notes:			**All Rounds In: Y / N**

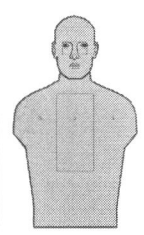

Date:	Location:	Weapon:	Holster:	Move To Cover: Y / N
Rep 1 Time:	Rep 2 Time:	Rep 3 Time:	Rep 4 Time:	Rep 5 Time:
Rep 1: Go / No Go	Rep 2: Go / No Go	Rep 3: Go / No Go	Rep 4: Go / No Go	Rep 5: Go / No Go
Rounds Per Rep:	Notes:			**All Rounds In: Y / N**

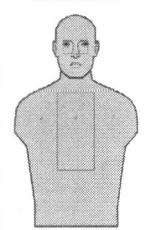

Date:	Location:	Weapon:	Holster:	Move To Cover: Y / N
Rep 1 Time:	Rep 2 Time:	Rep 3 Time:	Rep 4 Time:	Rep 5 Time:
Rep 1: Go / No Go	Rep 2: Go / No Go	Rep 3: Go / No Go	Rep 4: Go / No Go	Rep 5: Go / No Go
Rounds Per Rep:	Notes:			**All Rounds In: Y / N**

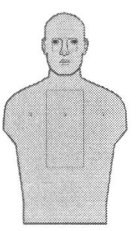

Advanced Pistol ©

IN A WORLD OF HURT

Date:	Location:	Weapon:	Holster:	Move To Cover: Y / N
Rep 1 Time:	Rep 2 Time:	Rep 3 Time:	Rep 4 Time:	Rep 5 Time:
Rep 1: Go / No Go	Rep 2: Go / No Go	Rep 3: Go / No Go	Rep 4: Go / No Go	Rep 5: Go / No Go
Rounds Per Rep:	Notes:			**All Rounds In: Y / N**

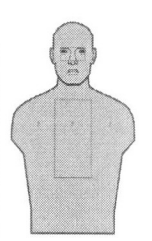

Date:	Location:	Weapon:	Holster:	Move To Cover: Y / N
Rep 1 Time:	Rep 2 Time:	Rep 3 Time:	Rep 4 Time:	Rep 5 Time:
Rep 1: Go / No Go	Rep 2: Go / No Go	Rep 3: Go / No Go	Rep 4: Go / No Go	Rep 5: Go / No Go
Rounds Per Rep:	Notes:			**All Rounds In: Y / N**

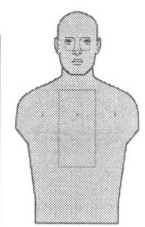

Date:	Location:	Weapon:	Holster:	Move To Cover: Y / N
Rep 1 Time:	Rep 2 Time:	Rep 3 Time:	Rep 4 Time:	Rep 5 Time:
Rep 1: Go / No Go	Rep 2: Go / No Go	Rep 3: Go / No Go	Rep 4: Go / No Go	Rep 5: Go / No Go
Rounds Per Rep:	Notes:			**All Rounds In: Y / N**

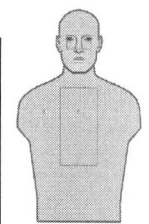

Date:	Location:	Weapon:	Holster:	Move To Cover: Y / N
Rep 1 Time:	Rep 2 Time:	Rep 3 Time:	Rep 4 Time:	Rep 5 Time:
Rep 1: Go / No Go	Rep 2: Go / No Go	Rep 3: Go / No Go	Rep 4: Go / No Go	Rep 5: Go / No Go
Rounds Per Rep:	Notes:			**All Rounds In: Y / N**

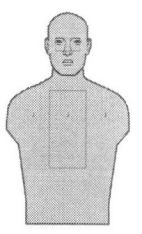

IN A WORLD OF HURT

Date:	Location:	Weapon:	Holster:	Move To Cover: Y / N
Rep 1 Time:	Rep 2 Time:	Rep 3 Time:	Rep 4 Time:	Rep 5 Time:
Rep 1: Go / No Go	Rep 2: Go / No Go	Rep 3: Go / No Go	Rep 4: Go / No Go	Rep 5: Go / No Go
Rounds Per Rep:	Notes:			All Rounds In: Y / N

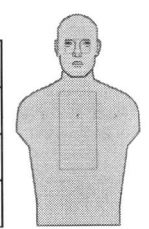

Date:	Location:	Weapon:	Holster:	Move To Cover: Y / N
Rep 1 Time:	Rep 2 Time:	Rep 3 Time:	Rep 4 Time:	Rep 5 Time:
Rep 1: Go / No Go	Rep 2: Go / No Go	Rep 3: Go / No Go	Rep 4: Go / No Go	Rep 5: Go / No Go
Rounds Per Rep:	Notes:			All Rounds In: Y / N

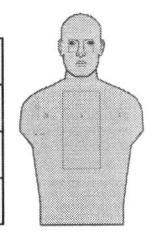

Date:	Location:	Weapon:	Holster:	Move To Cover: Y / N
Rep 1 Time:	Rep 2 Time:	Rep 3 Time:	Rep 4 Time:	Rep 5 Time:
Rep 1: Go / No Go	Rep 2: Go / No Go	Rep 3: Go / No Go	Rep 4: Go / No Go	Rep 5: Go / No Go
Rounds Per Rep:	Notes:			All Rounds In: Y / N

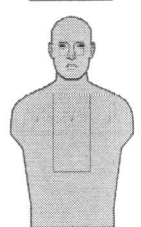

Date:	Location:	Weapon:	Holster:	Move To Cover: Y / N
Rep 1 Time:	Rep 2 Time:	Rep 3 Time:	Rep 4 Time:	Rep 5 Time:
Rep 1: Go / No Go	Rep 2: Go / No Go	Rep 3: Go / No Go	Rep 4: Go / No Go	Rep 5: Go / No Go
Rounds Per Rep:	Notes:			All Rounds In: Y / N

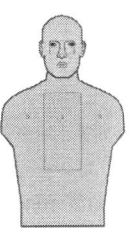

Advanced Pistol ©

IN A WORLD OF HURT

Date:	Location:	Weapon:	Holster:	Move To Cover: Y / N
Rep 1 Time:	Rep 2 Time:	Rep 3 Time:	Rep 4 Time:	Rep 5 Time:
Rep 1: Go / No Go	Rep 2: Go / No Go	Rep 3: Go / No Go	Rep 4: Go / No Go	Rep 5: Go / No Go
Rounds Per Rep:	Notes:			All Rounds In: Y / N

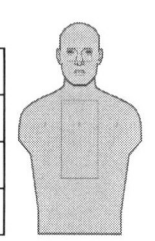

Date:	Location:	Weapon:	Holster:	Move To Cover: Y / N
Rep 1 Time:	Rep 2 Time:	Rep 3 Time:	Rep 4 Time:	Rep 5 Time:
Rep 1: Go / No Go	Rep 2: Go / No Go	Rep 3: Go / No Go	Rep 4: Go / No Go	Rep 5: Go / No Go
Rounds Per Rep:	Notes:			All Rounds In: Y / N

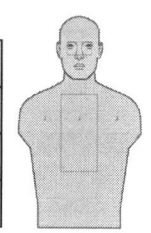

Date:	Location:	Weapon:	Holster:	Move To Cover: Y / N
Rep 1 Time:	Rep 2 Time:	Rep 3 Time:	Rep 4 Time:	Rep 5 Time:
Rep 1: Go / No Go	Rep 2: Go / No Go	Rep 3: Go / No Go	Rep 4: Go / No Go	Rep 5: Go / No Go
Rounds Per Rep:	Notes:			All Rounds In: Y / N

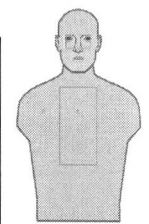

Date:	Location:	Weapon:	Holster:	Move To Cover: Y / N
Rep 1 Time:	Rep 2 Time:	Rep 3 Time:	Rep 4 Time:	Rep 5 Time:
Rep 1: Go / No Go	Rep 2: Go / No Go	Rep 3: Go / No Go	Rep 4: Go / No Go	Rep 5: Go / No Go
Rounds Per Rep:	Notes:			All Rounds In: Y / N

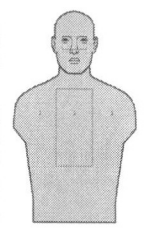

IN A WORLD OF HURT

Date:	Location:	Weapon:	Holster:	Move To Cover: Y / N
Rep 1 Time:	Rep 2 Time:	Rep 3 Time:	Rep 4 Time:	Rep 5 Time:
Rep 1: Go / No Go	Rep 2: Go / No Go	Rep 3: Go / No Go	Rep 4: Go / No Go	Rep 5: Go / No Go
Rounds Per Rep:	Notes:			All Rounds In: Y / N

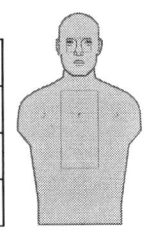

Date:	Location:	Weapon:	Holster:	Move To Cover: Y / N
Rep 1 Time:	Rep 2 Time:	Rep 3 Time:	Rep 4 Time:	Rep 5 Time:
Rep 1: Go / No Go	Rep 2: Go / No Go	Rep 3: Go / No Go	Rep 4: Go / No Go	Rep 5: Go / No Go
Rounds Per Rep:	Notes:			All Rounds In: Y / N

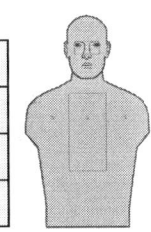

Date:	Location:	Weapon:	Holster:	Move To Cover: Y / N
Rep 1 Time:	Rep 2 Time:	Rep 3 Time:	Rep 4 Time:	Rep 5 Time:
Rep 1: Go / No Go	Rep 2: Go / No Go	Rep 3: Go / No Go	Rep 4: Go / No Go	Rep 5: Go / No Go
Rounds Per Rep:	Notes:			All Rounds In: Y / N

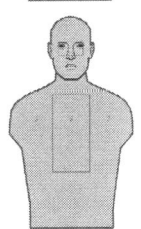

Date:	Location:	Weapon:	Holster:	Move To Cover: Y / N
Rep 1 Time:	Rep 2 Time:	Rep 3 Time:	Rep 4 Time:	Rep 5 Time:
Rep 1: Go / No Go	Rep 2: Go / No Go	Rep 3: Go / No Go	Rep 4: Go / No Go	Rep 5: Go / No Go
Rounds Per Rep:	Notes:			All Rounds In: Y / N

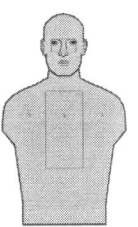

Advanced Pistol ©

DOUBLE KNEELING

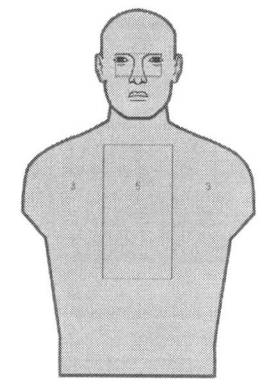

Purpose: Develop efficiency and accuracy using the double kneeling position.

Distance: 25 Yards.

Target: JD-QUAL1

Par Time: 15 Seconds.

Extra Equipment Required: Shot timer.

Rounds Fired Per Rep: 5 Rounds.

Total Rounds Fired: 15 Rounds.

Point Penalty: Time plus time penalties.

Repetitions: 3 Reps.

Starting Position & Condition: Standing – Surrender / Interview. Weapon Condition 1.

Description: At the timer beep, draw your pistol, take up a good double kneeling position and fire 5 rounds into the (5 point) A Zone body box. Put pistol on safe if applicable and stand up safely, while keeping the pistol pointed downrange. Once standing, holster pistol. Record time. Repeat drill 2 more times. Record time plus time penalties. For every hit in the 3 scoring zone, add 2 seconds to your time. For every hit in the 0 scoring zone, add 5 seconds to your time.

The double kneeling position is where you are kneeling on both of your knees. You may or may not be placing your butt on top of your heels, depending on the cover you are using in a real-life situation, practice both. As you become more familiar with the double kneeling position, your times will decrease, and your accuracy will increase.

Goal: 65 Seconds.   **Expert:** 55 Seconds.   **Gunfighter:** 45 Seconds.

Variations: Add distance or lower your personal par time.

DOUBLE KNEELING

Date:	Weapon:	Sights:	Holster:
Rep 1 Time:	Rep 2 Time:	Rep 3 Time:	Notes:
Combined Time:	+ Penalties:	**Total Time Score:**	

Date:	Weapon:	Sights:	Holster:
Rep 1 Time:	Rep 2 Time:	Rep 3 Time:	Notes:
Combined Time:	+ Penalties:	**Total Time Score:**	

Date:	Weapon:	Sights:	Holster:
Rep 1 Time:	Rep 2 Time:	Rep 3 Time:	Notes:
Combined Time:	+ Penalties:	**Total Time Score:**	

Date:	Weapon:	Sights:	Holster:
Rep 1 Time:	Rep 2 Time:	Rep 3 Time:	Notes:
Combined Time:	+ Penalties:	**Total Time Score:**	

Date:	Weapon:	Sights:	Holster:
Rep 1 Time:	Rep 2 Time:	Rep 3 Time:	Notes:
Combined Time:	+ Penalties:	**Total Time Score:**	

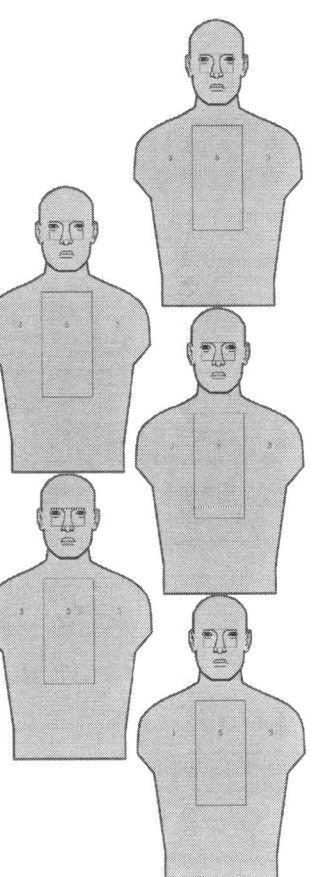

Advanced Pistol ©

DOUBLE KNEELING

Date:	Weapon:	Sights:	Holster:
Rep 1 Time:	Rep 2 Time:	Rep 3 Time:	Notes:
Combined Time:	+ Penalties:	**Total Time Score:**	

Date:	Weapon:	Sights:	Holster:
Rep 1 Time:	Rep 2 Time:	Rep 3 Time:	Notes:
Combined Time:	+ Penalties:	**Total Time Score:**	

Date:	Weapon:	Sights:	Holster:
Rep 1 Time:	Rep 2 Time:	Rep 3 Time:	Notes:
Combined Time:	+ Penalties:	**Total Time Score:**	

Date:	Weapon:	Sights:	Holster:
Rep 1 Time:	Rep 2 Time:	Rep 3 Time:	Notes:
Combined Time:	+ Penalties:	**Total Time Score:**	

Date:	Weapon:	Sights:	Holster:
Rep 1 Time:	Rep 2 Time:	Rep 3 Time:	Notes:
Combined Time:	+ Penalties:	**Total Time Score:**	

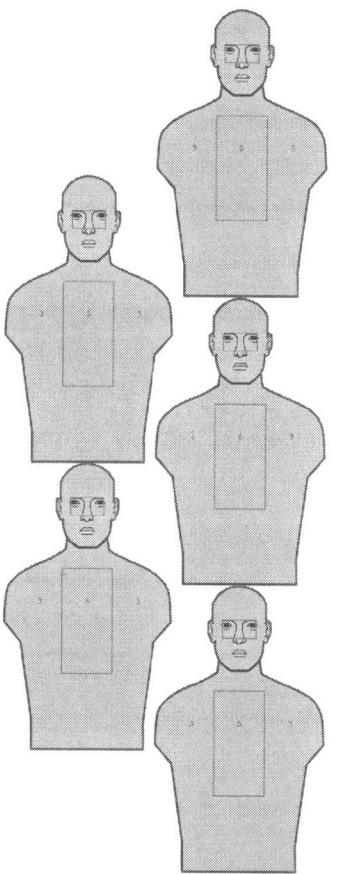

DOUBLE KNEELING

Date:	Weapon:	Sights:	Holster:
Rep 1 Time:	Rep 2 Time:	Rep 3 Time:	Notes:
Combined Time:	+ Penalties:	**Total Time Score:**	

Date:	Weapon:	Sights:	Holster:
Rep 1 Time:	Rep 2 Time:	Rep 3 Time:	Notes:
Combined Time:	+ Penalties:	**Total Time Score:**	

Date:	Weapon:	Sights:	Holster:
Rep 1 Time:	Rep 2 Time:	Rep 3 Time:	Notes:
Combined Time:	+ Penalties:	**Total Time Score:**	

Date:	Weapon:	Sights:	Holster:
Rep 1 Time:	Rep 2 Time:	Rep 3 Time:	Notes:
Combined Time:	+ Penalties:	**Total Time Score:**	

Date:	Weapon:	Sights:	Holster:
Rep 1 Time:	Rep 2 Time:	Rep 3 Time:	Notes:
Combined Time:	+ Penalties:	**Total Time Score:**	

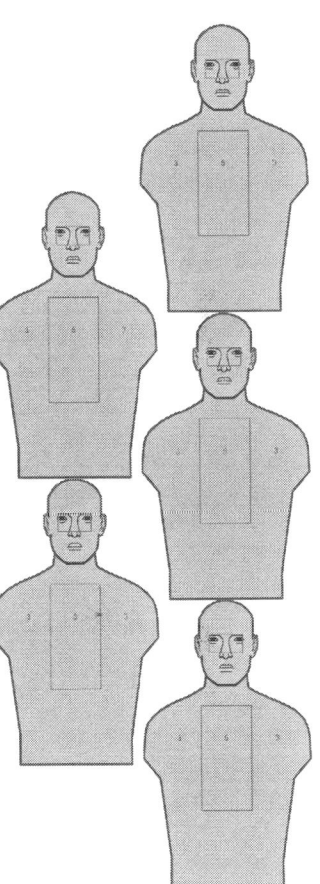

Positional Drills - 1

DOUBLE KNEELING

Date:	Weapon:	Sights:	Holster:
Rep 1 Time:	Rep 2 Time:	Rep 3 Time:	Notes:
Combined Time:	+ Penalties:	**Total Time Score:**	

Date:	Weapon:	Sights:	Holster:
Rep 1 Time:	Rep 2 Time:	Rep 3 Time:	Notes:
Combined Time:	+ Penalties:	**Total Time Score:**	

Date:	Weapon:	Sights:	Holster:
Rep 1 Time:	Rep 2 Time:	Rep 3 Time:	Notes:
Combined Time:	+ Penalties:	**Total Time Score:**	

Date:	Weapon:	Sights:	Holster:
Rep 1 Time:	Rep 2 Time:	Rep 3 Time:	Notes:
Combined Time:	+ Penalties:	**Total Time Score:**	

Date:	Weapon:	Sights:	Holster:
Rep 1 Time:	Rep 2 Time:	Rep 3 Time:	Notes:
Combined Time:	+ Penalties:	**Total Time Score:**	

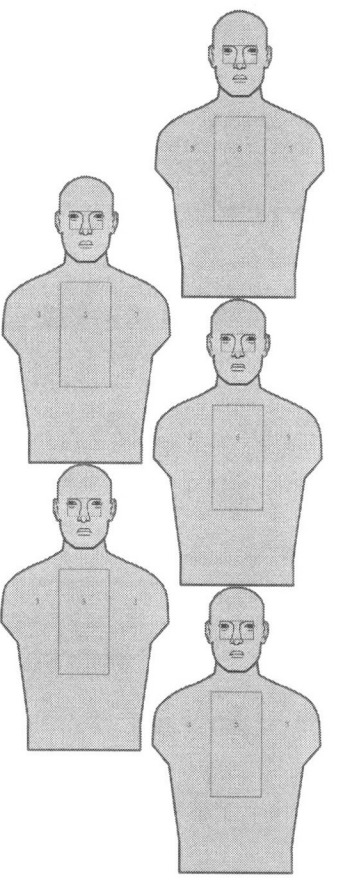

DOUBLE KNEELING

Date:	Weapon:	Sights:	Holster:
Rep 1 Time:	Rep 2 Time:	Rep 3 Time:	Notes:
Combined Time:	+ Penalties:	**Total Time Score:**	

Date:	Weapon:	Sights:	Holster:
Rep 1 Time:	Rep 2 Time:	Rep 3 Time:	Notes:
Combined Time:	+ Penalties:	**Total Time Score:**	

Date:	Weapon:	Sights:	Holster:
Rep 1 Time:	Rep 2 Time:	Rep 3 Time:	Notes:
Combined Time:	+ Penalties:	**Total Time Score:**	

Date:	Weapon:	Sights:	Holster:
Rep 1 Time:	Rep 2 Time:	Rep 3 Time:	Notes:
Combined Time:	+ Penalties:	**Total Time Score:**	

Date:	Weapon:	Sights:	Holster:
Rep 1 Time:	Rep 2 Time:	Rep 3 Time:	Notes:
Combined Time:	+ Penalties:	**Total Time Score:**	

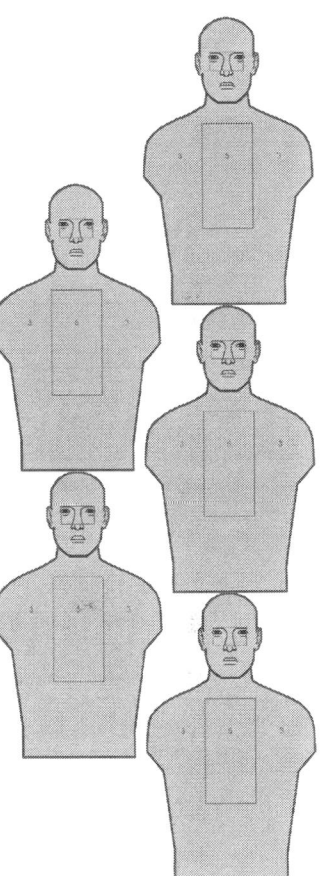

SUPINE

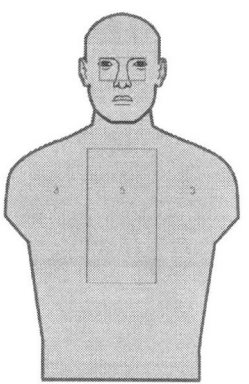

Purpose: Develop efficiency and accuracy using the supine position.

Distance: 7 Yards.

Target: JD-QUAL1

Extra Equipment Required: Shot timer.

Rounds Fired Per Rep: 5 Rounds.

Total Rounds Fired: 15 Rounds.

Point Penalty: Go / No Go.

Repetitions: 3 Reps.

Starting Position & Condition: Sitting with feet extended to the front – Surrender. Weapon Condition 1.

Description: At the timer beep, lean back so you are in a reclined position, rotate your toes away from your holster side and lean to clear your holster, draw your pistol, rotate your feet so they are pointing outboard, aim and fire 3 rounds into the (5 point) A Zone body box and 2 rounds into the (5 point) A Zone head box. Put pistol on safe if applicable and stand up safely, while keeping the pistol pointed downrange. Once standing, holster pistol. Record time. Repeat drill 2 more times. All rounds must be in or touching the (5 point) A Zone boxes for the drill to be a go. Make sure your rounds have a back stop and are not being shot up in the air.

The supine position is where you are laying on your back with your chest raised up enough that you can shoot at the target safely, without shooting any of your body parts. As you become more familiar with the supine position, your times will decrease, and your accuracy will increase.

Variations: Add distance. Try Head A Zone Box, if you have a tall enough impact berm behind the target.

SUPINE

Date:	Weapon:	Sights:	Holster:	Distance:
Rep 1 Time:	Rep 2 Time:	Rep 3 Time:	Head / Body	Notes:
Rep 1: Go / No Go	Rep 2: Go / No Go	Rep 3: Go / No Go	All In: Y / N	

Date:	Weapon:	Sights:	Holster:	Distance:
Rep 1 Time:	Rep 2 Time:	Rep 3 Time:	Head / Body	Notes:
Rep 1: Go / No Go	Rep 2: Go / No Go	Rep 3: Go / No Go	All In: Y / N	

Date:	Weapon:	Sights:	Holster:	Distance:
Rep 1 Time:	Rep 2 Time:	Rep 3 Time:	Head / Body	Notes:
Rep 1: Go / No Go	Rep 2: Go / No Go	Rep 3: Go / No Go	All In: Y / N	

Date:	Weapon:	Sights:	Holster:	Distance:
Rep 1 Time:	Rep 2 Time:	Rep 3 Time:	Head / Body	Notes:
Rep 1: Go / No Go	Rep 2: Go / No Go	Rep 3: Go / No Go	All In: Y / N	

Date:	Weapon:	Sights:	Holster:	Distance:
Rep 1 Time:	Rep 2 Time:	Rep 3 Time:	Head / Body	Notes:
Rep 1: Go / No Go	Rep 2: Go / No Go	Rep 3: Go / No Go	All In: Y / N	

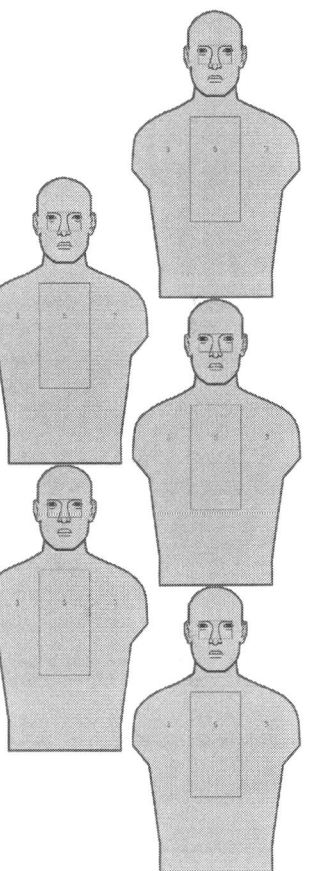

Advanced Pistol ©

SUPINE

Date:	Weapon:	Sights:	Holster:	Distance:
Rep 1 Time:	Rep 2 Time:	Rep 3 Time:	Head / Body	Notes:
Rep 1: Go / No Go	Rep 2: Go / No Go	Rep 3: Go / No Go	All In: Y / N	

Date:	Weapon:	Sights:	Holster:	Distance:
Rep 1 Time:	Rep 2 Time:	Rep 3 Time:	Head / Body	Notes:
Rep 1: Go / No Go	Rep 2: Go / No Go	Rep 3: Go / No Go	All In: Y / N	

Date:	Weapon:	Sights:	Holster:	Distance:
Rep 1 Time:	Rep 2 Time:	Rep 3 Time:	Head / Body	Notes:
Rep 1: Go / No Go	Rep 2: Go / No Go	Rep 3: Go / No Go	All In: Y / N	

Date:	Weapon:	Sights:	Holster:	Distance:
Rep 1 Time:	Rep 2 Time:	Rep 3 Time:	Head / Body	Notes:
Rep 1: Go / No Go	Rep 2: Go / No Go	Rep 3: Go / No Go	All In: Y / N	

Date:	Weapon:	Sights:	Holster:	Distance:
Rep 1 Time:	Rep 2 Time:	Rep 3 Time:	Head / Body	Notes:
Rep 1: Go / No Go	Rep 2: Go / No Go	Rep 3: Go / No Go	All In: Y / N	

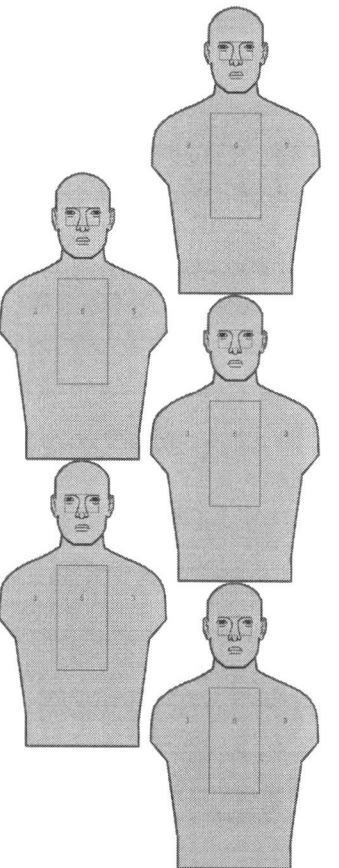

SUPINE

Date:	Weapon:	Sights:	Holster:	Distance:
Rep 1 Time:	Rep 2 Time:	Rep 3 Time:	Head / Body	Notes:
Rep 1: Go / No Go	Rep 2: Go / No Go	Rep 3: Go / No Go	**All In: Y / N**	

Date:	Weapon:	Sights:	Holster:	Distance:
Rep 1 Time:	Rep 2 Time:	Rep 3 Time:	Head / Body	Notes:
Rep 1: Go / No Go	Rep 2: Go / No Go	Rep 3: Go / No Go	**All In: Y / N**	

Date:	Weapon:	Sights:	Holster:	Distance:
Rep 1 Time:	Rep 2 Time:	Rep 3 Time:	Head / Body	Notes:
Rep 1: Go / No Go	Rep 2: Go / No Go	Rep 3: Go / No Go	**All In: Y / N**	

Date:	Weapon:	Sights:	Holster:	Distance:
Rep 1 Time:	Rep 2 Time:	Rep 3 Time:	Head / Body	Notes:
Rep 1: Go / No Go	Rep 2: Go / No Go	Rep 3: Go / No Go	**All In: Y / N**	

Date:	Weapon:	Sights:	Holster:	Distance:
Rep 1 Time:	Rep 2 Time:	Rep 3 Time:	Head / Body	Notes:
Rep 1: Go / No Go	Rep 2: Go / No Go	Rep 3: Go / No Go	**All In: Y / N**	

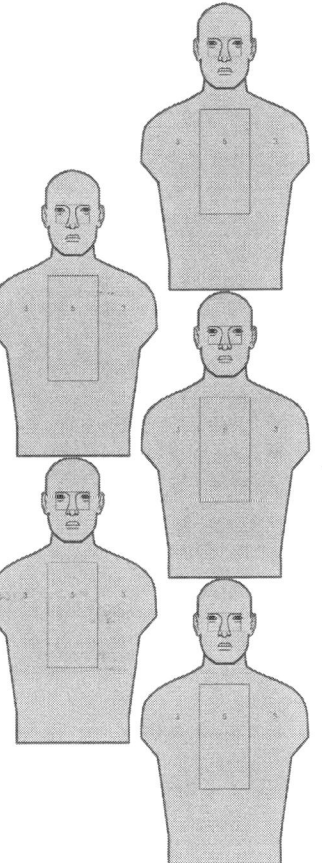

SUPINE

Date:	Weapon:	Sights:	Holster:	Distance:
Rep 1 Time:	Rep 2 Time:	Rep 3 Time:	Head / Body	Notes:
Rep 1: Go / No Go	Rep 2: Go / No Go	Rep 3: Go / No Go	**All In:** **Y** / **N**	

Date:	Weapon:	Sights:	Holster:	Distance:
Rep 1 Time:	Rep 2 Time:	Rep 3 Time:	Head / Body	Notes:
Rep 1: Go / No Go	Rep 2: Go / No Go	Rep 3: Go / No Go	**All In:** **Y** / **N**	

Date:	Weapon:	Sights:	Holster:	Distance:
Rep 1 Time:	Rep 2 Time:	Rep 3 Time:	Head / Body	Notes:
Rep 1: Go / No Go	Rep 2: Go / No Go	Rep 3: Go / No Go	**All In:** **Y** / **N**	

Date:	Weapon:	Sights:	Holster:	Distance:
Rep 1 Time:	Rep 2 Time:	Rep 3 Time:	Head / Body	Notes:
Rep 1: Go / No Go	Rep 2: Go / No Go	Rep 3: Go / No Go	**All In:** **Y** / **N**	

Date:	Weapon:	Sights:	Holster:	Distance:
Rep 1 Time:	Rep 2 Time:	Rep 3 Time:	Head / Body	Notes:
Rep 1: Go / No Go	Rep 2: Go / No Go	Rep 3: Go / No Go	**All In:** **Y** / **N**	

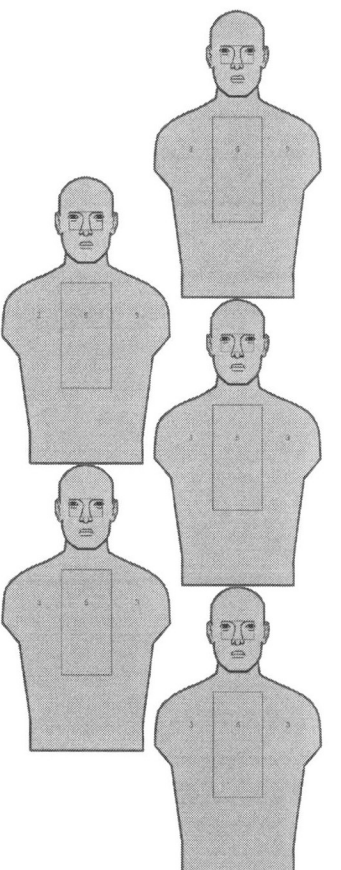

SUPINE

Date:	Weapon:	Sights:	Holster:	Distance:
Rep 1 Time:	Rep 2 Time:	Rep 3 Time:	Head / Body	Notes:
Rep 1: Go / No Go	Rep 2: Go / No Go	Rep 3: Go / No Go	All In: Y / N	

Date:	Weapon:	Sights:	Holster:	Distance:
Rep 1 Time:	Rep 2 Time:	Rep 3 Time:	Head / Body	Notes:
Rep 1: Go / No Go	Rep 2: Go / No Go	Rep 3: Go / No Go	All In: Y / N	

Date:	Weapon:	Sights:	Holster:	Distance:
Rep 1 Time:	Rep 2 Time:	Rep 3 Time:	Head / Body	Notes:
Rep 1: Go / No Go	Rep 2: Go / No Go	Rep 3: Go / No Go	All In: Y / N	

Date:	Weapon:	Sights:	Holster:	Distance:
Rep 1 Time:	Rep 2 Time:	Rep 3 Time:	Head / Body	Notes:
Rep 1: Go / No Go	Rep 2: Go / No Go	Rep 3: Go / No Go	All In: Y / N	

Date:	Weapon:	Sights:	Holster:	Distance:
Rep 1 Time:	Rep 2 Time:	Rep 3 Time:	Head / Body	Notes:
Rep 1: Go / No Go	Rep 2: Go / No Go	Rep 3: Go / No Go	All In: Y / N	

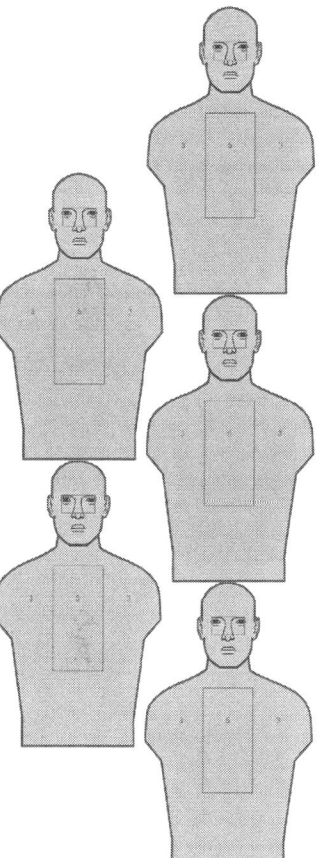

URBAN PRONE

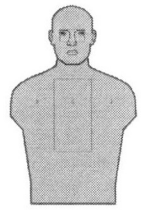

Purpose: Develop efficiency and accuracy using the urban prone position.

Distance: 15 Yards.   **Target:** JD-QUAL1

Extra Equipment Required: Shot timer and barrier or barricade to use as cover.

Rounds Fired Per Side: 5 Rounds.   **Total Rounds Fired:** 10 Rounds.

Point Penalty: Time plus penalties.

Repetitions: 2 Reps (1 Rep each side).

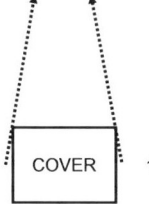

Starting Position & Condition: Sitting with feet extended to the front – Surrender. Weapon Condition 1.

Description: At the timer beep, rotate your toes away from your holster side and lean to clear your holster, draw your pistol, take up a safe urban prone position and fire 5 rounds into the (5 point) A Zone body box. Put pistol on safe if applicable and stand up safely, while keeping the pistol pointed downrange. Once standing, holster pistol. Record time. Repeat drill laying in urban prone on the opposite side. One repetition on one side, one repetition on the other side. All rounds must be in or touching the (5 point) A Zone body box for the drill to be a go. Record time plus time penalties. For every hit in the 3 scoring zone, add 2 seconds to your time. For every hit in the 0 scoring zone, add 5 seconds to your time.

The urban prone involves lying on your side, in basically a fetal position for shooting around and under low cover. The pistol is in a two handed grip, and your hands are between your knees. Your knees are steadying the pistol grip and your heels should be pointed towards your butt, and you must take great care to get them out of the way and not to shoot them. As you become more familiar with the urban prone position, your times will decrease, and your accuracy will increase.

Variations: Use different types of cover. Add distance.

URBAN PRONE

Date:	Weapon:	Sights:	Holster:
Distance:	Type Of Cover:	Notes:	
Left Time:	Right Time:	Penalties:	**Total Time Score:**

Date:	Weapon:	Sights:	Holster:
Distance:	Type Of Cover:	Notes:	
Left Time:	Right Time:	Penalties:	**Total Time Score:**

Date:	Weapon:	Sights:	Holster:
Distance:	Type Of Cover:	Notes:	
Left Time:	Right Time:	Penalties:	**Total Time Score:**

Date:	Weapon:	Sights:	Holster:
Distance:	Type Of Cover:	Notes:	
Left Time:	Right Time:	Penalties:	**Total Time Score:**

Date:	Weapon:	Sights:	Holster:
Distance:	Type Of Cover:	Notes:	Notes:
Left Time:	Right Time:	Penalties:	**Total Time Score:**

Advanced Pistol ©

Positional Drills - 3

URBAN PRONE

Date:	Weapon:	Sights:	Holster:
Distance:	Type Of Cover:	Notes:	
Left Time:	Right Time:	Penalties:	**Total Time Score:**

Date:	Weapon:	Sights:	Holster:
Distance:	Type Of Cover:	Notes:	
Left Time:	Right Time:	Penalties:	**Total Time Score:**

Date:	Weapon:	Sights:	Holster:
Distance:	Type Of Cover:	Notes:	
Left Time:	Right Time:	Penalties:	**Total Time Score:**

Date:	Weapon:	Sights:	Holster:
Distance:	Type Of Cover:	Notes:	
Left Time:	Right Time:	Penalties:	**Total Time Score:**

Date:	Weapon:	Sights:	Holster:
Distance:	Type Of Cover:	Notes:	Notes:
Left Time:	Right Time:	Penalties:	**Total Time Score:**

URBAN PRONE

Date:	Weapon:	Sights:	Holster:
Distance:	Type Of Cover:	Notes:	
Left Time:	Right Time:	Penalties:	**Total Time Score:**

Date:	Weapon:	Sights:	Holster:
Distance:	Type Of Cover:	Notes:	
Left Time:	Right Time:	Penalties:	**Total Time Score:**

Date:	Weapon:	Sights:	Holster:
Distance:	Type Of Cover:	Notes:	
Left Time:	Right Time:	Penalties:	**Total Time Score:**

Date:	Weapon:	Sights:	Holster:
Distance:	Type Of Cover:	Notes:	
Left Time:	Right Time:	Penalties:	**Total Time Score:**

Date:	Weapon:	Sights:	Holster:
Distance:	Type Of Cover:	Notes:	Notes:
Left Time:	Right Time:	Penalties:	**Total Time Score:**

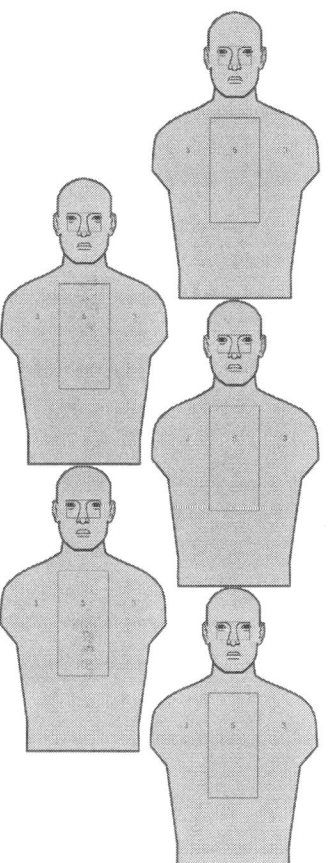

Advanced Pistol ©

Positional Drills - 1

URBAN PRONE

Date:	Weapon:	Sights:	Holster:
Distance:	Type Of Cover:	Notes:	
Left Time:	Right Time:	Penalties:	**Total Time Score:**

Date:	Weapon:	Sights:	Holster:
Distance:	Type Of Cover:	Notes:	
Left Time:	Right Time:	Penalties:	**Total Time Score:**

Date:	Weapon:	Sights:	Holster:
Distance:	Type Of Cover:	Notes:	
Left Time:	Right Time:	Penalties:	**Total Time Score:**

Date:	Weapon:	Sights:	Holster:
Distance:	Type Of Cover:	Notes:	
Left Time:	Right Time:	Penalties:	**Total Time Score:**

Date:	Weapon:	Sights:	Holster:
Distance:	Type Of Cover:	Notes:	Notes:
Left Time:	Right Time:	Penalties:	**Total Time Score:**

URBAN PRONE

Date:	Weapon:	Sights:	Holster:
Distance:	Type Of Cover:	Notes:	
Left Time:	Right Time:	Penalties:	**Total Time Score:**

Date:	Weapon:	Sights:	Holster:
Distance:	Type Of Cover:	Notes:	
Left Time:	Right Time:	Penalties:	**Total Time Score:**

Date:	Weapon:	Sights:	Holster:
Distance:	Type Of Cover:	Notes:	
Left Time:	Right Time:	Penalties:	**Total Time Score:**

Date:	Weapon:	Sights:	Holster:
Distance:	Type Of Cover:	Notes:	
Left Time:	Right Time:	Penalties:	**Total Time Score:**

Date:	Weapon:	Sights:	Holster:
Distance:	Type Of Cover:	Notes:	Notes:
Left Time:	Right Time:	Penalties:	**Total Time Score:**

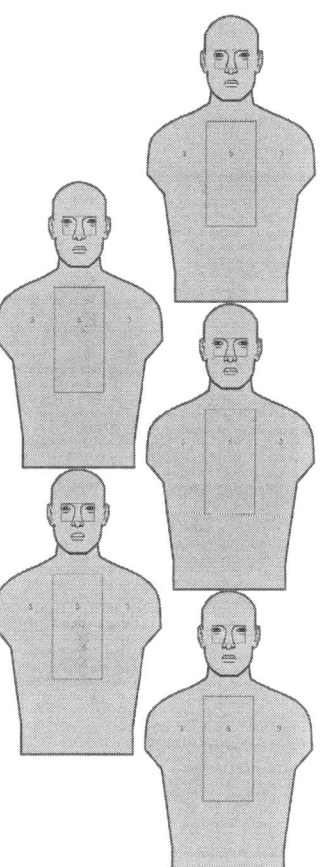

Advanced Pistol ©

STEPPING OUT

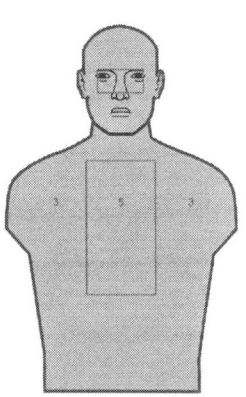

Purpose: Develop nervous system memory of getting off the X after retention shooting.

Distance: Arms length from target.   **Target:** JD-QUAL1

Extra Equipment Required: Shot timer.

Rounds Fired Per Rep: 5 Rounds.   **Total Rounds Fired:** 20 Rounds.   **Repetitions:** 4 Reps.

Point Penalty: As per target score.

Starting Position & Condition: Standing – Surrender / Interview. Weapon Condition 1.

Description: At your own personal go, take your dominant firing hand/arm, bring your elbow straight back and clear your concealment garment (if you have one) with your firing hand and establish a good grip on the pistol. As your bring your firing to establish a good pistol grip, move your support hand to the side and just in front of your face with your palm facing to your dominant side, at the same time draw your pistol straight up just under your arm pit and rotate pistol towards target (5 point) A Zone body box. When you point your pistol at the target, lean the slide away from your body just enough so when fired from that position, it will not contact your clothing or chest causing a malfunction.

Fire 2 rounds from retention, take 2 steps diagonally back to the left or right, taking up a two-handed grip, fire 3 more rounds in the (5 point) A Zone body box while moving back. Record time for each rep and score. Perform drill moving in each direction twice, 2 right, 2 left. Make sure at no point, does your pistol point at any body part while performing drill. Start out slow and work your speed up over time.

Goal: To safely perform shooting from retention and getting off the X smoothly and deliberately.

Variations: Immediately before the start of the drill, run 50 yards or do 2X25 yard shuttle runs, do 10 push-ups or 10 jumping jacks to get your heart rate up.   Wear a concealment over garment.

STEPPING OUT

Date:	Location:	Weapon:	Sights:	Holster:
Heart Rate Stress: Y / N	Cover Garment: Y / N	Notes:		
Left 1 Time:	Left 2 Time:	Right 1 Time:	Right 2 Time:	**Total Score:**

Date:	Location:	Weapon:	Sights:	Holster:
Heart Rate Stress: Y / N	Cover Garment: Y / N	Notes:		
Left 1 Time:	Left 2 Time:	Right 1 Time:	Right 2 Time:	**Total Score:**

Date:	Location:	Weapon:	Sights:	Holster:
Heart Rate Stress: Y / N	Cover Garment: Y / N	Notes:		
Left 1 Time:	Left 2 Time:	Right 1 Time:	Right 2 Time:	**Total Score:**

Date:	Location:	Weapon:	Sights:	Holster:
Heart Rate Stress: Y / N	Cover Garment: Y / N	Notes:		
Left 1 Time:	Left 2 Time:	Right 1 Time:	Right 2 Time:	**Total Score:**

Date:	Location:	Weapon:	Sights:	Holster:
Heart Rate Stress: Y / N	Cover Garment: Y / N	Notes:		
Left 1 Time:	Left 2 Time:	Right 1 Time:	Right 2 Time:	**Total Score:**

STEPPING OUT

Date:	Location:	Weapon:	Sights:	Holster:
Heart Rate Stress: Y / N	Cover Garment: Y / N	Notes:		
Left 1 Time:	Left 2 Time:	Right 1 Time:	Right 2 Time:	**Total Score:**

Date:	Location:	Weapon:	Sights:	Holster:
Heart Rate Stress: Y / N	Cover Garment: Y / N	Notes:		
Left 1 Time:	Left 2 Time:	Right 1 Time:	Right 2 Time:	**Total Score:**

Date:	Location:	Weapon:	Sights:	Holster:
Heart Rate Stress: Y / N	Cover Garment: Y / N	Notes:		
Left 1 Time:	Left 2 Time:	Right 1 Time:	Right 2 Time:	**Total Score:**

Date:	Location:	Weapon:	Sights:	Holster:
Heart Rate Stress: Y / N	Cover Garment: Y / N	Notes:		
Left 1 Time:	Left 2 Time:	Right 1 Time:	Right 2 Time:	**Total Score:**

Date:	Location:	Weapon:	Sights:	Holster:
Heart Rate Stress: Y / N	Cover Garment: Y / N	Notes:		
Left 1 Time:	Left 2 Time:	Right 1 Time:	Right 2 Time:	**Total Score:**

STEPPING OUT

Date:	Location:	Weapon:	Sights:	Holster:
Heart Rate Stress: Y / N	Cover Garment: Y / N	Notes:		
Left 1 Time:	Left 2 Time:	Right 1 Time:	Right 2 Time:	**Total Score:**

Date:	Location:	Weapon:	Sights:	Holster:
Heart Rate Stress: Y / N	Cover Garment: Y / N	Notes:		
Left 1 Time:	Left 2 Time:	Right 1 Time:	Right 2 Time:	**Total Score:**

Date:	Location:	Weapon:	Sights:	Holster:
Heart Rate Stress: Y / N	Cover Garment: Y / N	Notes:		
Left 1 Time:	Left 2 Time:	Right 1 Time:	Right 2 Time:	**Total Score:**

Date:	Location:	Weapon:	Sights:	Holster:
Heart Rate Stress: Y / N	Cover Garment: Y / N	Notes:		
Left 1 Time:	Left 2 Time:	Right 1 Time:	Right 2 Time:	**Total Score:**

Date:	Location:	Weapon:	Sights:	Holster:
Heart Rate Stress: Y / N	Cover Garment: Y / N	Notes:		
Left 1 Time:	Left 2 Time:	Right 1 Time:	Right 2 Time:	**Total Score:**

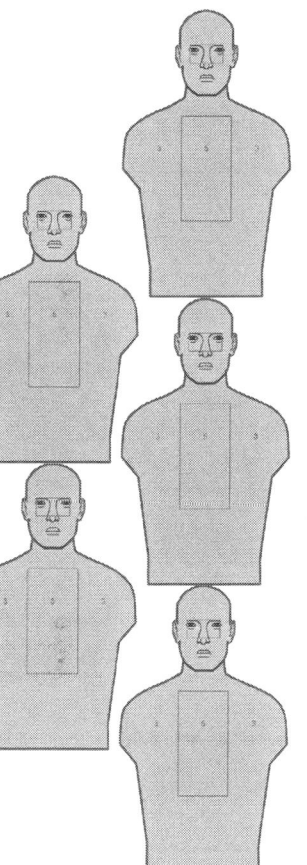

Movement Drills - 1

STEPPING OUT

Date:	Location:	Weapon:	Sights:	Holster:
Heart Rate Stress: Y / N	Cover Garment: Y / N	Notes:		
Left 1 Time:	Left 2 Time:	Right 1 Time:	Right 2 Time:	**Total Score:**

Date:	Location:	Weapon:	Sights:	Holster:
Heart Rate Stress: Y / N	Cover Garment: Y / N	Notes:		
Left 1 Time:	Left 2 Time:	Right 1 Time:	Right 2 Time:	**Total Score:**

Date:	Location:	Weapon:	Sights:	Holster:
Heart Rate Stress: Y / N	Cover Garment: Y / N	Notes:		
Left 1 Time:	Left 2 Time:	Right 1 Time:	Right 2 Time:	**Total Score:**

Date:	Location:	Weapon:	Sights:	Holster:
Heart Rate Stress: Y / N	Cover Garment: Y / N	Notes:		
Left 1 Time:	Left 2 Time:	Right 1 Time:	Right 2 Time:	**Total Score:**

Date:	Location:	Weapon:	Sights:	Holster:
Heart Rate Stress: Y / N	Cover Garment: Y / N	Notes:		
Left 1 Time:	Left 2 Time:	Right 1 Time:	Right 2 Time:	**Total Score:**

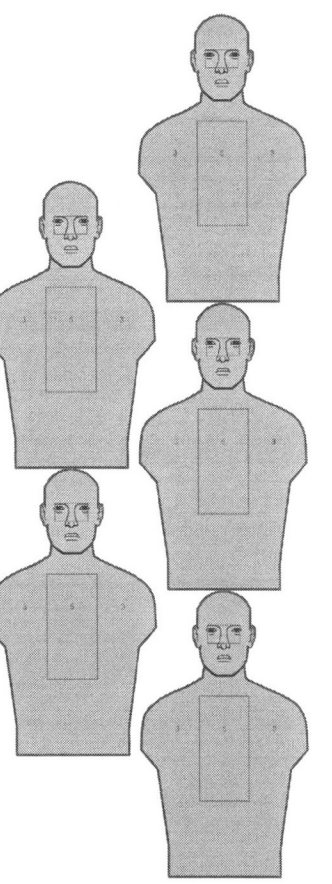

STEPPING OUT

Date:	Location:	Weapon:	Sights:	Holster:
Heart Rate Stress: Y / N	Cover Garment: Y / N	Notes:		
Left 1 Time:	Left 2 Time:	Right 1 Time:	Right 2 Time:	**Total Score:**

Date:	Location:	Weapon:	Sights:	Holster:
Heart Rate Stress: Y / N	Cover Garment: Y / N	Notes:		
Left 1 Time:	Left 2 Time:	Right 1 Time:	Right 2 Time:	**Total Score:**

Date:	Location:	Weapon:	Sights:	Holster:
Heart Rate Stress: Y / N	Cover Garment: Y / N	Notes:		
Left 1 Time:	Left 2 Time:	Right 1 Time:	Right 2 Time:	**Total Score:**

Date:	Location:	Weapon:	Sights:	Holster:
Heart Rate Stress: Y / N	Cover Garment: Y / N	Notes:		
Left 1 Time:	Left 2 Time:	Right 1 Time:	Right 2 Time:	**Total Score:**

Date:	Location:	Weapon:	Sights:	Holster:
Heart Rate Stress: Y / N	Cover Garment: Y / N	Notes:		
Left 1 Time:	Left 2 Time:	Right 1 Time:	Right 2 Time:	**Total Score:**

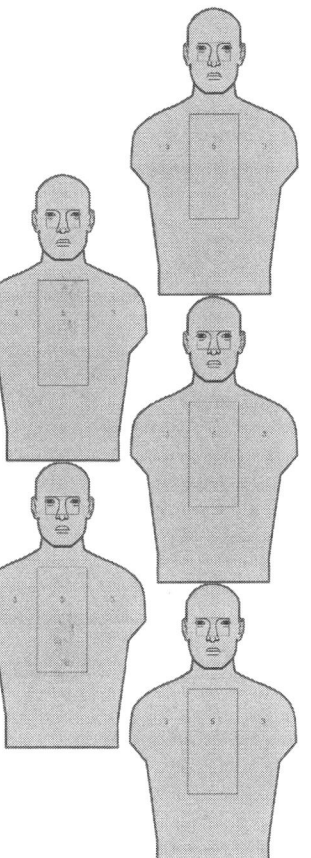

Advanced Pistol ©

SARG

Purpose: Develop nervous system memory of getting off the X and moving to cover and increase pistol draw under stress understanding.

By: Conceptual idea of Charlotte Police Sargent Paul Brentar.

Distance: 10 Yards. **Target:** JD-QUAL1

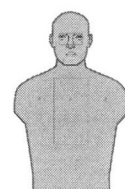

Extra Equipment Required: Shot timer. 2 Barriers / barricades to use as cover.

Rounds Fired Per Rep: 5 Rounds. **Total Rounds Fired:** 10 Rounds.

Point Penalty: Go / No Go.

Repetitions: 1 Rep of 2 stages.

Starting Position & Condition: Standing – Hands to side or interview. Weapon Condition 1.

Description:

Stage 1 - At the timer beep, quickly move left to cover, from the use of cover, fire 5 rounds into the (5 point) A Zone body box. Record time and score.

Stage 2 - At the timer beep, quickly move right to cover, from the use of cover, fire 5 rounds into the (5 point) A Zone body box. Record time and score.

Drawing on the move or after stopping at cover is shooters choice. Remember to use the firearm safety rules and don't break them. Start slow and work up to a smooth and deliberate speed.

Goal: Be smooth and deliberate with your movement and to understand if drawing while moving or at cover works best for a situation. .

Variations: Create cover with different objects, use what simulates walls, cars etc. Use the cover to the best of your ability.

SARG

Date	Weapon	Type of Cover	5 Reps Left?	5 Reps Right?	All in Body Box	Shooting Position Used
			Y / N	Y / N	Y / N	
			Y / N	Y / N	Y / N	
			Y / N	Y / N	Y / N	
			Y / N	Y / N	Y / N	
			Y / N	Y / N	Y / N	
			Y / N	Y / N	Y / N	
			Y / N	Y / N	Y / N	
			Y / N	Y / N	Y / N	
			Y / N	Y / N	Y / N	
			Y / N	Y / N	Y / N	
			Y / N	Y / N	Y / N	
			Y / N	Y / N	Y / N	
			Y / N	Y / N	Y / N	
			Y / N	Y / N	Y / N	
			Y / N	Y / N	Y / N	
			Y / N	Y / N	Y / N	
			Y / N	Y / N	Y / N	

SARG

Date	Weapon	Type of Cover	5 Reps Left?	5 Reps Right?	All in Body Box	Shooting Position Used
			Y / N	Y / N	Y / N	
			Y / N	Y / N	Y / N	
			Y / N	Y / N	Y / N	
			Y / N	Y / N	Y / N	
			Y / N	Y / N	Y / N	
			Y / N	Y / N	Y / N	
			Y / N	Y / N	Y / N	
			Y / N	Y / N	Y / N	
			Y / N	Y / N	Y / N	
			Y / N	Y / N	Y / N	
			Y / N	Y / N	Y / N	
			Y / N	Y / N	Y / N	
			Y / N	Y / N	Y / N	
			Y / N	Y / N	Y / N	
			Y / N	Y / N	Y / N	
			Y / N	Y / N	Y / N	
			Y / N	Y / N	Y / N	

SARG

Date	Weapon	Type of Cover	5 Reps Left?	5 Reps Right?	All in Body Box	Shooting Position Used
			Y / N	Y / N	Y / N	
			Y / N	Y / N	Y / N	
			Y / N	Y / N	Y / N	
			Y / N	Y / N	Y / N	
			Y / N	Y / N	Y / N	
			Y / N	Y / N	Y / N	
			Y / N	Y / N	Y / N	
			Y / N	Y / N	Y / N	
			Y / N	Y / N	Y / N	
			Y / N	Y / N	Y / N	
			Y / N	Y / N	Y / N	
			Y / N	Y / N	Y / N	
			Y / N	Y / N	Y / N	
			Y / N	Y / N	Y / N	
			Y / N	Y / N	Y / N	
			Y / N	Y / N	Y / N	
			Y / N	Y / N	Y / N	

www.GUNFIGHTERSERIES.com ©

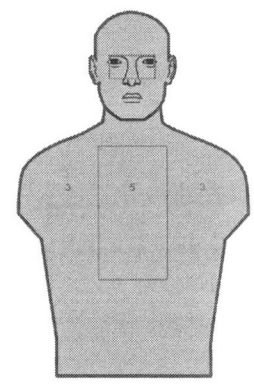

PISTOL SPRINTS

Purpose: Accuracy with stress.

Distance: 25, 20, 15, 10, and 5 Yards.

Target: JD-Qual1

Par Time: As per goal standard.

Extra Equipment Needed: Shot timer, position markers.

Total Rounds Fired: 15 Rounds.

Rounds Fired Per Yard Line: 3 Rounds.

Point Penalty: Add 2 seconds for each round outside A box. Add 5 seconds for each round outside body.

Starting Position & Condition: Standing - Surrender / Interview position. Condition 1.

Description: From the 25 yard line, at the timer beep, run to the target then back to the 25 yard line. Draw, fire 3 rounds into the A Zone (5 point) body box. Holster your pistol, run to the target then back to the 20 yard line. Draw, fire 3 rounds into the A Zone (5 point) body box. Holster your pistol, run to the target then back to the 15 yard line. Draw, fire 3 rounds into the A Zone (5 point) body box. Holster your pistol, run to the target then back to the 10 yard line. Draw, fire 3 rounds into the A Zone (5 point) body box. Holster your pistol, run to the target then back to the 5 yard line. Draw, fire 3 rounds into the A Zone (5 point) body box. Record last shot time plus penalties.

Goals: 125 Seconds.   Expert: 100 Seconds.   Gunfighter: 75 Seconds.

PISTOL SPRINTS

Date:	Weapon:	Sights:	Notes:		
Time: Secs	# in A Zone:	# in 3 Zone:	# Outside Body:	Total Score:	Sec

Date:	Weapon:	Sights:	Notes:		
Time: Secs	# in A Zone:	# in 3 Zone:	# Outside Body:	Total Score:	Sec

Date:	Weapon:	Sights:	Notes:		
Time: Secs	# in A Zone:	# in 3 Zone:	# Outside Body:	Total Score:	Sec

Date:	Weapon:	Sights:	Notes:		
Time: Secs	# in A Zone:	# in 3 Zone:	# Outside Body:	Total Score:	Sec

Date:	Weapon:	Sights:	Notes:		
Time: Secs	# in A Zone:	# in 3 Zone:	# Outside Body:	Total Score:	Sec

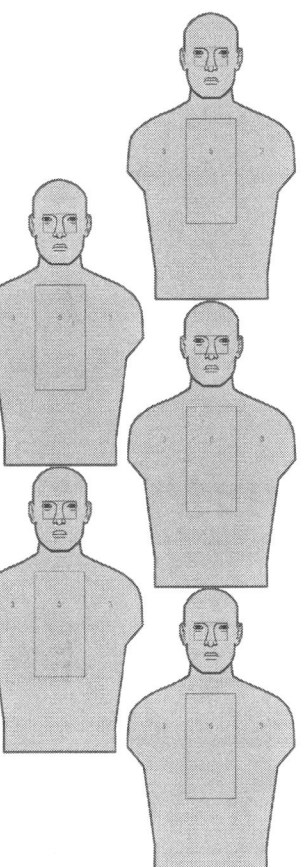

PISTOL SPRINTS

Date:	Weapon:	Sights:	Notes:		
Time: Secs	# in A Zone:	# in 3 Zone:	# Outside Body:	Total Score:	Sec

Date:	Weapon:	Sights:	Notes:		
Time: Secs	# in A Zone:	# in 3 Zone:	# Outside Body:	Total Score:	Sec

Date:	Weapon:	Sights:	Notes:		
Time: Secs	# in A Zone:	# in 3 Zone:	# Outside Body:	Total Score:	Sec

Date:	Weapon:	Sights:	Notes:		
Time: Secs	# in A Zone:	# in 3 Zone:	# Outside Body:	Total Score:	Sec

Date:	Weapon:	Sights:	Notes:		
Time: Secs	# in A Zone:	# in 3 Zone:	# Outside Body:	Total Score:	Sec

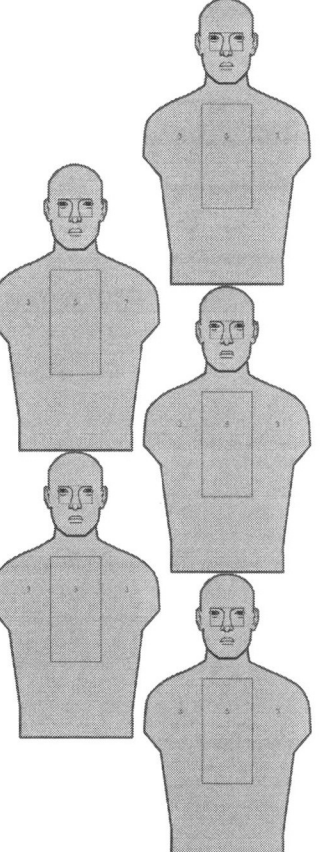

www.GUNFIGHTERSERIES.com ©

PISTOL SPRINTS

Date:	Weapon:	Sights:	Notes:		
Time: Secs	# in A Zone:	# in 3 Zone:	# Outside Body:	Total Score:	Sec

Date:	Weapon:	Sights:	Notes:		
Time: Secs	# in A Zone:	# in 3 Zone:	# Outside Body:	Total Score:	Sec

Date:	Weapon:	Sights:	Notes:		
Time: Secs	# in A Zone:	# in 3 Zone:	# Outside Body:	Total Score:	Sec

Date:	Weapon:	Sights:	Notes:		
Time: Secs	# in A Zone:	# in 3 Zone:	# Outside Body:	Total Score:	Sec

Date:	Weapon:	Sights:	Notes:		
Time: Secs	# in A Zone:	# in 3 Zone:	# Outside Body:	Total Score:	Sec

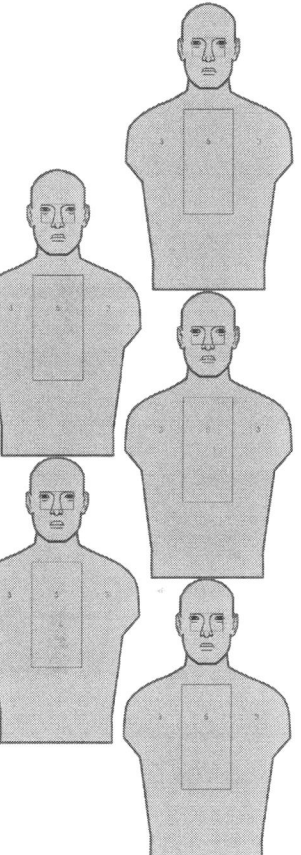

Movement Drills - 3

PISTOL SPRINTS

Date:	Weapon:	Sights:	Notes:		
Time: Secs	# in A Zone:	# in 3 Zone:	# Outside Body:	Total Score:	Sec

Date:	Weapon:	Sights:	Notes:		
Time: Secs	# in A Zone:	# in 3 Zone:	# Outside Body:	Total Score:	Sec

Date:	Weapon:	Sights:	Notes:		
Time: Secs	# in A Zone:	# in 3 Zone:	# Outside Body:	Total Score:	Sec

Date:	Weapon:	Sights:	Notes:		
Time: Secs	# in A Zone:	# in 3 Zone:	# Outside Body:	Total Score:	Sec

Date:	Weapon:	Sights:	Notes:		
Time: Secs	# in A Zone:	# in 3 Zone:	# Outside Body:	Total Score:	Sec

PISTOL SPRINTS

Date:	Weapon:	Sights:	Notes:		
Time: Secs	# in A Zone:	# in 3 Zone:	# Outside Body:	Total Score:	Sec

Date:	Weapon:	Sights:	Notes:		
Time: Secs	# in A Zone:	# in 3 Zone:	# Outside Body:	Total Score:	Sec

Date:	Weapon:	Sights:	Notes:		
Time: Secs	# in A Zone:	# in 3 Zone:	# Outside Body:	Total Score:	Sec

Date:	Weapon:	Sights:	Notes:		
Time: Secs	# in A Zone:	# in 3 Zone:	# Outside Body:	Total Score:	Sec

Date:	Weapon:	Sights:	Notes:		
Time: Secs	# in A Zone:	# in 3 Zone:	# Outside Body:	Total Score:	Sec

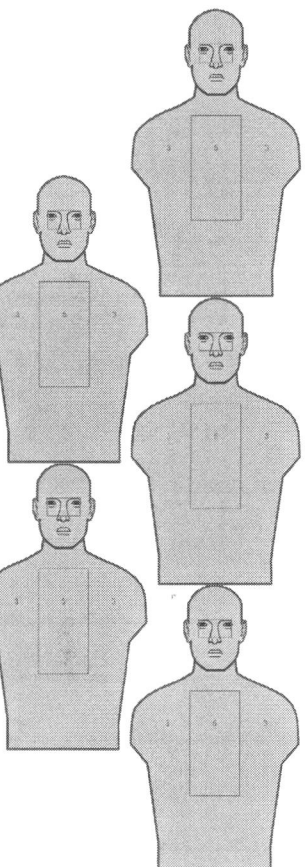

Movement Drills - 3

SHIELD

Purpose: Increase speed, accuracy and understanding of shooting on the move with a pistol.

Distance: Moving 15 to 5 yards and laterally at 7 yards.   **Target:** JD-Qual1

Extra Equipment Needed: Position markers, shot timer (optional).

Rounds Fired Per Stage: 5 Rounds.   **Total Rounds Fired:** 15 Rounds.

Point Penalty: As per target score.

Repetitions: 1 Rep of 3 stages.

Starting Position & Condition: Standing – Hands to side or interview. Weapon Condition 1.

Description:

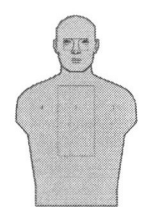
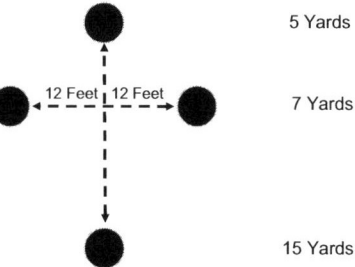

Stage 1: Starting at the 15 yard marker, at your own personal go, draw and fire 5 rounds into the (5 point) A Zone body box, while moving towards the 5 yard marker. Holster.

Stage 2 and 3: Starting at the left 7 yard marker, at your own personal go, draw and fire 5 rounds into the (5 point) A Zone body box, while moving left to right 7 yard marker. Holster. Repeat 7 yard rep moving from the right 7 to left marker. Holster. Score target. Any stop in movement to shoot makes the drill a No Go. The shooter has the choice to shoot one handed or two handed. Find what makes you move smoothly and shoot the most accurately.

Goals: 59 points.   Expert: 67 points.   Gunfighter: 75 Points.

Variations: Time reps. Add round count. Shoot A Zone head box.

SHIELD

Date:	Weapon:	Sights:	Body / Head	Cover Garment: Y / N
Rounds Per Rep:	Stage 1 Time:	Stage 2 Time:	Stage 3 Time:	**Total Score:**
Notes:				
Date:	Weapon:	Sights:	Body / Head	Cover Garment: Y / N
Rounds Per Rep:	Stage 1 Time:	Stage 2 Time:	Stage 3 Time:	**Total Score:**
Notes:				
Date:	Weapon:	Sights:	Body / Head	Cover Garment: Y / N
Rounds Per Rep:	Stage 1 Time:	Stage 2 Time:	Stage 3 Time:	**Total Score:**
Notes:				
Date:	Weapon:	Sights:	Body / Head	Cover Garment: Y / N
Rounds Per Rep:	Stage 1 Time:	Stage 2 Time:	Stage 3 Time:	**Total Score:**
Notes:				
Date:	Weapon:	Sights:	Body / Head	Cover Garment: Y / N
Rounds Per Rep:	Stage 1 Time:	Stage 2 Time:	Stage 3 Time:	**Total Score:**
Notes:				

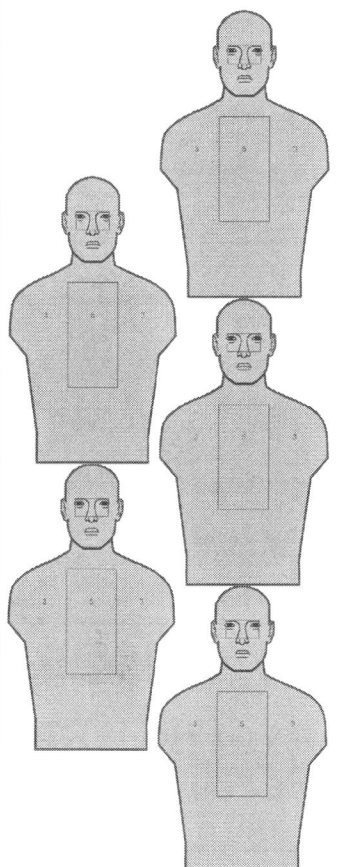

Advanced Pistol ©

Movement Drills - 4

SHIELD

Date:	Weapon:	Sights:	Body / Head	Cover Garment: Y / N
Rounds Per Rep:	Stage 1 Time:	Stage 2 Time:	Stage 3 Time:	**Total Score:**
Notes:				
Date:	Weapon:	Sights:	Body / Head	Cover Garment: Y / N
Rounds Per Rep:	Stage 1 Time:	Stage 2 Time:	Stage 3 Time:	**Total Score:**
Notes:				
Date:	Weapon:	Sights:	Body / Head	Cover Garment: Y / N
Rounds Per Rep:	Stage 1 Time:	Stage 2 Time:	Stage 3 Time:	**Total Score:**
Notes:				
Date:	Weapon:	Sights:	Body / Head	Cover Garment: Y / N
Rounds Per Rep:	Stage 1 Time:	Stage 2 Time:	Stage 3 Time:	**Total Score:**
Notes:				
Date:	Weapon:	Sights:	Body / Head	Cover Garment: Y / N
Rounds Per Rep:	Stage 1 Time:	Stage 2 Time:	Stage 3 Time:	**Total Score:**
Notes:				

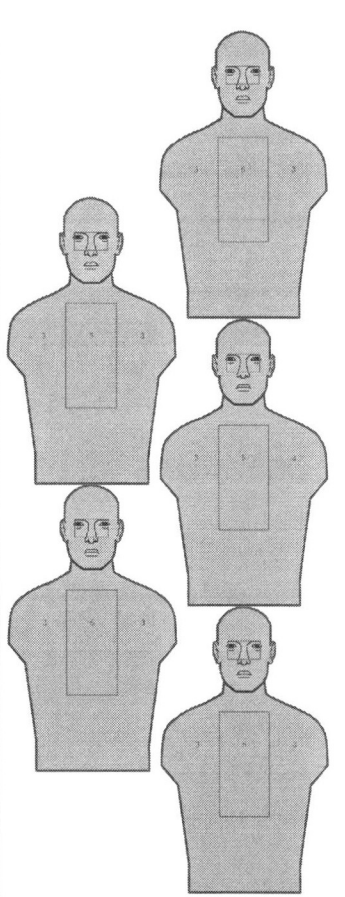

SHIELD

Date:	Weapon:	Sights:	Body / Head	Cover Garment: Y / N
Rounds Per Rep:	Stage 1 Time:	Stage 2 Time:	Stage 3 Time:	**Total Score:**
Notes:				
Date:	Weapon:	Sights:	Body / Head	Cover Garment: Y / N
Rounds Per Rep:	Stage 1 Time:	Stage 2 Time:	Stage 3 Time:	**Total Score:**
Notes:				
Date:	Weapon:	Sights:	Body / Head	Cover Garment: Y / N
Rounds Per Rep:	Stage 1 Time:	Stage 2 Time:	Stage 3 Time:	**Total Score:**
Notes:				
Date:	Weapon:	Sights:	Body / Head	Cover Garment: Y / N
Rounds Per Rep:	Stage 1 Time:	Stage 2 Time:	Stage 3 Time:	**Total Score:**
Notes:				
Date:	Weapon:	Sights:	Body / Head	Cover Garment: Y / N
Rounds Per Rep:	Stage 1 Time:	Stage 2 Time:	Stage 3 Time:	**Total Score:**
Notes:				

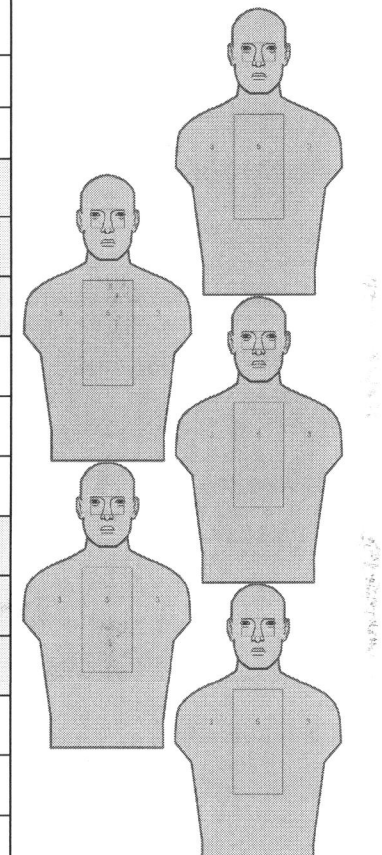

Movement Drills - 4

SHIELD

Date:	Weapon:	Sights:	Body / Head	Cover Garment: Y / N
Rounds Per Rep:	Stage 1 Time:	Stage 2 Time:	Stage 3 Time:	**Total Score:**
Notes:				
Date:	Weapon:	Sights:	Body / Head	Cover Garment: Y / N
Rounds Per Rep:	Stage 1 Time:	Stage 2 Time:	Stage 3 Time:	**Total Score:**
Notes:				
Date:	Weapon:	Sights:	Body / Head	Cover Garment: Y / N
Rounds Per Rep:	Stage 1 Time:	Stage 2 Time:	Stage 3 Time:	**Total Score:**
Notes:				
Date:	Weapon:	Sights:	Body / Head	Cover Garment: Y / N
Rounds Per Rep:	Stage 1 Time:	Stage 2 Time:	Stage 3 Time:	**Total Score:**
Notes:				
Date:	Weapon:	Sights:	Body / Head	Cover Garment: Y / N
Rounds Per Rep:	Stage 1 Time:	Stage 2 Time:	Stage 3 Time:	**Total Score:**
Notes:				

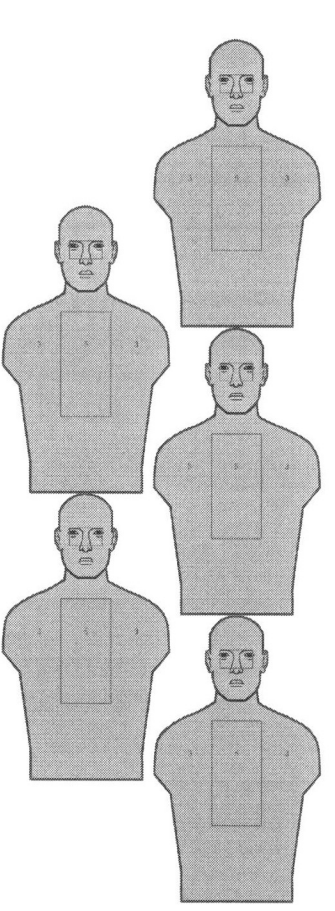

SHIELD

Date:	Weapon:	Sights:	Body / Head	Cover Garment: Y / N
Rounds Per Rep:	Stage 1 Time:	Stage 2 Time:	Stage 3 Time:	**Total Score:**
Notes:				
Date:	Weapon:	Sights:	Body / Head	Cover Garment: Y / N
Rounds Per Rep:	Stage 1 Time:	Stage 2 Time:	Stage 3 Time:	**Total Score:**
Notes:				
Date:	Weapon:	Sights:	Body / Head	Cover Garment: Y / N
Rounds Per Rep:	Stage 1 Time:	Stage 2 Time:	Stage 3 Time:	**Total Score:**
Notes:				
Date:	Weapon:	Sights:	Body / Head	Cover Garment: Y / N
Rounds Per Rep:	Stage 1 Time:	Stage 2 Time:	Stage 3 Time:	**Total Score:**
Notes:				
Date:	Weapon:	Sights:	Body / Head	Cover Garment: Y / N
Rounds Per Rep:	Stage 1 Time:	Stage 2 Time:	Stage 3 Time:	**Total Score:**
Notes:				

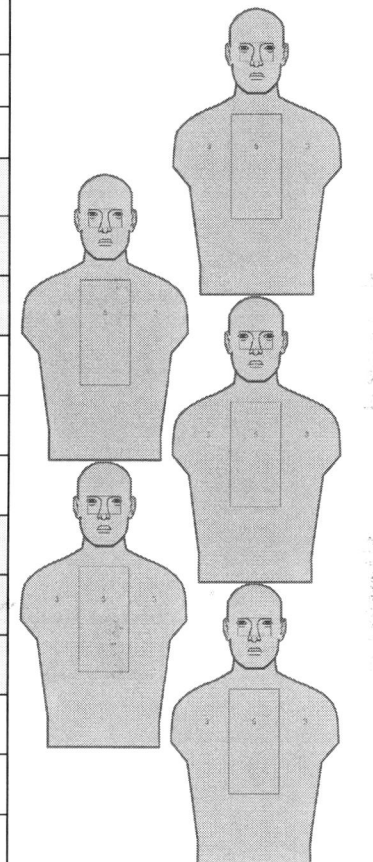

Advanced Pistol ©

Movement Drills - 4

ZIG ZAG

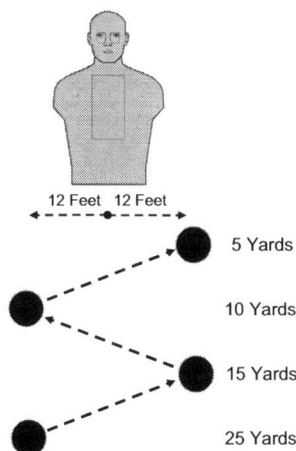

Purpose: Develop accuracy and speed from moving at a high rate of speed to stopping to shoot.

Distance: 25, 15, 10, 5 Yards.   **Target:** JD-Qual1

Par Time: Per goal standard.

Extra Equipment Needed: Shot timer, 2 magazines, position markers or optional barriers/barricades.

Rounds Fired Per Yard Marker: 4 Rounds.   **Total Rounds Fired:** 16 Rounds.

Point Penalty: Time plus 2 seconds for every hit in the 3 scoring zone, add plus 5 seconds for any misses off silhouette.

Starting Position & Condition: Standing – Hands to side or interview. Weapon Condition 1.

Description: Load 1st mag with 2 to 8 rounds (have someone load for you, if possible). Second magazine stored in pouch to be loaded full.

Starting at the 25 yard maker, at the timer beep, draw and fire 4 rounds into the (5 point) A Zone body box. Move to the 15 yard marker, fire 4 rounds into the (5 point) A Zone body box. Move to the 10 yard marker, fire 4 rounds into the (5 point) A Zone body box. Move to the 5 yard marker, fire 4 rounds into the (5 point) A Zone body box. Reload as needed. Record repetition time, score and penalties. For every hit in the 3 scoring zone, add 2 seconds to your time. For every hit in the 0 scoring zone, add 5 seconds to your time.

Follow the firearm safety rules, keep your pistol pointed in the direction of the target during movement or in a safe position.

Goals: 54 seconds.   Expert: 40 Seconds.   Gunfighter: All rounds in A Zone body box within 27 seconds.

Variations: Immediately before the start of the drill, run 50 yards or do 2X25 yard shuttle runs, do 10 push-ups or 10 jumping jacks to get your heart rate up. Add barriers to shoot behind cover.

ZIG ZAG

Date:	Weapon:	Sights:	Holster:	Cover Garment: Y / N	
Heart Rate Stress: Y / N		Notes:			
Time: Secs	# in A Zone:	# in 3 Zone:	# Outside Body:	**Total Score:**	**Secs**

Date:	Weapon:	Sights:	Holster:	Cover Garment: Y / N	
Heart Rate Stress: Y / N		Notes:			
Time: Secs	# in A Zone:	# in 3 Zone:	# Outside Body:	**Total Score:**	**Secs**

Date:	Weapon:	Sights:	Holster:	Cover Garment: Y / N	
Heart Rate Stress: Y / N		Notes:			
Time: Secs	# in A Zone:	# in 3 Zone:	# Outside Body:	**Total Score:**	**Secs**

Date:	Weapon:	Sights:	Holster:	Cover Garment: Y / N	
Heart Rate Stress: Y / N		Notes:			
Time: Secs	# in A Zone:	# in 3 Zone:	# Outside Body:	**Total Score:**	**Secs**

Date:	Weapon:	Sights:	Holster:	Cover Garment: Y / N	
Heart Rate Stress: Y / N		Notes:			
Time: Secs	# in A Zone:	# in 3 Zone:	# Outside Body:	**Total Score:**	**Secs**

Advanced Pistol ©

www.GUNFIGHTERSERIES.com ©

ZIG ZAG

Date:	Weapon:	Sights:	Holster:	Cover Garment: Y / N
Heart Rate Stress: Y / N		Notes:		
Time: Secs	# in A Zone:	# in 3 Zone:	# Outside Body:	Total Score: Secs

Date:	Weapon:	Sights:	Holster:	Cover Garment: Y / N
Heart Rate Stress: Y / N		Notes:		
Time: Secs	# in A Zone:	# in 3 Zone:	# Outside Body:	Total Score: Secs

Date:	Weapon:	Sights:	Holster:	Cover Garment: Y / N
Heart Rate Stress: Y / N		Notes:		
Time: Secs	# in A Zone:	# in 3 Zone:	# Outside Body:	Total Score: Secs

Date:	Weapon:	Sights:	Holster:	Cover Garment: Y / N
Heart Rate Stress: Y / N		Notes:		
Time: Secs	# in A Zone:	# in 3 Zone:	# Outside Body:	Total Score: Secs

Date:	Weapon:	Sights:	Holster:	Cover Garment: Y / N
Heart Rate Stress: Y / N		Notes:		
Time: Secs	# in A Zone:	# in 3 Zone:	# Outside Body:	Total Score: Secs

ZIG ZAG

Date:	Weapon:	Sights:	Holster:	Cover Garment: Y / N
Heart Rate Stress: Y / N		Notes:		
Time: Secs	# in A Zone:	# in 3 Zone:	# Outside Body:	Total Score: Secs

Date:	Weapon:	Sights:	Holster:	Cover Garment: Y / N
Heart Rate Stress: Y / N		Notes:		
Time: Secs	# in A Zone:	# in 3 Zone:	# Outside Body:	Total Score: Secs

Date:	Weapon:	Sights:	Holster:	Cover Garment: Y / N
Heart Rate Stress: Y / N		Notes:		
Time: Secs	# in A Zone:	# in 3 Zone:	# Outside Body:	Total Score: Secs

Date:	Weapon:	Sights:	Holster:	Cover Garment: Y / N
Heart Rate Stress: Y / N		Notes:		
Time: Secs	# in A Zone:	# in 3 Zone:	# Outside Body:	Total Score: Secs

Date:	Weapon:	Sights:	Holster:	Cover Garment: Y / N
Heart Rate Stress: Y / N		Notes:		
Time: Secs	# in A Zone:	# in 3 Zone:	# Outside Body:	Total Score: Secs

Advanced Pistol ©

ZIG ZAG

www.GUNFIGHTERSERIES.com ©

Date:	Weapon:	Sights:	Holster:	Cover Garment: Y / N	
Heart Rate Stress: Y / N		Notes:			
Time: Secs	# in A Zone:	# in 3 Zone:	# Outside Body:	Total Score:	Secs

Date:	Weapon:	Sights:	Holster:	Cover Garment: Y / N	
Heart Rate Stress: Y / N		Notes:			
Time: Secs	# in A Zone:	# in 3 Zone:	# Outside Body:	Total Score:	Secs

Date:	Weapon:	Sights:	Holster:	Cover Garment: Y / N	
Heart Rate Stress: Y / N		Notes:			
Time: Secs	# in A Zone:	# in 3 Zone:	# Outside Body:	Total Score:	Secs

Date:	Weapon:	Sights:	Holster:	Cover Garment: Y / N	
Heart Rate Stress: Y / N		Notes:			
Time: Secs	# in A Zone:	# in 3 Zone:	# Outside Body:	Total Score:	Secs

Date:	Weapon:	Sights:	Holster:	Cover Garment: Y / N	
Heart Rate Stress: Y / N		Notes:			
Time: Secs	# in A Zone:	# in 3 Zone:	# Outside Body:	Total Score:	Secs

ZIG ZAG

Date:	Weapon:	Sights:	Holster:	Cover Garment: Y / N
Heart Rate Stress: Y / N		Notes:		
Time: Secs	# in A Zone:	# in 3 Zone:	# Outside Body:	**Total Score:** **Secs**

Date:	Weapon:	Sights:	Holster:	Cover Garment: Y / N
Heart Rate Stress: Y / N		Notes:		
Time: Secs	# in A Zone:	# in 3 Zone:	# Outside Body:	**Total Score:** **Secs**

Date:	Weapon:	Sights:	Holster:	Cover Garment: Y / N
Heart Rate Stress: Y / N		Notes:		
Time: Secs	# in A Zone:	# in 3 Zone:	# Outside Body:	**Total Score:** **Secs**

Date:	Weapon:	Sights:	Holster:	Cover Garment: Y / N
Heart Rate Stress: Y / N		Notes:		
Time: Secs	# in A Zone:	# in 3 Zone:	# Outside Body:	**Total Score:** **Secs**

Date:	Weapon:	Sights:	Holster:	Cover Garment: Y / N
Heart Rate Stress: Y / N		Notes:		
Time: Secs	# in A Zone:	# in 3 Zone:	# Outside Body:	**Total Score:** **Secs**

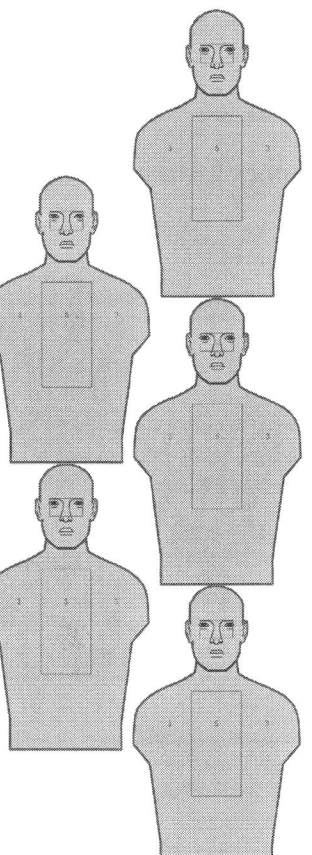

Advanced Pistol ©

ELBOWS

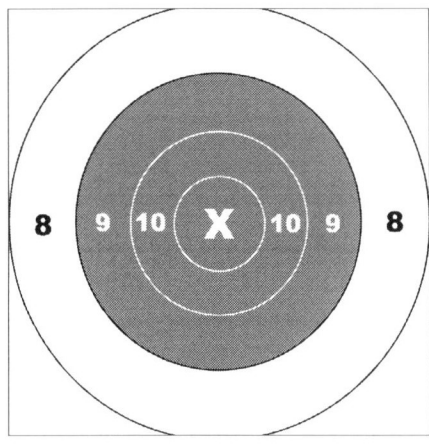

Purpose: Develop consistent arm position for accuracy and efficient recoil management.

Distance: 5 Yards.

Target: GF-1

Par Time: 4 Seconds.

Extra Equipment Needed: Shot timer.

Rounds Fired Per Rep: 5 Rounds.   **Total Rounds Fired:** 15 Rounds.

Point Penalty: As per target score.

Repetitions: 3 Reps.

Starting Position & Condition: Standing – Surrender / Interview. Weapon Condition 1.

Description: At the timer beep, fire 5 rounds into the GF-1 target at 5 yards. Set drill back up and repeat. Being solid and rolling your elbows up slightly about 10 degrees during firing is essential to master this drill. Rotate your arms bringing your elbows up slightly, but not so much to put a bend in your arms.

Goals: 135 points within a 4 second par time (All in 9 ring or better).   **Expert:** 145 points within a 3.5 second par time (All in 9 ring or better).

Gunfighter: 150 points within a 3.25 second par time.

ELBOWS

Date:	Weapon:	Sights:	Notes:	
Rep 1 Time:	Rep 2 Time:	Rep 3 Time:		
# of 8's:	# of 9's:	# of 10's:	Total Score:	X's
Date:	Weapon:	Sights:	Notes:	
Rep 1 Time:	Rep 2 Time:	Rep 3 Time:		
# of 8's:	# of 9's:	# of 10's:	Total Score:	X's
Date:	Weapon:	Sights:	Notes:	
Rep 1 Time:	Rep 2 Time:	Rep 3 Time:		
# of 8's:	# of 9's:	# of 10's:	Total Score:	X's
Date:	Weapon:	Sights:	Notes:	
Rep 1 Time:	Rep 2 Time:	Rep 3 Time:		
# of 8's:	# of 9's:	# of 10's:	Total Score:	X's
Date:	Weapon:	Sights:	Notes:	
Rep 1 Time:	Rep 2 Time:	Rep 3 Time:		
# of 8's:	# of 9's:	# of 10's:	Total Score:	X's

ELBOWS

Date:	Weapon:	Sights:	Notes:	
Rep 1 Time:	Rep 2 Time:	Rep 3 Time:		
# of 8's:	# of 9's:	# of 10's:	Total Score: X's	
Date:	Weapon:	Sights:	Notes:	
Rep 1 Time:	Rep 2 Time:	Rep 3 Time:		
# of 8's:	# of 9's:	# of 10's:	Total Score: X's	
Date:	Weapon:	Sights:	Notes:	
Rep 1 Time:	Rep 2 Time:	Rep 3 Time:		
# of 8's:	# of 9's:	# of 10's:	Total Score: X's	
Date:	Weapon:	Sights:	Notes:	
Rep 1 Time:	Rep 2 Time:	Rep 3 Time:		
# of 8's:	# of 9's:	# of 10's:	Total Score: X's	
Date:	Weapon:	Sights:	Notes:	
Rep 1 Time:	Rep 2 Time:	Rep 3 Time:		
# of 8's:	# of 9's:	# of 10's:	Total Score: X's	

ELBOWS

Date:	Weapon:	Sights:	Notes:	
Rep 1 Time:	Rep 2 Time:	Rep 3 Time:		
# of 8's:	# of 9's:	# of 10's:	Total Score:	X's
Date:	Weapon:	Sights:	Notes:	
Rep 1 Time:	Rep 2 Time:	Rep 3 Time:		
# of 8's:	# of 9's:	# of 10's:	Total Score:	X's
Date:	Weapon:	Sights:	Notes:	
Rep 1 Time:	Rep 2 Time:	Rep 3 Time:		
# of 8's:	# of 9's:	# of 10's:	Total Score:	X's
Date:	Weapon:	Sights:	Notes:	
Rep 1 Time:	Rep 2 Time:	Rep 3 Time:		
# of 8's:	# of 9's:	# of 10's:	Total Score:	X's
Date:	Weapon:	Sights:	Notes:	
Rep 1 Time:	Rep 2 Time:	Rep 3 Time:		
# of 8's:	# of 9's:	# of 10's:	Total Score:	X's

Recoil Management Drills - 1

ELBOWS

Date:	Weapon:	Sights:	Notes:	
Rep 1 Time:	Rep 2 Time:	Rep 3 Time:		
# of 8's:	# of 9's:	# of 10's:	Total Score: X's	
Date:	Weapon:	Sights:	Notes:	
Rep 1 Time:	Rep 2 Time:	Rep 3 Time:		
# of 8's:	# of 9's:	# of 10's:	Total Score: X's	
Date:	Weapon:	Sights:	Notes:	
Rep 1 Time:	Rep 2 Time:	Rep 3 Time:		
# of 8's:	# of 9's:	# of 10's:	Total Score: X's	
Date:	Weapon:	Sights:	Notes:	
Rep 1 Time:	Rep 2 Time:	Rep 3 Time:		
# of 8's:	# of 9's:	# of 10's:	Total Score: X's	
Date:	Weapon:	Sights:	Notes:	
Rep 1 Time:	Rep 2 Time:	Rep 3 Time:		
# of 8's:	# of 9's:	# of 10's:	Total Score: X's	

ELBOWS

Date:	Weapon:	Sights:	Notes:
Rep 1 Time:	Rep 2 Time:	Rep 3 Time:	
# of 8's:	# of 9's:	# of 10's:	Total Score: X's
Date:	Weapon:	Sights:	Notes:
Rep 1 Time:	Rep 2 Time:	Rep 3 Time:	
# of 8's:	# of 9's:	# of 10's:	Total Score: X's
Date:	Weapon:	Sights:	Notes:
Rep 1 Time:	Rep 2 Time:	Rep 3 Time:	
# of 8's:	# of 9's:	# of 10's:	Total Score: X's
Date:	Weapon:	Sights:	Notes:
Rep 1 Time:	Rep 2 Time:	Rep 3 Time:	
# of 8's:	# of 9's:	# of 10's:	Total Score: X's
Date:	Weapon:	Sights:	Notes:
Rep 1 Time:	Rep 2 Time:	Rep 3 Time:	
# of 8's:	# of 9's:	# of 10's:	Total Score: X's

Advanced Pistol ©

Recoil Management Drills - 1

2 TO 5

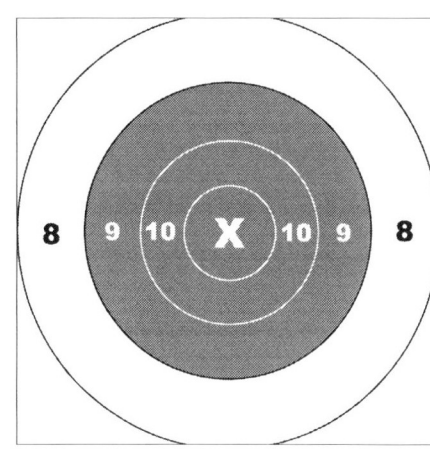

Purpose: Develop controlled fire recoil management.

Distance: 7 Yards.   **Target:** GF-1

Par Time: Varies per repetition round count.   **Extra Equipment Needed:** Shot timer.

Total Rounds Fired: 14 Rounds.

Point Penalty: As per target score.

Repetitions: 1 Rep of 4 stages.

Starting Position & Condition: Standing – Pistol aimed at target. Weapon Condition 1.

Description: At the timer beep, fire the prescribed number of rounds into the GF-1 target within the listed stage par time. Record time. Repeat drill with 2, 3, 4 and 5 rounds fired. Having good sight alignment, sight picture, a solid stance and trigger control is essential to master this drill.

Stage 1 – 2 rounds in 2 seconds.   Gunfighter par time: 1.5 seconds.

Stage 2 – 3 rounds in 2.75 seconds.   Gunfighter par time: 2 seconds.

Stage 3 – 4 rounds in 3.5 seconds.   Gunfighter par time: 2.5 seconds.

Stage 4 – 5 rounds in 4.25 seconds.   Gunfighter par time: 3 seconds.

Goals: 126 points with all rounds in or touching the black.   Expert: 140 points within listed par time.   Gunfighter: 140 points within listed par time.

2 TO 5

Date:	Location:	Weapon:	Sights:	Notes:
Rep 1 Time:	Rep 2 Time:	Rep 3 Time:	Rep 4 Time:	
# Out of Black:	# of 9's:	# of 10's:	Total Score: X's	
Date:	Location:	Weapon:	Sights:	Notes:
Rep 1 Time:	Rep 2 Time:	Rep 3 Time:	Rep 4 Time:	
# Out of Black:	# of 9's:	# of 10's:	Total Score: X's	
Date:	Location:	Weapon:	Sights:	Notes:
Rep 1 Time:	Rep 2 Time:	Rep 3 Time:	Rep 4 Time:	
# Out of Black:	# of 9's:	# of 10's:	Total Score: X's	
Date:	Location:	Weapon:	Sights:	Notes:
Rep 1 Time:	Rep 2 Time:	Rep 3 Time:	Rep 4 Time:	
# Out of Black:	# of 9's:	# of 10's:	Total Score: X's	
Date:	Location:	Weapon:	Sights:	Notes:
Rep 1 Time:	Rep 2 Time:	Rep 3 Time:	Rep 4 Time:	
# Out of Black:	# of 9's:	# of 10's:	Total Score: X's	

2 TO 5

Date:	Location:	Weapon:	Sights:	Notes:
Rep 1 Time:	Rep 2 Time:	Rep 3 Time:	Rep 4 Time:	
# Out of Black:	# of 9's:	# of 10's:	Total Score: X's	
Date:	Location:	Weapon:	Sights:	Notes:
Rep 1 Time:	Rep 2 Time:	Rep 3 Time:	Rep 4 Time:	
# Out of Black:	# of 9's:	# of 10's:	Total Score: X's	
Date:	Location:	Weapon:	Sights:	Notes:
Rep 1 Time:	Rep 2 Time:	Rep 3 Time:	Rep 4 Time:	
# Out of Black:	# of 9's:	# of 10's:	Total Score: X's	
Date:	Location:	Weapon:	Sights:	Notes:
Rep 1 Time:	Rep 2 Time:	Rep 3 Time:	Rep 4 Time:	
# Out of Black:	# of 9's:	# of 10's:	Total Score: X's	
Date:	Location:	Weapon:	Sights:	Notes:
Rep 1 Time:	Rep 2 Time:	Rep 3 Time:	Rep 4 Time:	
# Out of Black:	# of 9's:	# of 10's:	Total Score: X's	

2 TO 5

Date:	Location:	Weapon:	Sights:	Notes:
Rep 1 Time:	Rep 2 Time:	Rep 3 Time:	Rep 4 Time:	
# Out of Black:	# of 9's:	# of 10's:	**Total Score:** X's	
Date:	Location:	Weapon:	Sights:	Notes:
Rep 1 Time:	Rep 2 Time:	Rep 3 Time:	Rep 4 Time:	
# Out of Black:	# of 9's:	# of 10's:	**Total Score:** X's	
Date:	Location:	Weapon:	Sights:	Notes:
Rep 1 Time:	Rep 2 Time:	Rep 3 Time:	Rep 4 Time:	
# Out of Black:	# of 9's:	# of 10's:	**Total Score:** X's	
Date:	Location:	Weapon:	Sights:	Notes:
Rep 1 Time:	Rep 2 Time:	Rep 3 Time:	Rep 4 Time:	
# Out of Black:	# of 9's:	# of 10's:	**Total Score:** X's	
Date:	Location:	Weapon:	Sights:	Notes:
Rep 1 Time:	Rep 2 Time:	Rep 3 Time:	Rep 4 Time:	
# Out of Black:	# of 9's:	# of 10's:	**Total Score:** X's	

Advanced Pistol ©

Recoil Management Drills - 2

2 TO 5

Date:	Location:	Weapon:	Sights:	Notes:
Rep 1 Time:	Rep 2 Time:	Rep 3 Time:	Rep 4 Time:	
# Out of Black:	# of 9's:	# of 10's:	**Total Score:** **X's**	
Date:	Location:	Weapon:	Sights:	Notes:
Rep 1 Time:	Rep 2 Time:	Rep 3 Time:	Rep 4 Time:	
# Out of Black:	# of 9's:	# of 10's:	**Total Score:** **X's**	
Date:	Location:	Weapon:	Sights:	Notes:
Rep 1 Time:	Rep 2 Time:	Rep 3 Time:	Rep 4 Time:	
# Out of Black:	# of 9's:	# of 10's:	**Total Score:** **X's**	
Date:	Location:	Weapon:	Sights:	Notes:
Rep 1 Time:	Rep 2 Time:	Rep 3 Time:	Rep 4 Time:	
# Out of Black:	# of 9's:	# of 10's:	**Total Score:** **X's**	
Date:	Location:	Weapon:	Sights:	Notes:
Rep 1 Time:	Rep 2 Time:	Rep 3 Time:	Rep 4 Time:	
# Out of Black:	# of 9's:	# of 10's:	**Total Score:** **X's**	

2 TO 5

Date:	Location:	Weapon:	Sights:	Notes:	
Rep 1 Time:	Rep 2 Time:	Rep 3 Time:	Rep 4 Time:		
# Out of Black:	# of 9's:	# of 10's:	**Total Score:** **X's**		
Date:	Location:	Weapon:	Sights:	Notes:	
Rep 1 Time:	Rep 2 Time:	Rep 3 Time:	Rep 4 Time:		
# Out of Black:	# of 9's:	# of 10's:	**Total Score:** **X's**		
Date:	Location:	Weapon:	Sights:	Notes:	
Rep 1 Time:	Rep 2 Time:	Rep 3 Time:	Rep 4 Time:		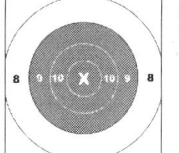
# Out of Black:	# of 9's:	# of 10's:	**Total Score:** **X's**		
Date:	Location:	Weapon:	Sights:	Notes:	
Rep 1 Time:	Rep 2 Time:	Rep 3 Time:	Rep 4 Time:		
# Out of Black:	# of 9's:	# of 10's:	**Total Score:** **X's**		
Date:	Location:	Weapon:	Sights:	Notes:	
Rep 1 Time:	Rep 2 Time:	Rep 3 Time:	Rep 4 Time:		
# Out of Black:	# of 9's:	# of 10's:	**Total Score:** **X's**		

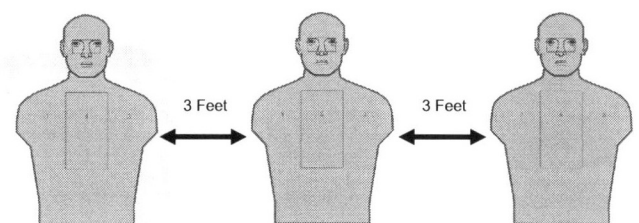

MULTIPLICITY

Purpose: Develop efficient recoil management during one-handed multiple target engagements.

Distance: 7 Yards.

Target: JD-QUAL1 X 3 Targets 3 feet apart.

Par Time: 12 Seconds.

Extra Equipment Needed: Shot timer, weighted bag with handle.

Total Rounds Fired: 15 Rounds.

Point Penalty: As per target score.

Repetitions: 1 Rep.

Starting Position & Condition: Standing - Hands at side, bag in support hand. Weapon Condition 1.

Description: At the timer beep, draw your pistol and fire 5 rounds into each of the (5 point) A Zone body boxes using only one-handed fire. The bag must stay in your support hand during entire drill. If you have a malfunction, you must clear it while keeping the bag in your support hand. Good hand placement during the draw and trigger control is essential to master this drill.

Goals: 66 Points under 12 seconds.   Expert: 73 Points under 10 seconds.   Gunfighter: 75 Points under 8 seconds.

Variations: Stagger distance of targets from each other and/or add distance.   Replace weighted bag with child simulator, wounded dummy or cuffed brief case.

MULTIPLICITY

Date:	Weapon:	Sights:	Left to Right / Right to Left
Holster:	Over Garment: Y / N	Bag Type:	Notes:
Rep Time:	# Out of A Box:	Total Score:	

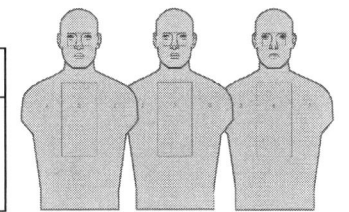

Date:	Weapon:	Sights:	Left to Right / Right to Left
Holster:	Over Garment: Y / N	Bag Type:	Notes:
Rep Time:	# Out of A Box:	Total Score:	

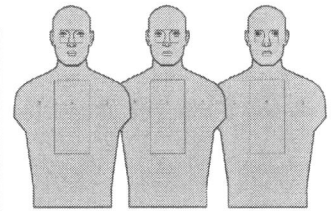

Date:	Weapon:	Sights:	Left to Right / Right to Left
Holster:	Over Garment: Y / N	Bag Type:	Notes:
Rep Time:	# Out of A Box:	Total Score:	

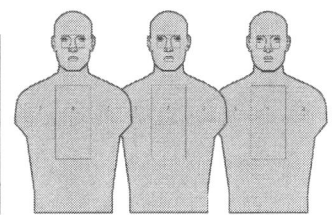

Date:	Weapon:	Sights:	Left to Right / Right to Left
Holster:	Over Garment: Y / N	Bag Type:	Notes:
Rep Time:	# Out of A Box:	Total Score:	

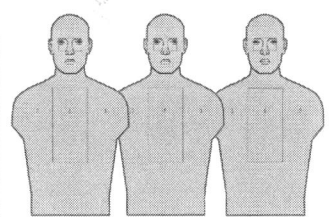

MULTIPLICITY

Date:	Weapon:	Sights:	Left to Right / Right to Left
Holster:	Over Garment: Y / N	Bag Type:	Notes:
Rep Time:	# Out of A Box:	**Total Score:**	

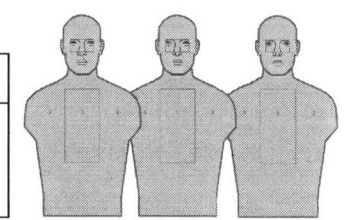

Date:	Weapon:	Sights:	Left to Right / Right to Left
Holster:	Over Garment: Y / N	Bag Type:	Notes:
Rep Time:	# Out of A Box:	**Total Score:**	

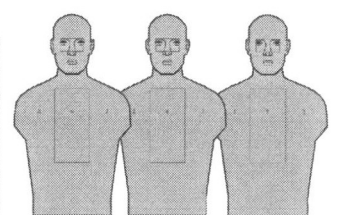

Date:	Weapon:	Sights:	Left to Right / Right to Left
Holster:	Over Garment: Y / N	Bag Type:	Notes:
Rep Time:	# Out of A Box:	**Total Score:**	

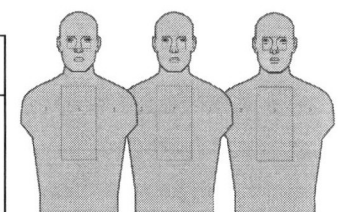

Date:	Weapon:	Sights:	Left to Right / Right to Left
Holster:	Over Garment: Y / N	Bag Type:	Notes:
Rep Time:	# Out of A Box:	**Total Score:**	

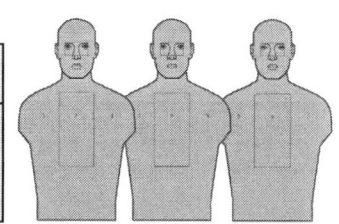

MULTIPLICITY

Date:	Weapon:	Sights:	Left to Right / Right to Left
Holster:	Over Garment: Y / N	Bag Type:	Notes:
Rep Time:	# Out of A Box:	**Total Score:**	

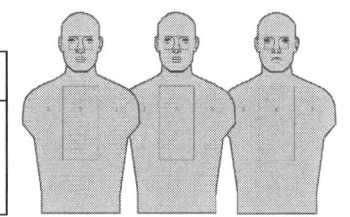

Date:	Weapon:	Sights:	Left to Right / Right to Left
Holster:	Over Garment: Y / N	Bag Type:	Notes:
Rep Time:	# Out of A Box:	**Total Score:**	

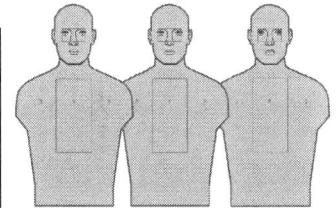

Date:	Weapon:	Sights:	Left to Right / Right to Left
Holster:	Over Garment: Y / N	Bag Type:	Notes:
Rep Time:	# Out of A Box:	**Total Score:**	

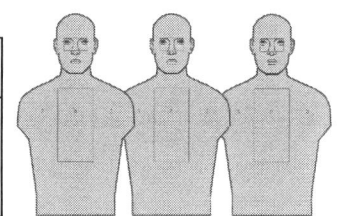

Date:	Weapon:	Sights:	Left to Right / Right to Left
Holster:	Over Garment: Y / N	Bag Type:	Notes:
Rep Time:	# Out of A Box:	**Total Score:**	

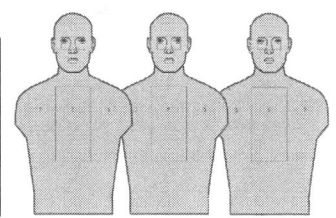

Recoil Management Drills - 3

MULTIPLICITY

Date:	Weapon:	Sights:	Left to Right / Right to Left
Holster:	Over Garment: Y / N	Bag Type:	Notes:
Rep Time:	# Out of A Box:	**Total Score:**	

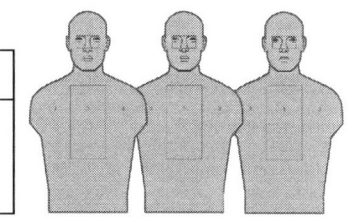

Date:	Weapon:	Sights:	Left to Right / Right to Left
Holster:	Over Garment: Y / N	Bag Type:	Notes:
Rep Time:	# Out of A Box:	**Total Score:**	

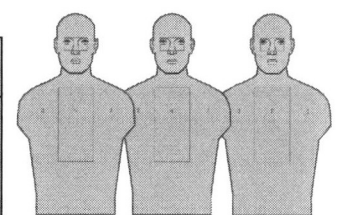

Date:	Weapon:	Sights:	Left to Right / Right to Left
Holster:	Over Garment: Y / N	Bag Type:	Notes:
Rep Time:	# Out of A Box:	**Total Score:**	

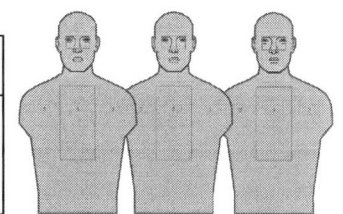

Date:	Weapon:	Sights:	Left to Right / Right to Left
Holster:	Over Garment: Y / N	Bag Type:	Notes:
Rep Time:	# Out of A Box:	**Total Score:**	

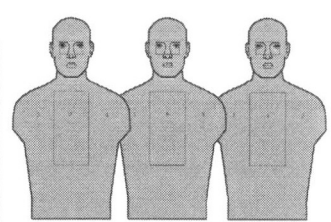

MULTIPLICITY

Date:	Weapon:	Sights:	Left to Right / Right to Left
Holster:	Over Garment: Y / N	Bag Type:	Notes:
Rep Time:	# Out of A Box:	**Total Score:**	

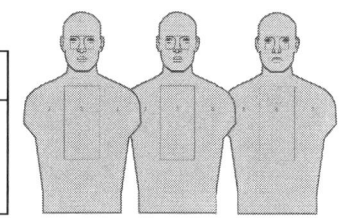

Date:	Weapon:	Sights:	Left to Right / Right to Left
Holster:	Over Garment: Y / N	Bag Type:	Notes:
Rep Time:	# Out of A Box:	**Total Score:**	

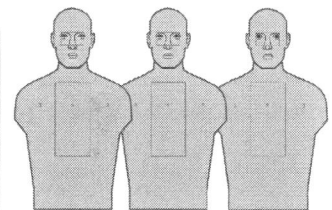

Date:	Weapon:	Sights:	Left to Right / Right to Left
Holster:	Over Garment: Y / N	Bag Type:	Notes:
Rep Time:	# Out of A Box:	**Total Score:**	

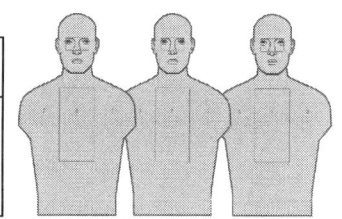

Date:	Weapon:	Sights:	Left to Right / Right to Left
Holster:	Over Garment: Y / N	Bag Type:	Notes:
Rep Time:	# Out of A Box:	**Total Score:**	

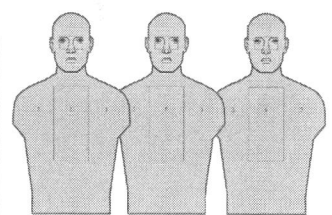

TEST YOURSELF

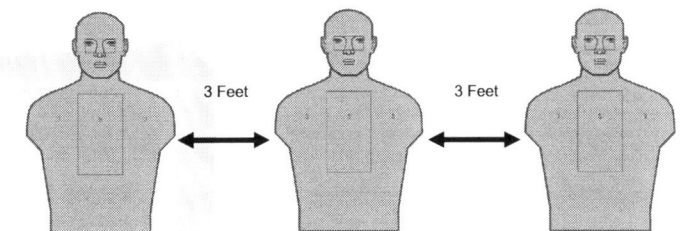

Purpose: Increase multiple target eye tracking skill.

Distance: 3, 7, 10, 15 Yards.   **Target:** JD-QUAL1 X 3 Targets 3 feet apart.

Extra Equipment Needed: Shot timer, weighted bag with handle.

Rounds Fired Per Stage: 3 Rounds.   **Total Rounds Fired:** 24 Rounds.

Point Penalty: Go / No Go.

Repetitions: 1 Rep of 8 stages.

Starting Position & Condition: Standing - Dominate hand at surrender, bag in support hand. Weapon Condition 1.

Description: At the timer beep, draw your pistol and fire 1 round into each of the (5 point) A Zone body boxes <u>left to right</u> using only one-handed fire. Put pistol on safe if applicable and holster it safely. Record time. Repeat drill shooting <u>right to left</u>. Put pistol on safe if applicable and holster it safely and record time after each stage. Move back to 7 yards. Repeat drill at 7, 10 and 15 yards. Record your time after every stage.

If you have a malfunction, you must clear it while keeping the bag in your support hand. The bag must stay in your support hand during entire stage. Good hand placement during the draw, trigger control and tracking the eye to the next target before the pistol gets there is essential to master this skill. As your efficiency increases, your times will decrease.

Goals: All rounds in (5 point) A Zone body box.

Variations: Stagger distance of targets from each other and/or add distance.   Replace weighted bag with child simulator, wounded dummy or cuffed brief case. Immediately before the start of the drill, run 50 yards or do 2X25 yard shuttle runs, do 10 push-ups or 10 jumping jacks to get your heart rate up.

TEST YOURSELF

Date:	Weapon:	Sights:	Holster:
3Y L to R Time:	7Y L to R Time:	10Y L to R Time:	15Y L to R Time:
3Y R to L Time:	7Y R to L Time:	10Y R to L Time:	15Y R to L Time:
Heart Rate Stress: Y / N	Bag Type:	# Out of A Box:	**Total Score:**

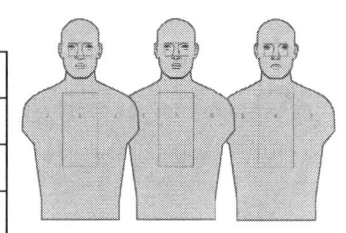

Date:	Weapon:	Sights:	Holster:
3Y L to R Time:	7Y L to R Time:	10Y L to R Time:	15Y L to R Time:
3Y R to L Time:	7Y R to L Time:	10Y R to L Time:	15Y R to L Time:
Heart Rate Stress: Y / N	Bag Type:	# Out of A Box:	**Total Score:**

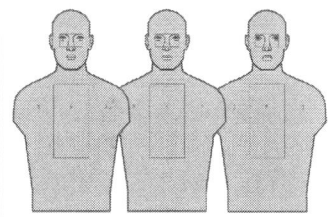

Date:	Weapon:	Sights:	Holster:
3Y L to R Time:	7Y L to R Time:	10Y L to R Time:	15Y L to R Time:
3Y R to L Time:	7Y R to L Time:	10Y R to L Time:	15Y R to L Time:
Heart Rate Stress: Y / N	Bag Type:	# Out of A Box:	**Total Score:**

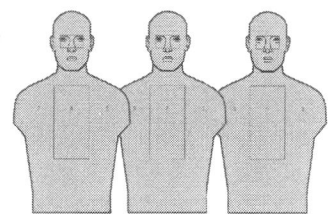

Date:	Weapon:	Sights:	Holster:
3Y L to R Time:	7Y L to R Time:	10Y L to R Time:	15Y L to R Time:
3Y R to L Time:	7Y R to L Time:	10Y R to L Time:	15Y R to L Time:
Heart Rate Stress: Y / N	Bag Type:	# Out of A Box:	**Total Score:**

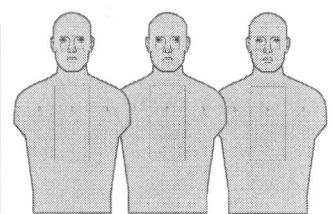

Advanced Pistol ©

TEST YOURSELF

Date:	Weapon:	Sights:	Holster:
3Y L to R Time:	7Y L to R Time:	10Y L to R Time:	15Y L to R Time:
3Y R to L Time:	7Y R to L Time:	10Y R to L Time:	15Y R to L Time:
Heart Rate Stress: Y / N	Bag Type:	# Out of A Box:	**Total Score:**

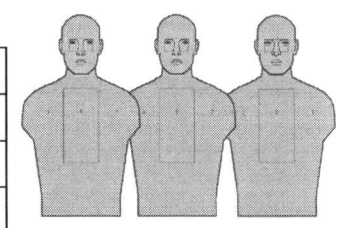

Date:	Weapon:	Sights:	Holster:
3Y L to R Time:	7Y L to R Time:	10Y L to R Time:	15Y L to R Time:
3Y R to L Time:	7Y R to L Time:	10Y R to L Time:	15Y R to L Time:
Heart Rate Stress: Y / N	Bag Type:	# Out of A Box:	**Total Score:**

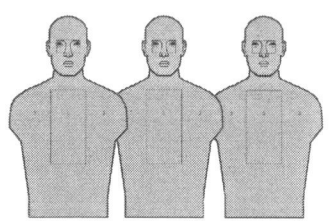

Date:	Weapon:	Sights:	Holster:
3Y L to R Time:	7Y L to R Time:	10Y L to R Time:	15Y L to R Time:
3Y R to L Time:	7Y R to L Time:	10Y R to L Time:	15Y R to L Time:
Heart Rate Stress: Y / N	Bag Type:	# Out of A Box:	**Total Score:**

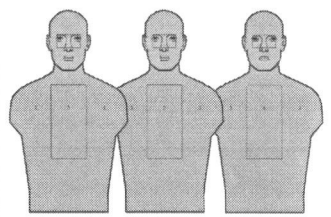

Date:	Weapon:	Sights:	Holster:
3Y L to R Time:	7Y L to R Time:	10Y L to R Time:	15Y L to R Time:
3Y R to L Time:	7Y R to L Time:	10Y R to L Time:	15Y R to L Time:
Heart Rate Stress: Y / N	Bag Type:	# Out of A Box:	**Total Score:**

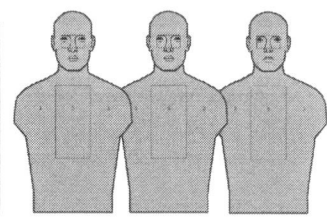

TEST YOURSELF

Date:	Weapon:	Sights:	Holster:
3Y L to R Time:	7Y L to R Time:	10Y L to R Time:	15Y L to R Time:
3Y R to L Time:	7Y R to L Time:	10Y R to L Time:	15Y R to L Time:
Heart Rate Stress: Y / N	Bag Type:	# Out of A Box:	**Total Score:**

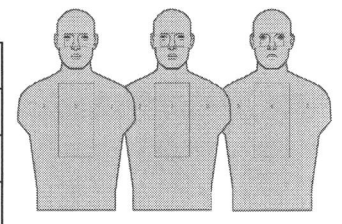

Date:	Weapon:	Sights:	Holster:
3Y L to R Time:	7Y L to R Time:	10Y L to R Time:	15Y L to R Time:
3Y R to L Time:	7Y R to L Time:	10Y R to L Time:	15Y R to L Time:
Heart Rate Stress: Y / N	Bag Type:	# Out of A Box:	**Total Score:**

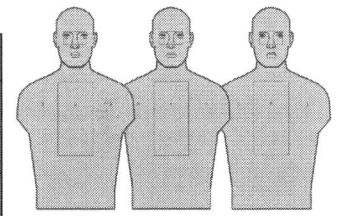

Date:	Weapon:	Sights:	Holster:
3Y L to R Time:	7Y L to R Time:	10Y L to R Time:	15Y L to R Time:
3Y R to L Time:	7Y R to L Time:	10Y R to L Time:	15Y R to L Time:
Heart Rate Stress: Y / N	Bag Type:	# Out of A Box:	**Total Score:**

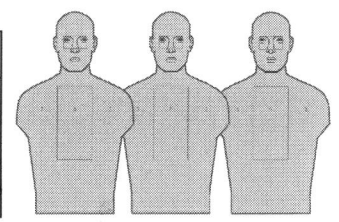

Date:	Weapon:	Sights:	Holster:
3Y L to R Time:	7Y L to R Time:	10Y L to R Time:	15Y L to R Time:
3Y R to L Time:	7Y R to L Time:	10Y R to L Time:	15Y R to L Time:
Heart Rate Stress: Y / N	Bag Type:	# Out of A Box:	**Total Score:**

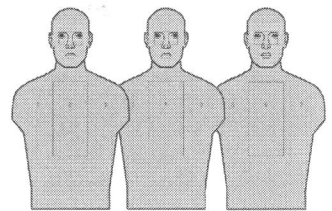

Advanced Pistol ©

Recoil Management Drills - 4

TEST YOURSELF

Date:	Weapon:	Sights:	Holster:
3Y L to R Time:	7Y L to R Time:	10Y L to R Time:	15Y L to R Time:
3Y R to L Time:	7Y R to L Time:	10Y R to L Time:	15Y R to L Time:
Heart Rate Stress: Y / N	Bag Type:	# Out of A Box:	**Total Score:**

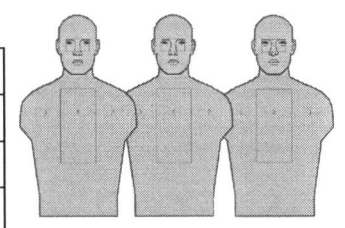

Date:	Weapon:	Sights:	Holster:
3Y L to R Time:	7Y L to R Time:	10Y L to R Time:	15Y L to R Time:
3Y R to L Time:	7Y R to L Time:	10Y R to L Time:	15Y R to L Time:
Heart Rate Stress: Y / N	Bag Type:	# Out of A Box:	**Total Score:**

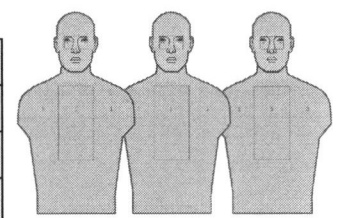

Date:	Weapon:	Sights:	Holster:
3Y L to R Time:	7Y L to R Time:	10Y L to R Time:	15Y L to R Time:
3Y R to L Time:	7Y R to L Time:	10Y R to L Time:	15Y R to L Time:
Heart Rate Stress: Y / N	Bag Type:	# Out of A Box:	**Total Score:**

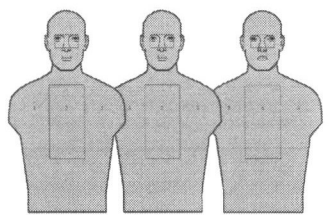

Date:	Weapon:	Sights:	Holster:
3Y L to R Time:	7Y L to R Time:	10Y L to R Time:	15Y L to R Time:
3Y R to L Time:	7Y R to L Time:	10Y R to L Time:	15Y R to L Time:
Heart Rate Stress: Y / N	Bag Type:	# Out of A Box:	**Total Score:**

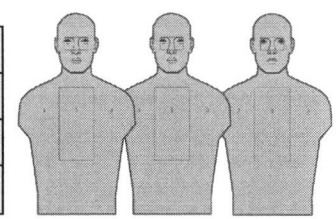

TEST YOURSELF

Date:	Weapon:	Sights:	Holster:
3Y L to R Time:	7Y L to R Time:	10Y L to R Time:	15Y L to R Time:
3Y R to L Time:	7Y R to L Time:	10Y R to L Time:	15Y R to L Time:
Heart Rate Stress: Y / N	Bag Type:	# Out of A Box:	**Total Score:**

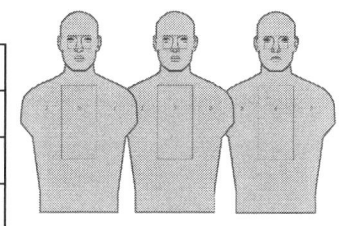

Date:	Weapon:	Sights:	Holster:
3Y L to R Time:	7Y L to R Time:	10Y L to R Time:	15Y L to R Time:
3Y R to L Time:	7Y R to L Time:	10Y R to L Time:	15Y R to L Time:
Heart Rate Stress: Y / N	Bag Type:	# Out of A Box:	**Total Score:**

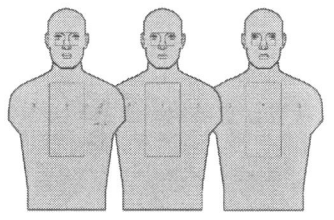

Date:	Weapon:	Sights:	Holster:
3Y L to R Time:	7Y L to R Time:	10Y L to R Time:	15Y L to R Time:
3Y R to L Time:	7Y R to L Time:	10Y R to L Time:	15Y R to L Time:
Heart Rate Stress: Y / N	Bag Type:	# Out of A Box:	**Total Score:**

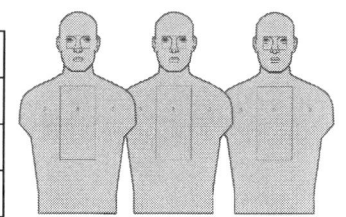

Date:	Weapon:	Sights:	Holster:
3Y L to R Time:	7Y L to R Time:	10Y L to R Time:	15Y L to R Time:
3Y R to L Time:	7Y R to L Time:	10Y R to L Time:	15Y R to L Time:
Heart Rate Stress: Y / N	Bag Type:	# Out of A Box:	**Total Score:**

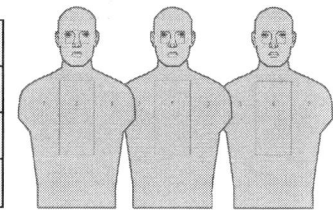

PROTECTOR

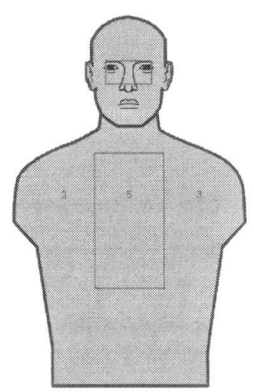

Purpose: Pistol multi-tasking familiarization.

Distance: 5, 10, 15, 20, 25 Yards.   **Target:** JD-Qual1

Par Time: As per distance par time.

Extra Equipment Needed: Shot timer, and weighted bag, child simulator, wounded dummy, etc.

Rounds Fired Per Yard Line: 3 Rounds.   **Total Rounds Fired:** 15 Rounds.

Point Penalty: As per target score.   **Repetitions:** 1 Rep.

Starting Position & Condition: Standing - Surrender with object in support hand. Weapon Condition 1.

Description: Pick up your selected object, place against chest or hang from hand. At the timer beep, draw your pistol and fire three rounds into the (5 point) A Zone body box from 5 yards. Put pistol on safe if applicable and holster it safely. Move back to 10 yards. Repeat drill at 10, 15, 20 and 25 yards.

Distance par times:

    5 yards – 3 seconds.   10 yards – 4 seconds.   15 yards – 5 seconds.   20 yards – 6 seconds.   25 yards – 7 seconds.

Your weighted object needs to be held through the entire drill. Putting down object or not making the par time per distance will make the drill a No Go. Management of holding an object, good hand placement during the draw and trigger control is essential to master this drill.

Goals: 60 points.   **Expert:** 65 points.   **Gunfighter:** 75 points.

Note: If you are really good, you will shoot farther distances in roughly half the allowed par time. Track to see your speed increase while keeping your accuracy.

PROTECTOR

Date:	Weapon:	Sights:	Notes	
5 Yard Time:	10 Yard Time:	15 Yard Time:	20 Yard Time:	25 Yard Time:
Holster:	Over Garment: Y / N	Bag Type:	# Out of A Box:	**Total Score:**

Date:	Weapon:	Sights:	Notes	
5 Yard Time:	10 Yard Time:	15 Yard Time:	20 Yard Time:	25 Yard Time:
Holster:	Over Garment: Y / N	Bag Type:	# Out of A Box:	**Total Score:**

Date:	Weapon:	Sights:	Notes	
5 Yard Time:	10 Yard Time:	15 Yard Time:	20 Yard Time:	25 Yard Time:
Holster:	Over Garment: Y / N	Bag Type:	# Out of A Box:	**Total Score:**

Date:	Weapon:	Sights:	Notes	
5 Yard Time:	10 Yard Time:	15 Yard Time:	20 Yard Time:	25 Yard Time:
Holster:	Over Garment: Y / N	Bag Type:	# Out of A Box:	**Total Score:**

Date:	Weapon:	Sights:	Notes	
5 Yard Time:	10 Yard Time:	15 Yard Time:	20 Yard Time:	25 Yard Time:
Holster:	Over Garment: Y / N	Bag Type:	# Out of A Box:	**Total Score:**

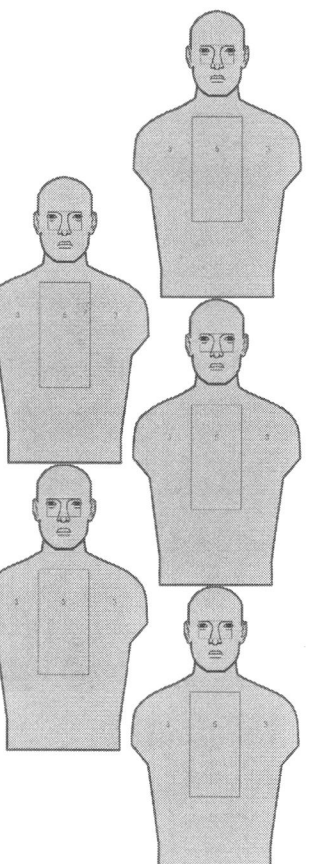

Advanced Pistol ©

Gunfighter Drills - 1

PROTECTOR

Date:	Weapon:	Sights:	Notes	
5 Yard Time:	10 Yard Time:	15 Yard Time:	20 Yard Time:	25 Yard Time:
Holster:	Over Garment: Y / N	Bag Type:	# Out of A Box:	**Total Score:**

Date:	Weapon:	Sights:	Notes	
5 Yard Time:	10 Yard Time:	15 Yard Time:	20 Yard Time:	25 Yard Time:
Holster:	Over Garment: Y / N	Bag Type:	# Out of A Box:	**Total Score:**

Date:	Weapon:	Sights:	Notes	
5 Yard Time:	10 Yard Time:	15 Yard Time:	20 Yard Time:	25 Yard Time:
Holster:	Over Garment: Y / N	Bag Type:	# Out of A Box:	**Total Score:**

Date:	Weapon:	Sights:	Notes	
5 Yard Time:	10 Yard Time:	15 Yard Time:	20 Yard Time:	25 Yard Time:
Holster:	Over Garment: Y / N	Bag Type:	# Out of A Box:	**Total Score:**

Date:	Weapon:	Sights:	Notes	
5 Yard Time:	10 Yard Time:	15 Yard Time:	20 Yard Time:	25 Yard Time:
Holster:	Over Garment: Y / N	Bag Type:	# Out of A Box:	**Total Score:**

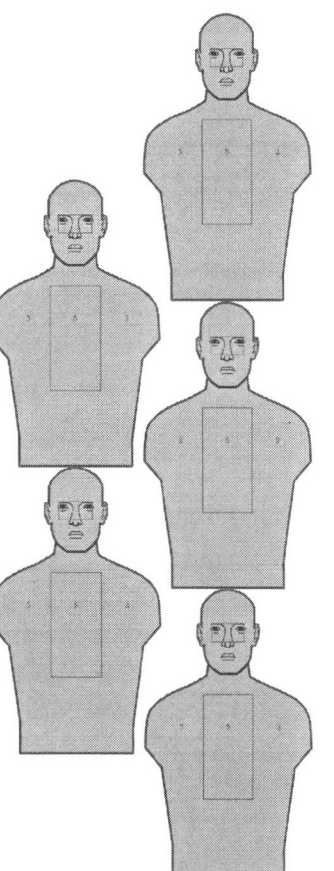

PROTECTOR

Date:	Weapon:	Sights:	Notes	
5 Yard Time:	10 Yard Time:	15 Yard Time:	20 Yard Time:	25 Yard Time:
Holster:	Over Garment: Y / N	Bag Type:	# Out of A Box:	**Total Score:**

Date:	Weapon:	Sights:	Notes	
5 Yard Time:	10 Yard Time:	15 Yard Time:	20 Yard Time:	25 Yard Time:
Holster:	Over Garment: Y / N	Bag Type:	# Out of A Box:	**Total Score:**

Date:	Weapon:	Sights:	Notes	
5 Yard Time:	10 Yard Time:	15 Yard Time:	20 Yard Time:	25 Yard Time:
Holster:	Over Garment: Y / N	Bag Type:	# Out of A Box:	**Total Score:**

Date:	Weapon:	Sights:	Notes	
5 Yard Time:	10 Yard Time:	15 Yard Time:	20 Yard Time:	25 Yard Time:
Holster:	Over Garment: Y / N	Bag Type:	# Out of A Box:	**Total Score:**

Date:	Weapon:	Sights:	Notes	
5 Yard Time:	10 Yard Time:	15 Yard Time:	20 Yard Time:	25 Yard Time:
Holster:	Over Garment: Y / N	Bag Type:	# Out of A Box:	**Total Score:**

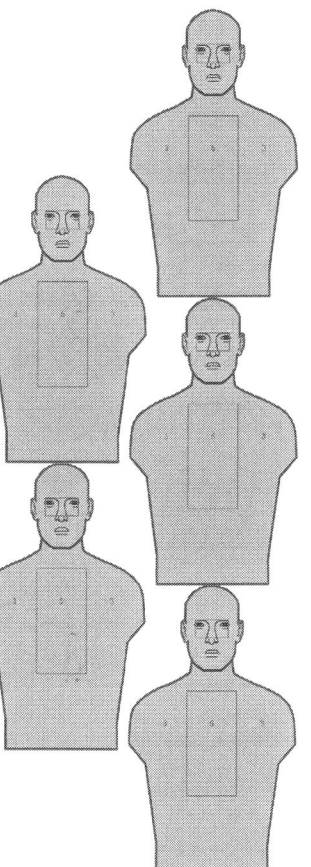

Advanced Pistol ©

Gunfighter Drills - 1

PROTECTOR

Date:	Weapon:	Sights:	Notes	
5 Yard Time:	10 Yard Time:	15 Yard Time:	20 Yard Time:	25 Yard Time:
Holster:	Over Garment: Y / N	Bag Type:	# Out of A Box:	**Total Score:**

Date:	Weapon:	Sights:	Notes	
5 Yard Time:	10 Yard Time:	15 Yard Time:	20 Yard Time:	25 Yard Time:
Holster:	Over Garment: Y / N	Bag Type:	# Out of A Box:	**Total Score:**

Date:	Weapon:	Sights:	Notes	
5 Yard Time:	10 Yard Time:	15 Yard Time:	20 Yard Time:	25 Yard Time:
Holster:	Over Garment: Y / N	Bag Type:	# Out of A Box:	**Total Score:**

Date:	Weapon:	Sights:	Notes	
5 Yard Time:	10 Yard Time:	15 Yard Time:	20 Yard Time:	25 Yard Time:
Holster:	Over Garment: Y / N	Bag Type:	# Out of A Box:	**Total Score:**

Date:	Weapon:	Sights:	Notes	
5 Yard Time:	10 Yard Time:	15 Yard Time:	20 Yard Time:	25 Yard Time:
Holster:	Over Garment: Y / N	Bag Type:	# Out of A Box:	**Total Score:**

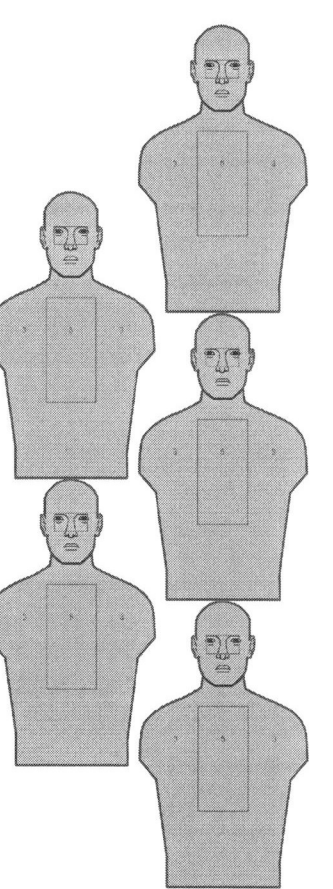

PROTECTOR

Date:	Weapon:	Sights:	Notes	
5 Yard Time:	10 Yard Time:	15 Yard Time:	20 Yard Time:	25 Yard Time:
Holster:	Over Garment: Y / N	Bag Type:	# Out of A Box:	**Total Score:**

Date:	Weapon:	Sights:	Notes	
5 Yard Time:	10 Yard Time:	15 Yard Time:	20 Yard Time:	25 Yard Time:
Holster:	Over Garment: Y / N	Bag Type:	# Out of A Box:	**Total Score:**

Date:	Weapon:	Sights:	Notes	
5 Yard Time:	10 Yard Time:	15 Yard Time:	20 Yard Time:	25 Yard Time:
Holster:	Over Garment: Y / N	Bag Type:	# Out of A Box:	**Total Score:**

Date:	Weapon:	Sights:	Notes	
5 Yard Time:	10 Yard Time:	15 Yard Time:	20 Yard Time:	25 Yard Time:
Holster:	Over Garment: Y / N	Bag Type:	# Out of A Box:	**Total Score:**

Date:	Weapon:	Sights:	Notes	
5 Yard Time:	10 Yard Time:	15 Yard Time:	20 Yard Time:	25 Yard Time:
Holster:	Over Garment: Y / N	Bag Type:	# Out of A Box:	**Total Score:**

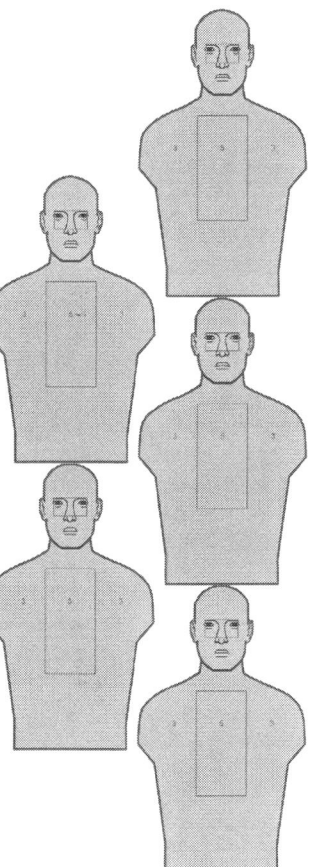

Advanced Pistol ©

Gunfighter Drills - 1

TOO BUSY

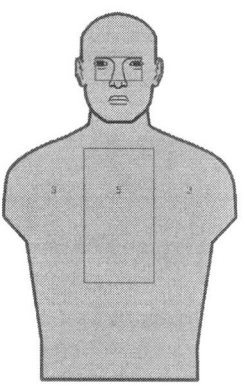

Purpose: Pistol multi-tasking familiarization.

Distance: 5, 10, 15, 25 Yards.   **Target**: JD-Qual1

Extra Equipment Needed: 3 Pistol mags and mag pouches, shot timer, and weighted bag, child simulator, wounded dummy, etc.

Rounds Fired Per Distance: 5 Rounds.   **Total Rounds Fired:** 20 Rounds.

Point Penalty: As per target score.

Repetitions: 1 Rep of 4 distances.

Starting Position & Condition: Standing - Surrender with object in support hand. Weapon Condition 1.

Description: Load 1st mag with between 3 to 6 rounds (have someone load for you or load multiple mags with different counts and mix them up). 2nd magazine with between 5 to 6 rounds. 3rd magazine to be loaded with 12 rounds.

Pick up your selected object, place against chest or hang from hand. At the timer beep, draw your pistol and fire 5 rounds into the (5 point) A Zone body box at 5 yards. Reload as needed with dominate hand only. Put pistol on safe if applicable and holster it safely. Move back to 10 yards. Repeat drill at 10, 15 and 25 yards. Record in your notes if you felt smooth and deliberate with whole drill or if you messed up any reloads, etc. Your weighted object needs to be held through the entire drill. All emergency reloads must be done one handed.

Goals: 80 points.   Expert: 90 points.   Gunfighter: 100 points with no reloading mistakes

Variation: Have someone load a dummy round in one of the two magazines to be used first. Use barriers/barricades for cover.   Time the entire drill.

TOO BUSY

Date:	Weapon:	Sights:	Holster:
Carry Object:	Dummy Rounds: Y / N	Notes:	
Cover Used: Y / N	Drill Time:	# Out of A Box:	**Total Score:**

Date:	Weapon:	Sights:	Holster:
Carry Object:	Dummy Rounds: Y / N	Notes:	
Cover Used: Y / N	Drill Time:	# Out of A Box:	**Total Score:**

Date:	Weapon:	Sights:	Holster:
Carry Object:	Dummy Rounds: Y / N	Notes:	
Cover Used: Y / N	Drill Time:	# Out of A Box:	**Total Score:**

Date:	Weapon:	Sights:	Holster:
Carry Object:	Dummy Rounds: Y / N	Notes:	
Cover Used: Y / N	Drill Time:	# Out of A Box:	**Total Score:**

Date:	Weapon:	Sights:	Holster:
Carry Object:	Dummy Rounds: Y / N	Notes:	
Cover Used: Y / N	Drill Time:	# Out of A Box:	**Total Score:**

TOO BUSY

Date:	Weapon:	Sights:	Holster:
Carry Object:	Dummy Rounds: Y / N	Notes:	
Cover Used: Y / N	Drill Time:	# Out of A Box:	**Total Score:**

Date:	Weapon:	Sights:	Holster:
Carry Object:	Dummy Rounds: Y / N	Notes:	
Cover Used: Y / N	Drill Time:	# Out of A Box:	**Total Score:**

Date:	Weapon:	Sights:	Holster:
Carry Object:	Dummy Rounds: Y / N	Notes:	
Cover Used: Y / N	Drill Time:	# Out of A Box:	**Total Score:**

Date:	Weapon:	Sights:	Holster:
Carry Object:	Dummy Rounds: Y / N	Notes:	
Cover Used: Y / N	Drill Time:	# Out of A Box:	**Total Score:**

Date:	Weapon:	Sights:	Holster:
Carry Object:	Dummy Rounds: Y / N	Notes:	
Cover Used: Y / N	Drill Time:	# Out of A Box:	**Total Score:**

TOO BUSY

Date:	Weapon:	Sights:	Holster:
Carry Object:	Dummy Rounds: Y / N	Notes:	
Cover Used: Y / N	Drill Time:	# Out of A Box:	**Total Score:**

Date:	Weapon:	Sights:	Holster:
Carry Object:	Dummy Rounds: Y / N	Notes:	
Cover Used: Y / N	Drill Time:	# Out of A Box:	**Total Score:**

Date:	Weapon:	Sights:	Holster:
Carry Object:	Dummy Rounds: Y / N	Notes:	
Cover Used: Y / N	Drill Time:	# Out of A Box:	**Total Score:**

Date:	Weapon:	Sights:	Holster:
Carry Object:	Dummy Rounds: Y / N	Notes:	
Cover Used: Y / N	Drill Time:	# Out of A Box:	**Total Score:**

Date:	Weapon:	Sights:	Holster:
Carry Object:	Dummy Rounds: Y / N	Notes:	
Cover Used: Y / N	Drill Time:	# Out of A Box:	**Total Score:**

www.GUNFIGHTERSERIES.com ©

TOO BUSY

Date:	Weapon:	Sights:	Holster:
Carry Object:	Dummy Rounds: Y / N	Notes:	
Cover Used: Y / N	Drill Time:	# Out of A Box:	**Total Score:**

Date:	Weapon:	Sights:	Holster:
Carry Object:	Dummy Rounds: Y / N	Notes:	
Cover Used: Y / N	Drill Time:	# Out of A Box:	**Total Score:**

Date:	Weapon:	Sights:	Holster:
Carry Object:	Dummy Rounds: Y / N	Notes:	
Cover Used: Y / N	Drill Time:	# Out of A Box:	**Total Score:**

Date:	Weapon:	Sights:	Holster:
Carry Object:	Dummy Rounds: Y / N	Notes:	
Cover Used: Y / N	Drill Time:	# Out of A Box:	**Total Score:**

Date:	Weapon:	Sights:	Holster:
Carry Object:	Dummy Rounds: Y / N	Notes:	
Cover Used: Y / N	Drill Time:	# Out of A Box:	**Total Score:**

TOO BUSY

Date:	Weapon:	Sights:	Holster:
Carry Object:	Dummy Rounds: Y / N	Notes:	
Cover Used: Y / N	Drill Time:	# Out of A Box:	**Total Score:**

Date:	Weapon:	Sights:	Holster:
Carry Object:	Dummy Rounds: Y / N	Notes:	
Cover Used: Y / N	Drill Time:	# Out of A Box:	**Total Score:**

Date:	Weapon:	Sights:	Holster:
Carry Object:	Dummy Rounds: Y / N	Notes:	
Cover Used: Y / N	Drill Time:	# Out of A Box:	**Total Score:**

Date:	Weapon:	Sights:	Holster:
Carry Object:	Dummy Rounds: Y / N	Notes:	
Cover Used: Y / N	Drill Time:	# Out of A Box:	**Total Score:**

Date:	Weapon:	Sights:	Holster:
Carry Object:	Dummy Rounds: Y / N	Notes:	
Cover Used: Y / N	Drill Time:	# Out of A Box:	**Total Score:**

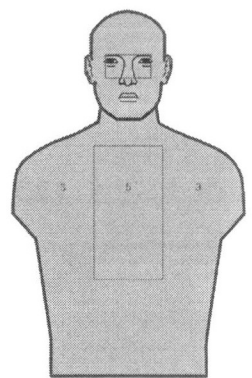

CAR JACK RIGHT & LEFT

Purpose: Develop non-standard real world position skill.

Distance: 5 Yards.

Par Time: 3 Seconds.

Rounds Fired Per Rep: 5 Rounds.

Point Penalty: Go / No Go.

Target: JD-Qual1

Extra Equipment Needed: Shot timer, a chair or vehicle.

Total Rounds Fired: 20 Rounds.

Repetitions: 4 Reps (2 each direction).

Starting Position & Condition: Seated – Surrender or on steering wheel. Weapon Condition 1.

Car Jack Right Description: Sit in the chair facing 90 degrees to your target with your <u>right shoulder</u> towards the target. At the timer beep, draw your pistol and fire 5 rounds into the JD-QUAL1 target from 5 yards. Stand keeping your pistol pointed in a safe direction. Put pistol on safe if applicable and holster it safely. Record time. Re-set drill 1 more time. Any rounds out of the (5 point) A Zone body box or going over par time is a drill No Go.

Car Jack Left Description: Sit in the chair facing 90 degrees to your target with your <u>left shoulder</u> towards the target. At the timer beep, draw your pistol and fire 5 rounds into the JD-QUAL1 target from 5 yards. Stand keeping your pistol pointed in a safe direction. Put pistol on safe if applicable and holster it safely. Record time. Re-set the drill 1 more time. Any rounds out of the (5 point) A Zone body box or going over par time is a drill No Go.

A safe draw, moving pistol as if you are in a car and good one-handed recoil management is essential to master this drill. Follow the firearm safety rules and don't point the pistol at anything you do not want to destroy to include your leg as your drawing and presenting your pistol to the target.

Variation: Immediately before the start of the drill, run 50 yards or do 2X25 yard shuttle runs, do 10 push-ups or 10 jumping jacks to get your heart rate up. Simulate releasing a seatbelt. If possible, live fire from the driver, passenger and rear seat of a designated training vehicle.

CAR JACK RIGHT & LEFT

Date:	Weapon:	Holster:	Chair / Vehicle
Right Rep 1 Time:	Right Rep 2 Time:	Heart Rate Stress: Y / N	Notes:
Left Rep 1 Time:	Left Rep 2 Time:	**All In Body Box: Y / N**	

Date:	Weapon:	Holster:	Chair / Vehicle
Right Rep 1 Time:	Right Rep 2 Time:	Heart Rate Stress: Y / N	Notes:
Left Rep 1 Time:	Left Rep 2 Time:	**All In Body Box: Y / N**	

Date:	Weapon:	Holster:	Chair / Vehicle
Right Rep 1 Time:	Right Rep 2 Time:	Heart Rate Stress: Y / N	Notes:
Left Rep 1 Time:	Left Rep 2 Time:	**All In Body Box: Y / N**	

Date:	Weapon:	Holster:	Chair / Vehicle
Right Rep 1 Time:	Right Rep 2 Time:	Heart Rate Stress: Y / N	Notes:
Left Rep 1 Time:	Left Rep 2 Time:	**All In Body Box: Y / N**	

Date:	Weapon:	Holster:	Chair / Vehicle
Right Rep 1 Time:	Right Rep 2 Time:	Heart Rate Stress: Y / N	Notes:
Left Rep 1 Time:	Left Rep 2 Time:	**All In Body Box: Y / N**	

Advanced Pistol ©

Gunfighter Drills - 3

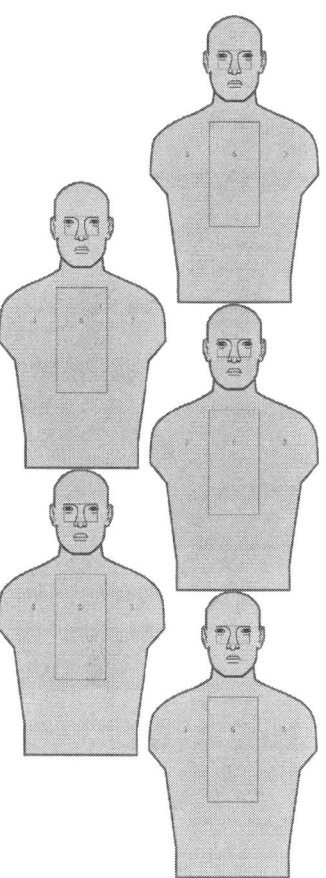

CAR JACK RIGHT & LEFT

Date:	Weapon:	Holster:	Chair / Vehicle
Right Rep 1 Time:	Right Rep 2 Time:	Heart Rate Stress: Y / N	Notes:
Left Rep 1 Time:	Left Rep 2 Time:	**All In Body Box: Y / N**	

Date:	Weapon:	Holster:	Chair / Vehicle
Right Rep 1 Time:	Right Rep 2 Time:	Heart Rate Stress: Y / N	Notes:
Left Rep 1 Time:	Left Rep 2 Time:	**All In Body Box: Y / N**	

Date:	Weapon:	Holster:	Chair / Vehicle
Right Rep 1 Time:	Right Rep 2 Time:	Heart Rate Stress: Y / N	Notes:
Left Rep 1 Time:	Left Rep 2 Time:	**All In Body Box: Y / N**	

Date:	Weapon:	Holster:	Chair / Vehicle
Right Rep 1 Time:	Right Rep 2 Time:	Heart Rate Stress: Y / N	Notes:
Left Rep 1 Time:	Left Rep 2 Time:	**All In Body Box: Y / N**	

Date:	Weapon:	Holster:	Chair / Vehicle
Right Rep 1 Time:	Right Rep 2 Time:	Heart Rate Stress: Y / N	Notes:
Left Rep 1 Time:	Left Rep 2 Time:	**All In Body Box: Y / N**	

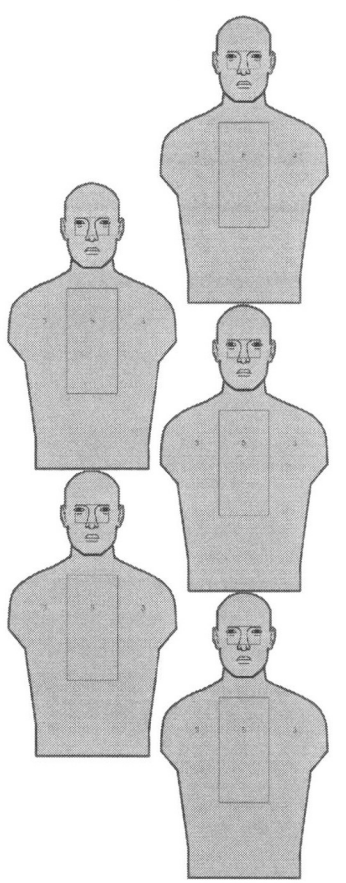

CAR JACK RIGHT & LEFT

Date:	Weapon:	Holster:	Chair / Vehicle
Right Rep 1 Time:	Right Rep 2 Time:	Heart Rate Stress: Y / N	Notes:
Left Rep 1 Time:	Left Rep 2 Time:	**All In Body Box: Y / N**	

Date:	Weapon:	Holster:	Chair / Vehicle
Right Rep 1 Time:	Right Rep 2 Time:	Heart Rate Stress: Y / N	Notes:
Left Rep 1 Time:	Left Rep 2 Time:	**All In Body Box: Y / N**	

Date:	Weapon:	Holster:	Chair / Vehicle
Right Rep 1 Time:	Right Rep 2 Time:	Heart Rate Stress: Y / N	Notes:
Left Rep 1 Time:	Left Rep 2 Time:	**All In Body Box: Y / N**	

Date:	Weapon:	Holster:	Chair / Vehicle
Right Rep 1 Time:	Right Rep 2 Time:	Heart Rate Stress: Y / N	Notes:
Left Rep 1 Time:	Left Rep 2 Time:	**All In Body Box: Y / N**	

Date:	Weapon:	Holster:	Chair / Vehicle
Right Rep 1 Time:	Right Rep 2 Time:	Heart Rate Stress: Y / N	Notes:
Left Rep 1 Time:	Left Rep 2 Time:	**All In Body Box: Y / N**	

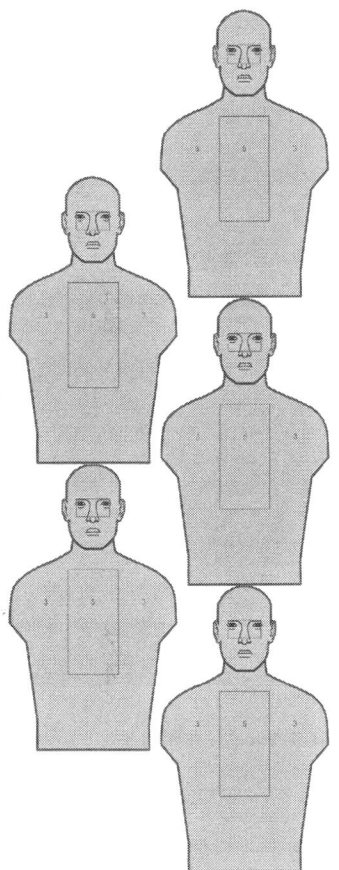

Advanced Pistol ©

CAR JACK RIGHT & LEFT

Date:	Weapon:	Holster:	Chair / Vehicle
Right Rep 1 Time:	Right Rep 2 Time:	Heart Rate Stress: Y / N	Notes:
Left Rep 1 Time:	Left Rep 2 Time:	**All In Body Box: Y / N**	

Date:	Weapon:	Holster:	Chair / Vehicle
Right Rep 1 Time:	Right Rep 2 Time:	Heart Rate Stress: Y / N	Notes:
Left Rep 1 Time:	Left Rep 2 Time:	**All In Body Box: Y / N**	

Date:	Weapon:	Holster:	Chair / Vehicle
Right Rep 1 Time:	Right Rep 2 Time:	Heart Rate Stress: Y / N	Notes:
Left Rep 1 Time:	Left Rep 2 Time:	**All In Body Box: Y / N**	

Date:	Weapon:	Holster:	Chair / Vehicle
Right Rep 1 Time:	Right Rep 2 Time:	Heart Rate Stress: Y / N	Notes:
Left Rep 1 Time:	Left Rep 2 Time:	**All In Body Box: Y / N**	

Date:	Weapon:	Holster:	Chair / Vehicle
Right Rep 1 Time:	Right Rep 2 Time:	Heart Rate Stress: Y / N	Notes:
Left Rep 1 Time:	Left Rep 2 Time:	**All In Body Box: Y / N**	

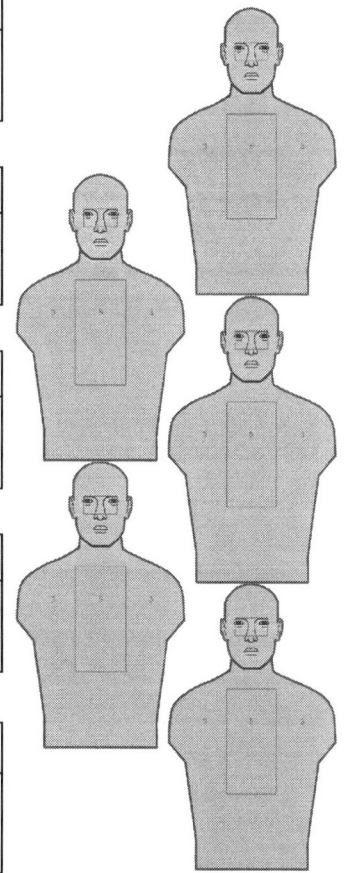

CAR JACK RIGHT & LEFT

Date:	Weapon:	Holster:	Chair / Vehicle
Right Rep 1 Time:	Right Rep 2 Time:	Heart Rate Stress: Y / N	Notes:
Left Rep 1 Time:	Left Rep 2 Time:	**All In Body Box: Y / N**	

Date:	Weapon:	Holster:	Chair / Vehicle
Right Rep 1 Time:	Right Rep 2 Time:	Heart Rate Stress: Y / N	Notes:
Left Rep 1 Time:	Left Rep 2 Time:	**All In Body Box: Y / N**	

Date:	Weapon:	Holster:	Chair / Vehicle
Right Rep 1 Time:	Right Rep 2 Time:	Heart Rate Stress: Y / N	Notes:
Left Rep 1 Time:	Left Rep 2 Time:	**All In Body Box: Y / N**	

Date:	Weapon:	Holster:	Chair / Vehicle
Right Rep 1 Time:	Right Rep 2 Time:	Heart Rate Stress: Y / N	Notes:
Left Rep 1 Time:	Left Rep 2 Time:	**All In Body Box: Y / N**	

Date:	Weapon:	Holster:	Chair / Vehicle
Right Rep 1 Time:	Right Rep 2 Time:	Heart Rate Stress: Y / N	Notes:
Left Rep 1 Time:	Left Rep 2 Time:	**All In Body Box: Y / N**	

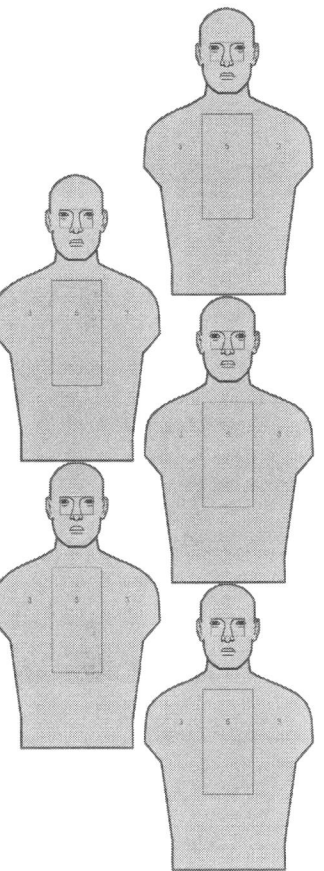

GUNDO RELOAD

Purpose: Accurate shooting under stress and unexpected pistol manipulation.

By: Greg Otto of Gundo Holsters.

Distance: 5 Yards.

Target: GF-3 X 2. Targets placed next to each other.

Extra Equipment Needed: Shot timer, 2 pistol magazines, 2 magazine pouches.

Rounds Fired Per Rep: 8 Rounds.

Total Rounds Fired: 24 Rounds.

Repetitions: 3 Reps.

Starting Position & Condition: Standing – Interview or hands relaxed at side. Weapon Condition 1.

Description: Load 1st mag with between 2 to 5 rounds (have someone load for you or load multiple mags with different counts and mix them up). 2nd magazine to be loaded full then placed in mag pouch.

At the timer beep, draw your pistol and fire 2 rounds into each of the 4 boxes of the two GF-3 targets. Reload as needed. Record your time. Repeat drill 2 more times. Record your times to track progress. If any of the shots fall outside of the boxes, the drill is a No Go.

Goals: To be smooth and deliberate, over time increased speed. The Gundo Holsters goal is 3 perfect repetitions, each under 5.5 seconds.

Variation: Add random dummy rounds to your magazines. Add distance.

GUNDO RELOAD

Date:	Weapon:	Sights:	Holster:
Rep 1 Reload Split:	Rep 2 Reload Split:	Rep 3 Reload Split:	Dummy Round: Y / N
Rep 1 Time:	Rep 2 Time:	Rep 3 Time:	Notes:
Rep 1 All In: **Go** / **No Go**	Rep 2 All In: **Go** / **No Go**	Rep 3 All In: **Go** / **No Go**	

Date:	Weapon:	Sights:	Holster:
Rep 1 Reload Split:	Rep 2 Reload Split:	Rep 3 Reload Split:	
Rep 1 Time:	Rep 2 Time:	Rep 3 Time:	Notes:
Rep 1 All In: **Go** / **No Go**	Rep 2 All In: **Go** / **No Go**	Rep 3 All In: **Go** / **No Go**	

Date:	Weapon:	Sights:	Holster:
Rep 1 Reload Split:	Rep 2 Reload Split:	Rep 3 Reload Split:	
Rep 1 Time:	Rep 2 Time:	Rep 3 Time:	Notes:
Rep 1 All In: **Go** / **No Go**	Rep 2 All In: **Go** / **No Go**	Rep 3 All In: **Go** / **No Go**	

Date:	Weapon:	Sights:	Holster:
Rep 1 Reload Split:	Rep 2 Reload Split:	Rep 3 Reload Split:	
Rep 1 Time:	Rep 2 Time:	Rep 3 Time:	Notes:
Rep 1 All In: **Go** / **No Go**	Rep 2 All In: **Go** / **No Go**	Rep 3 All In: **Go** / **No Go**	

Advanced Pistol ©

www.GUNFIGHTERSERIES.com ©

GUNDO RELOAD

Date:	Weapon:	Sights:	Holster:
Rep 1 Reload Split:	Rep 2 Reload Split:	Rep 3 Reload Split:	Dummy Round: Y / N
Rep 1 Time:	Rep 2 Time:	Rep 3 Time:	Notes:
Rep 1 All In: **Go** / **No Go**	Rep 2 All In: **Go** / **No Go**	Rep 3 All In: **Go** / **No Go**	

Date:	Weapon:	Sights:	Holster:
Rep 1 Reload Split:	Rep 2 Reload Split:	Rep 3 Reload Split:	
Rep 1 Time:	Rep 2 Time:	Rep 3 Time:	Notes:
Rep 1 All In: **Go** / **No Go**	Rep 2 All In: **Go** / **No Go**	Rep 3 All In: **Go** / **No Go**	

Date:	Weapon:	Sights:	Holster:
Rep 1 Reload Split:	Rep 2 Reload Split:	Rep 3 Reload Split:	
Rep 1 Time:	Rep 2 Time:	Rep 3 Time:	Notes:
Rep 1 All In: **Go** / **No Go**	Rep 2 All In: **Go** / **No Go**	Rep 3 All In: **Go** / **No Go**	

Date:	Weapon:	Sights:	Holster:
Rep 1 Reload Split:	Rep 2 Reload Split:	Rep 3 Reload Split:	
Rep 1 Time:	Rep 2 Time:	Rep 3 Time:	Notes:
Rep 1 All In: **Go** / **No Go**	Rep 2 All In: **Go** / **No Go**	Rep 3 All In: **Go** / **No Go**	

GUNDO RELOAD

Date:	Weapon:	Sights:	Holster:
Rep 1 Reload Split:	Rep 2 Reload Split:	Rep 3 Reload Split:	Dummy Round: Y / N
Rep 1 Time:	Rep 2 Time:	Rep 3 Time:	Notes:
Rep 1 All In: **Go** / **No Go**	Rep 2 All In: **Go** / **No Go**	Rep 3 All In: **Go** / **No Go**	

Date:	Weapon:	Sights:	Holster:
Rep 1 Reload Split:	Rep 2 Reload Split:	Rep 3 Reload Split:	
Rep 1 Time:	Rep 2 Time:	Rep 3 Time:	Notes:
Rep 1 All In: **Go** / **No Go**	Rep 2 All In: **Go** / **No Go**	Rep 3 All In: **Go** / **No Go**	

Date:	Weapon:	Sights:	Holster:
Rep 1 Reload Split:	Rep 2 Reload Split:	Rep 3 Reload Split:	
Rep 1 Time:	Rep 2 Time:	Rep 3 Time:	Notes:
Rep 1 All In: **Go** / **No Go**	Rep 2 All In: **Go** / **No Go**	Rep 3 All In: **Go** / **No Go**	

Date:	Weapon:	Sights:	Holster:
Rep 1 Reload Split:	Rep 2 Reload Split:	Rep 3 Reload Split:	
Rep 1 Time:	Rep 2 Time:	Rep 3 Time:	Notes:
Rep 1 All In: **Go** / **No Go**	Rep 2 All In: **Go** / **No Go**	Rep 3 All In: **Go** / **No Go**	

Advanced Pistol ©

GUNDO RELOAD

Date:	Weapon:	Sights:	Holster:
Rep 1 Reload Split:	Rep 2 Reload Split:	Rep 3 Reload Split:	Dummy Round: Y / N
Rep 1 Time:	Rep 2 Time:	Rep 3 Time:	Notes:
Rep 1 All In: **Go / No Go**	Rep 2 All In: **Go / No Go**	Rep 3 All In: **Go / No Go**	

Date:	Weapon:	Sights:	Holster:
Rep 1 Reload Split:	Rep 2 Reload Split:	Rep 3 Reload Split:	
Rep 1 Time:	Rep 2 Time:	Rep 3 Time:	Notes:
Rep 1 All In: **Go / No Go**	Rep 2 All In: **Go / No Go**	Rep 3 All In: **Go / No Go**	

Date:	Weapon:	Sights:	Holster:
Rep 1 Reload Split:	Rep 2 Reload Split:	Rep 3 Reload Split:	
Rep 1 Time:	Rep 2 Time:	Rep 3 Time:	Notes:
Rep 1 All In: **Go / No Go**	Rep 2 All In: **Go / No Go**	Rep 3 All In: **Go / No Go**	

Date:	Weapon:	Sights:	Holster:
Rep 1 Reload Split:	Rep 2 Reload Split:	Rep 3 Reload Split:	
Rep 1 Time:	Rep 2 Time:	Rep 3 Time:	Notes:
Rep 1 All In: **Go / No Go**	Rep 2 All In: **Go / No Go**	Rep 3 All In: **Go / No Go**	

GUNDO RELOAD

Date:	Weapon:	Sights:	Holster:
Rep 1 Reload Split:	Rep 2 Reload Split:	Rep 3 Reload Split:	Dummy Round: Y / N
Rep 1 Time:	Rep 2 Time:	Rep 3 Time:	Notes:
Rep 1 All In: **Go** / **No Go**	Rep 2 All In: **Go** / **No Go**	Rep 3 All In: **Go** / **No Go**	

Date:	Weapon:	Sights:	Holster:
Rep 1 Reload Split:	Rep 2 Reload Split:	Rep 3 Reload Split:	
Rep 1 Time:	Rep 2 Time:	Rep 3 Time:	Notes:
Rep 1 All In: **Go** / **No Go**	Rep 2 All In: **Go** / **No Go**	Rep 3 All In: **Go** / **No Go**	

Date:	Weapon:	Sights:	Holster:
Rep 1 Reload Split:	Rep 2 Reload Split:	Rep 3 Reload Split:	
Rep 1 Time:	Rep 2 Time:	Rep 3 Time:	Notes:
Rep 1 All In: **Go** / **No Go**	Rep 2 All In: **Go** / **No Go**	Rep 3 All In: **Go** / **No Go**	

Date:	Weapon:	Sights:	Holster:
Rep 1 Reload Split:	Rep 2 Reload Split:	Rep 3 Reload Split:	
Rep 1 Time:	Rep 2 Time:	Rep 3 Time:	Notes:
Rep 1 All In: **Go** / **No Go**	Rep 2 All In: **Go** / **No Go**	Rep 3 All In: **Go** / **No Go**	

Advanced Pistol ©

www.GUNFIGHTERSERIES.com ©

CRAP SHOOT

Purpose: Mental focus under stress.   **By:** Kevin Lippert of Jericho Defense

Distance: 5, 7, 9 Yards.   **Target:** JD-Qual1   **Par Time:** 30 Seconds.

Extra Equipment Needed: Shot timer, 2 magazines, magazine pouch, position markers, one large game die.

Rounds Fired Per Marker: 1 Round increase per each maker.   **Total Rounds Fired:** 21 Rounds.

Point Penalty: Go / No Go.   **Repetitions:** 1 Rep.

Starting Position & Condition: Standing – Surrender / Interview. Weapon Condition 1.

Rules: In this drill, you will shoot from 6 different markers with an ascending round count representing the numbers on a game die, from 1 to 6 rounds. Example, if you roll a 3, you shoot 3 rounds from the first marker, then 4, 5, 6, 1, and finally 2 at the last marker you pick. You must shoot from each of the 6 markers and you can not shoot from the same marker twice. Also, you may move diagonally or jump over a marker but you can not move to a marker that is directly right or left of you or the marker right in front of or behind you.

Description: Start at the 9 yard right marker. At the timer beep, drop dice and see what number you dropped, draw your pistol and fire the number of rounds on the game die into the (5 point) A Zone body box. Keep pistol pointed in a safe direction and move to another marker of your choice. Shoot the next ascending round number, move, repeat until you have gone through all 6 markers and shot all 21 rounds. Record your time and score. Any rounds out side of the (5 point) A Zone body box, if you shoot rounds out of numerical order, do not use all makers or if you go over 30 second par, the drill is a No Go. Good mental focus counting your rounds fired, remembering where you fired from and making quick decisions is essential to master this drill.

Goals: Shoot from all 6 maker positions, shoot in ascending round count and keep all rounds in (5 point) A Zone body box.

Variation: Add random dummy rounds to your magazines. Double the distance.

CRAP SHOOT

Date:	Weapon:	Sights:	Holster:
Distance Multiplier: X1 / X2	Game Time:	# Out of A Box:	**All In Body Box: Y / N**
Dummy Rounds: Y / N	Notes:		

Date:	Weapon:	Sights:	Holster:
Distance Multiplier: X1 / X2	Game Time:	# Out of A Box:	**All In Body Box: Y / N**
Dummy Rounds: Y / N	Notes:		

Date:	Weapon:	Sights:	Holster:
Distance Multiplier: X1 / X2	Game Time:	# Out of A Box:	**All In Body Box: Y / N**
Dummy Rounds: Y / N	Notes:		

Date:	Weapon:	Sights:	Holster:
Distance Multiplier: X1 / X2	Game Time:	# Out of A Box:	**All In Body Box: Y / N**
Dummy Rounds: Y / N	Notes:		

Date:	Weapon:	Sights:	Holster:
Distance Multiplier: X1 / X2	Game Time:	# Out of A Box:	**All In Body Box: Y / N**
Dummy Rounds: Y / N	Notes:		

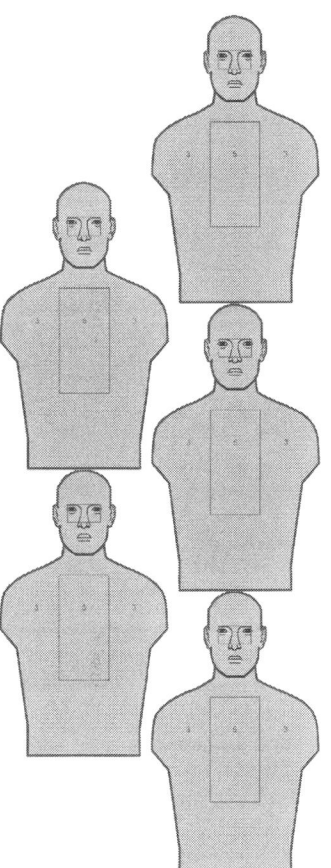

CRAP SHOOT

Date:	Weapon:	Sights:	Holster:
Distance Multiplier: X1 / X2	Game Time:	# Out of A Box:	**All In Body Box**: Y / N
Dummy Rounds: Y / N	Notes:		

Date:	Weapon:	Sights:	Holster:
Distance Multiplier: X1 / X2	Game Time:	# Out of A Box:	**All In Body Box**: Y / N
Dummy Rounds: Y / N	Notes:		

Date:	Weapon:	Sights:	Holster:
Distance Multiplier: X1 / X2	Game Time:	# Out of A Box:	**All In Body Box**: Y / N
Dummy Rounds: Y / N	Notes:		

Date:	Weapon:	Sights:	Holster:
Distance Multiplier: X1 / X2	Game Time:	# Out of A Box:	**All In Body Box**: Y / N
Dummy Rounds: Y / N	Notes:		

Date:	Weapon:	Sights:	Holster:
Distance Multiplier: X1 / X2	Game Time:	# Out of A Box:	**All In Body Box**: Y / N
Dummy Rounds: Y / N	Notes:		

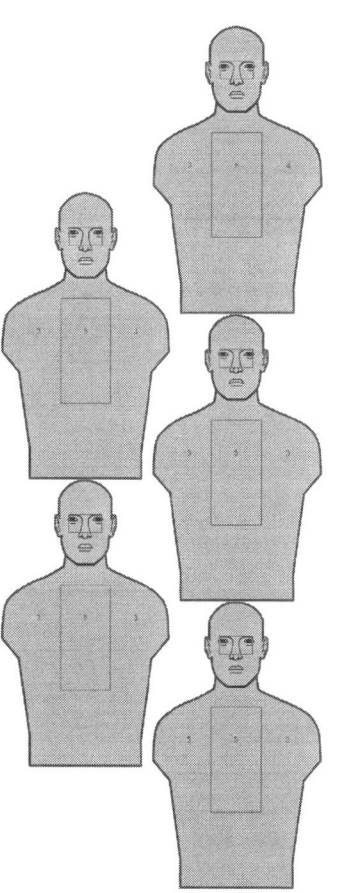

CRAP SHOOT

Date:	Weapon:	Sights:	Holster:
Distance Multiplier: X1 / X2	Game Time:	# Out of A Box:	**All In Body Box: Y / N**
Dummy Rounds: Y / N	Notes:		

Date:	Weapon:	Sights:	Holster:
Distance Multiplier: X1 / X2	Game Time:	# Out of A Box:	**All In Body Box: Y / N**
Dummy Rounds: Y / N	Notes:		

Date:	Weapon:	Sights:	Holster:
Distance Multiplier: X1 / X2	Game Time:	# Out of A Box:	**All In Body Box: Y / N**
Dummy Rounds: Y / N	Notes:		

Date:	Weapon:	Sights:	Holster:
Distance Multiplier: X1 / X2	Game Time:	# Out of A Box:	**All In Body Box: Y / N**
Dummy Rounds: Y / N	Notes:		

Date:	Weapon:	Sights:	Holster:
Distance Multiplier: X1 / X2	Game Time:	# Out of A Box:	**All In Body Box: Y / N**
Dummy Rounds: Y / N	Notes:		

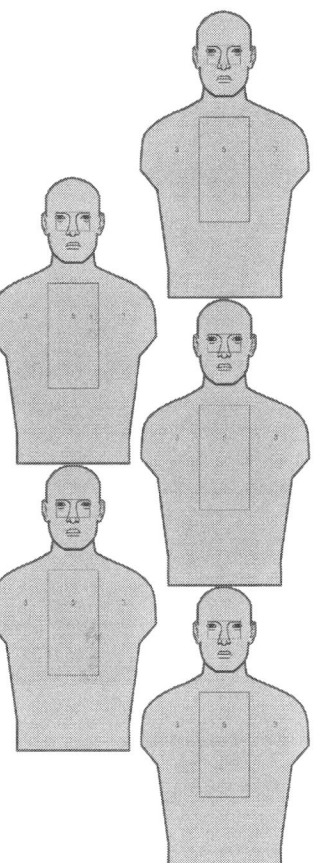

CRAP SHOOT

Date:	Weapon:	Sights:	Holster:
Distance Multiplier: X1 / X2	Game Time:	# Out of A Box:	**All In Body Box: Y / N**
Dummy Rounds: Y / N	Notes:		

Date:	Weapon:	Sights:	Holster:
Distance Multiplier: X1 / X2	Game Time:	# Out of A Box:	**All In Body Box: Y / N**
Dummy Rounds: Y / N	Notes:		

Date:	Weapon:	Sights:	Holster:
Distance Multiplier: X1 / X2	Game Time:	# Out of A Box:	**All In Body Box: Y / N**
Dummy Rounds: Y / N	Notes:		

Date:	Weapon:	Sights:	Holster:
Distance Multiplier: X1 / X2	Game Time:	# Out of A Box:	**All In Body Box: Y / N**
Dummy Rounds: Y / N	Notes:		

Date:	Weapon:	Sights:	Holster:
Distance Multiplier: X1 / X2	Game Time:	# Out of A Box:	**All In Body Box: Y / N**
Dummy Rounds: Y / N	Notes:		

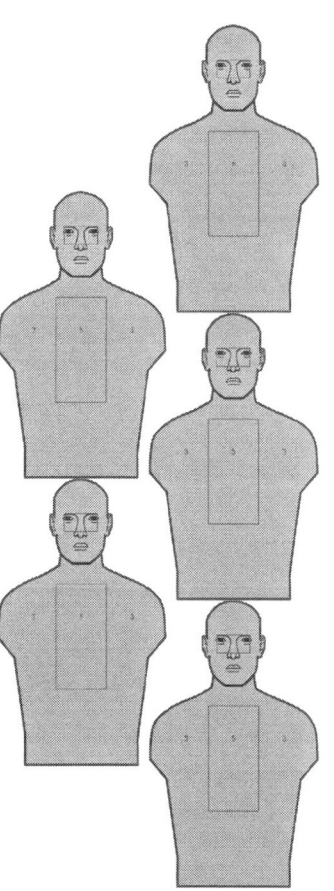

CRAP SHOOT

Date:	Weapon:	Sights:	Holster:
Distance Multiplier: X1 / X2	Game Time:	# Out of A Box:	**All In Body Box: Y / N**
Dummy Rounds: Y / N	Notes:		

Date:	Weapon:	Sights:	Holster:
Distance Multiplier: X1 / X2	Game Time:	# Out of A Box:	**All In Body Box: Y / N**
Dummy Rounds: Y / N	Notes:		

Date:	Weapon:	Sights:	Holster:
Distance Multiplier: X1 / X2	Game Time:	# Out of A Box:	**All In Body Box: Y / N**
Dummy Rounds: Y / N	Notes:		

Date:	Weapon:	Sights:	Holster:
Distance Multiplier: X1 / X2	Game Time:	# Out of A Box:	**All In Body Box: Y / N**
Dummy Rounds: Y / N	Notes:		

Date:	Weapon:	Sights:	Holster:
Distance Multiplier: X1 / X2	Game Time:	# Out of A Box:	**All In Body Box: Y / N**
Dummy Rounds: Y / N	Notes:		

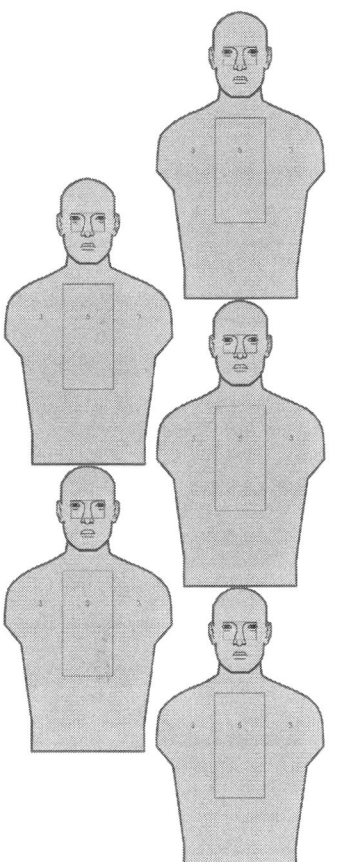

LEAN INTO IT

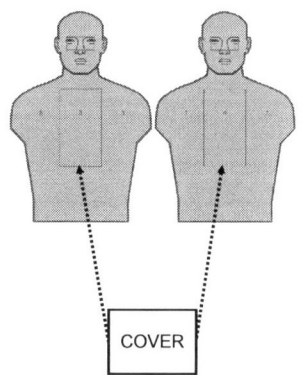

Purpose: Develop and increase efficient use of cover.

Distance: 7 Yards.

Target: JD-Qual1 X 2

Extra Equipment Needed: 5 Dummy rounds (optional), barrier/barricade for cover, extra magazines, and extra magazine pouches.

Rounds Fired Per Rep: 2 to 3 Rounds.

Total Rounds Fired: 12 to 36 Rounds.

Point Penalty: Go / No Go.

Repetitions: 6 Reps (3 per side).

Starting Position & Condition: Standing – Surrender / Interview. Weapon Condition 1.

Description: At your own personal go, draw your pistol properly using cover, fire 2 to 6 rounds into the (5 point) A Zone body box. Put pistol on safe if applicable and holster it safely. Repeat drill on other side of cover. Right target is for right side of cover. Left target is for left side of cover. Repeat this sequence until you have completed the drill on each side of cover 3 times. Reload and fix malfunctions as needed.

Dominant side use of cover: Start approximately 7 feet back completely behind cover. Assuming a regular stance, place your outside foot forward at the edge, but so it doesn't break cover. From behind cover, present your pistol towards the target while getting your sight alignment set, lean forward until your pistol just breaks cover, fire your shots, lean back behind cover. If the threat was looking back at your, they should only see a very small slice of your head, your pistol and a small part of your elbow.

Support side use of cover: Support use of cover is the same as the dominant side, however, you will have to turn your pistol sideway and use your support eye to sight the pistol on target. Closing your dominant eye is acceptable.

Goal: To be smooth and deliberate with your actions and present as small of a target to the threat while you are shooting from cover.

Variation: Have someone mix dummy rounds randomly in your magazines. Try different barricades/barriers for cover. Use different shooting positions.

LEAN INTO IT

Date:	Location:	Weapon:	Holster:
Dummy Rounds: Y / N	Left Side All In: Y / N	Right Side All In: Y / N	**All Rounds In:** Y / N
Standing / Kneeling	Rounds Per Rep:	Rounds Per Rep:	**Total Score:**
Cover Used:	Notes:		

Left Rep   Right Rep

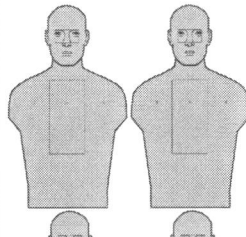

Date:	Location:	Weapon:	Holster:
Dummy Rounds: Y / N	Left Side All In: Y / N	Right Side All In: Y / N	**All Rounds In:** Y / N
Standing / Kneeling	Rounds Per Rep:	Rounds Per Rep:	**Total Score:**
Cover Used:	Notes:		

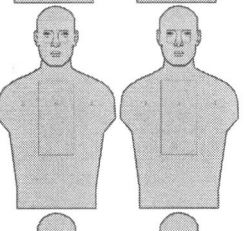

Date:	Location:	Weapon:	Holster:
Dummy Rounds: Y / N	Left Side All In: Y / N	Right Side All In: Y / N	**All Rounds In:** Y / N
Standing / Kneeling	Rounds Per Rep:	Rounds Per Rep:	**Total Score:**
Cover Used:	Notes:		

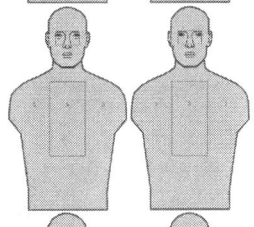

Date:	Location:	Weapon:	Holster:
Dummy Rounds: Y / N	Left Side All In: Y / N	Right Side All In: Y / N	**All Rounds In:** Y / N
Standing / Kneeling	Rounds Per Rep:	Rounds Per Rep:	**Total Score:**
Cover Used:	Notes:		

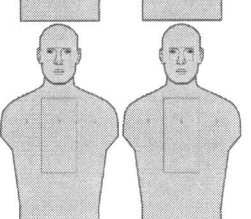

LEAN INTO IT

Date:	Location:	Weapon:	Holster:
Dummy Rounds: Y / N	Left Side All In: Y / N	Right Side All In: Y / N	**All Rounds In:** Y / N
Standing / Kneeling	Rounds Per Rep:	Rounds Per Rep:	**Total Score:**
Cover Used:	Notes:		

Date:	Location:	Weapon:	Holster:
Dummy Rounds: Y / N	Left Side All In: Y / N	Right Side All In: Y / N	**All Rounds In:** Y / N
Standing / Kneeling	Rounds Per Rep:	Rounds Per Rep:	**Total Score:**
Cover Used:	Notes:		

Date:	Location:	Weapon:	Holster:
Dummy Rounds: Y / N	Left Side All In: Y / N	Right Side All In: Y / N	**All Rounds In:** Y / N
Standing / Kneeling	Rounds Per Rep:	Rounds Per Rep:	**Total Score:**
Cover Used:	Notes:		

Date:	Location:	Weapon:	Holster:
Dummy Rounds: Y / N	Left Side All In: Y / N	Right Side All In: Y / N	**All Rounds In:** Y / N
Standing / Kneeling	Rounds Per Rep:	Rounds Per Rep:	**Total Score:**
Cover Used:	Notes:		

Left Rep   Right Rep

LEAN INTO IT

Date:	Location:	Weapon:	Holster:
Dummy Rounds: Y / N	Left Side All In: Y / N	Right Side All In: Y / N	**All Rounds In:** Y / N
Standing / Kneeling	Rounds Per Rep:	Rounds Per Rep:	**Total Score:**
Cover Used:	Notes:		

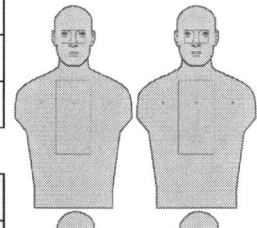

Left Rep   Right Rep

Date:	Location:	Weapon:	Holster:
Dummy Rounds: Y / N	Left Side All In: Y / N	Right Side All In: Y / N	**All Rounds In:** Y / N
Standing / Kneeling	Rounds Per Rep:	Rounds Per Rep:	**Total Score:**
Cover Used:	Notes:		

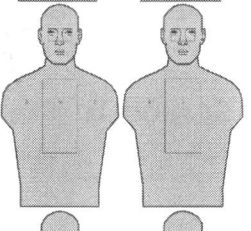

Date:	Location:	Weapon:	Holster:
Dummy Rounds: Y / N	Left Side All In: Y / N	Right Side All In: Y / N	**All Rounds In:** Y / N
Standing / Kneeling	Rounds Per Rep:	Rounds Per Rep:	**Total Score:**
Cover Used:	Notes:		

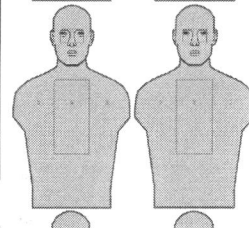

Date:	Location:	Weapon:	Holster:
Dummy Rounds: Y / N	Left Side All In: Y / N	Right Side All In: Y / N	**All Rounds In:** Y / N
Standing / Kneeling	Rounds Per Rep:	Rounds Per Rep:	**Total Score:**
Cover Used:	Notes:		

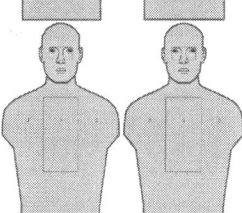

Advanced Pistol ©

LEAN INTO IT

Date:	Location:	Weapon:	Holster:
Dummy Rounds: Y / N	Left Side All In: Y / N	Right Side All In: Y / N	**All Rounds In:** Y / N
Standing / Kneeling	Rounds Per Rep:	Rounds Per Rep:	**Total Score:**
Cover Used:	Notes:		

Date:	Location:	Weapon:	Holster:
Dummy Rounds: Y / N	Left Side All In: Y / N	Right Side All In: Y / N	**All Rounds In:** Y / N
Standing / Kneeling	Rounds Per Rep:	Rounds Per Rep:	**Total Score:**
Cover Used:	Notes:		

Date:	Location:	Weapon:	Holster:
Dummy Rounds: Y / N	Left Side All In: Y / N	Right Side All In: Y / N	**All Rounds In:** Y / N
Standing / Kneeling	Rounds Per Rep:	Rounds Per Rep:	**Total Score:**
Cover Used:	Notes:		

Date:	Location:	Weapon:	Holster:
Dummy Rounds: Y / N	Left Side All In: Y / N	Right Side All In: Y / N	**All Rounds In:** Y / N
Standing / Kneeling	Rounds Per Rep:	Rounds Per Rep:	**Total Score:**
Cover Used:	Notes:		

Left Rep   Right Rep

LEAN INTO IT

Date:	Location:	Weapon:	Holster:
Dummy Rounds: Y / N	Left Side All In: Y / N	Right Side All In: Y / N	**All Rounds In:** Y / N
Standing / Kneeling	Rounds Per Rep:	Rounds Per Rep:	**Total Score:**
Cover Used:	Notes:		

Left Rep   Right Rep

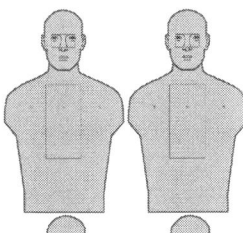

Date:	Location:	Weapon:	Holster:
Dummy Rounds: Y / N	Left Side All In: Y / N	Right Side All In: Y / N	**All Rounds In:** Y / N
Standing / Kneeling	Rounds Per Rep:	Rounds Per Rep:	**Total Score:**
Cover Used:	Notes:		

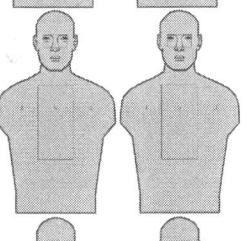

Date:	Location:	Weapon:	Holster:
Dummy Rounds: Y / N	Left Side All In: Y / N	Right Side All In: Y / N	**All Rounds In:** Y / N
Standing / Kneeling	Rounds Per Rep:	Rounds Per Rep:	**Total Score:**
Cover Used:	Notes:		

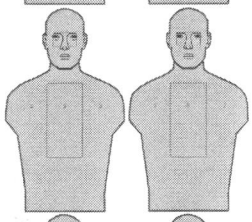

Date:	Location:	Weapon:	Holster:
Dummy Rounds: Y / N	Left Side All In: Y / N	Right Side All In: Y / N	**All Rounds In:** Y / N
Standing / Kneeling	Rounds Per Rep:	Rounds Per Rep:	**Total Score:**
Cover Used:	Notes:		

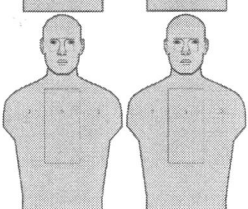

GUNFIGHTER PISTOL STANDARD 3

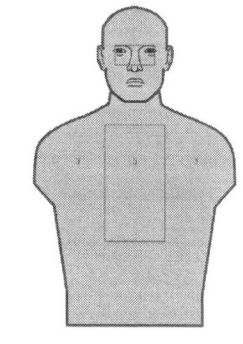

- **Target:** JD-QUAL1 target

- **Ammo:** 17 Rounds total.

- **Scoring:** Per target score. Subtract 5 points for any shot over time. Passing score is 75 out of 85 points.

- **Draw:** Each stage requires a Condition 1 draw from concealment. Holster after each stage.

Stage	Distance	#Rnds	Time	Position/Description
1	10 Yards	2	8 Sec	Empty chamber with full magazine inserted, clear type one malfunction one handed, 2 rounds to A zone BODY box.
2	10 Yards	5	5 Sec	Starting from low ready. 5 rounds to A zone BODY box using only dominant hand.
3	10 Yards	5	7 Sec	Starting from low ready. 5 rounds to A zone BODY box, using only support hand.
4	7 Yards	2	2.5 Sec	2 rounds to A zone BODY box, using only dominant hand.
5	7 Yards	2	7 Sec	2 rounds to A zone BODY box, using only support hand.
6	5 Yards	1	2 Sec	1 round to A zone HEAD box.

GUNFIGHTER PISTOL STANDARD 3

Date:	Location:	Holster: Concealed / Duty / Open	
Weapon:	Sights:	Ammo:	Day / Night
Stage 1: 2 Round - 8 Sec.	Draw Time:	Stage Time:	Score:
Stage 2: 5 Rounds - 5 Sec.	Draw Time:	Stage Time:	Score:
Stage 3: 5+1 Rounds - 7 Sec.	Draw Time:	Stage Time:	Score:
Stage 4: 2 Rounds - 2.5 Sec	Draw Time:	Stage Time:	Score:
Stage 5: 2 Rounds - 7 Sec.	Draw Time:	Stage Time:	Score:
Stage 6: 1 Rounds - 2 Sec.	Draw Time:	Stage Time:	Score:
Notes:			**Total Score:**

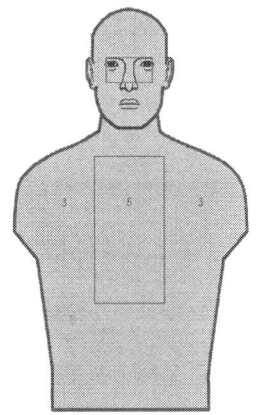

Passing score is 75 out of 85 points.

Date:	Location:	Holster: Concealed / Duty / Open	
Weapon:	Sights:	Ammo:	Day / Night
Stage 1: 2 Round - 8 Sec.	Draw Time:	Stage Time:	Score:
Stage 2: 5 Rounds - 5 Sec.	Draw Time:	Stage Time:	Score:
Stage 3: 5+1 Rounds - 7 Sec.	Draw Time:	Stage Time:	Score:
Stage 4: 2 Rounds - 2.5 Sec	Draw Time:	Stage Time:	Score:
Stage 5: 2 Rounds - 7 Sec.	Draw Time:	Stage Time:	Score:
Stage 6: 1 Rounds - 2 Sec.	Draw Time:	Stage Time:	Score:
Notes:			**Total Score:**

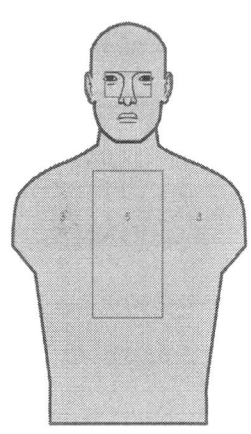

Advanced Pistol ©   Qualification COF - 3

www.GUNFIGHTERSERIES.com ©

GUNFIGHTER PISTOL STANDARD 3

Date:	Location:	Holster: Concealed / Duty / Open	
Weapon:	Sights:	Ammo:	Day / Night
Stage 1: 2 Round - 8 Sec.	Draw Time:	Stage Time:	Score:
Stage 2: 5 Rounds - 5 Sec.	Draw Time:	Stage Time:	Score:
Stage 3: 5+1 Rounds - 7 Sec.	Draw Time:	Stage Time:	Score:
Stage 4: 2 Rounds - 2.5 Sec	Draw Time:	Stage Time:	Score:
Stage 5: 2 Rounds - 7 Sec.	Draw Time:	Stage Time:	Score:
Stage 6: 1 Rounds - 2 Sec.	Draw Time:	Stage Time:	Score:
Notes:			**Total Score:**

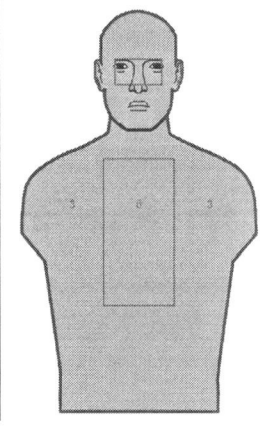

Passing score is 75 out of 85 points.

Date:	Location:	Holster: Concealed / Duty / Open	
Weapon:	Sights:	Ammo:	Day / Night
Stage 1: 2 Round - 8 Sec.	Draw Time:	Stage Time:	Score:
Stage 2: 5 Rounds - 5 Sec.	Draw Time:	Stage Time:	Score:
Stage 3: 5+1 Rounds - 7 Sec.	Draw Time:	Stage Time:	Score:
Stage 4: 2 Rounds - 2.5 Sec	Draw Time:	Stage Time:	Score:
Stage 5: 2 Rounds - 7 Sec.	Draw Time:	Stage Time:	Score:
Stage 6: 1 Rounds - 2 Sec.	Draw Time:	Stage Time:	Score:
Notes:			**Total Score:**

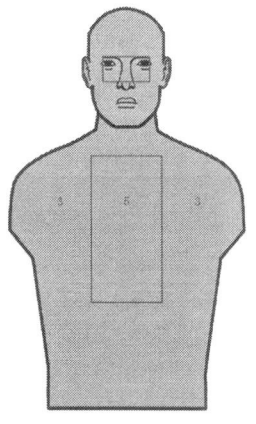

GUNFIGHTER PISTOL STANDARD 3

Date:	Location:	Holster: Concealed / Duty / Open	
Weapon:	Sights:	Ammo:	Day / Night
Stage 1: 2 Round - 8 Sec.	Draw Time:	Stage Time:	Score:
Stage 2: 5 Rounds - 5 Sec.	Draw Time:	Stage Time:	Score:
Stage 3: 5+1 Rounds - 7 Sec.	Draw Time:	Stage Time:	Score:
Stage 4: 2 Rounds - 2.5 Sec	Draw Time:	Stage Time:	Score:
Stage 5: 2 Rounds - 7 Sec.	Draw Time:	Stage Time:	Score:
Stage 6: 1 Rounds - 2 Sec.	Draw Time:	Stage Time:	Score:
Notes:			**Total Score:**

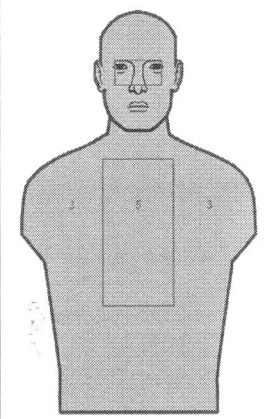

Passing score is 75 out of 85 points.

Date:	Location:	Holster: Concealed / Duty / Open	
Weapon:	Sights:	Ammo:	Day / Night
Stage 1: 2 Round - 8 Sec.	Draw Time:	Stage Time:	Score:
Stage 2: 5 Rounds - 5 Sec.	Draw Time:	Stage Time:	Score:
Stage 3: 5+1 Rounds - 7 Sec.	Draw Time:	Stage Time:	Score:
Stage 4: 2 Rounds - 2.5 Sec	Draw Time:	Stage Time:	Score:
Stage 5: 2 Rounds - 7 Sec.	Draw Time:	Stage Time:	Score:
Stage 6: 1 Rounds - 2 Sec.	Draw Time:	Stage Time:	Score:
Notes:			**Total Score:**

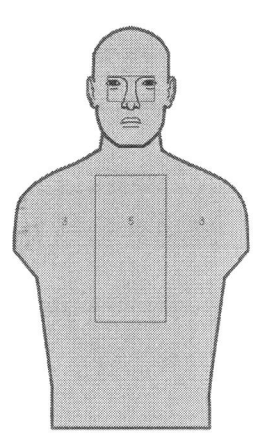

Advanced Pistol ©   Qualification COF - 3

GUNFIGHTER PISTOL STANDARD 3

Date:	Location:	Holster: Concealed / Duty / Open	
Weapon:	Sights:	Ammo:	Day / Night
Stage 1: 2 Round - 8 Sec.	Draw Time:	Stage Time:	Score:
Stage 2: 5 Rounds - 5 Sec.	Draw Time:	Stage Time:	Score:
Stage 3: 5+1 Rounds - 7 Sec.	Draw Time:	Stage Time:	Score:
Stage 4: 2 Rounds - 2.5 Sec	Draw Time:	Stage Time:	Score:
Stage 5: 2 Rounds - 7 Sec.	Draw Time:	Stage Time:	Score:
Stage 6: 1 Rounds - 2 Sec.	Draw Time:	Stage Time:	Score:
Notes:			**Total Score:**

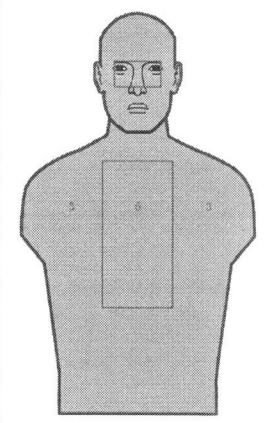

Passing score is 75 out of 85 points.

Date:	Location:	Holster: Concealed / Duty / Open	
Weapon:	Sights:	Ammo:	Day / Night
Stage 1: 2 Round - 8 Sec.	Draw Time:	Stage Time:	Score:
Stage 2: 5 Rounds - 5 Sec.	Draw Time:	Stage Time:	Score:
Stage 3: 5+1 Rounds - 7 Sec.	Draw Time:	Stage Time:	Score:
Stage 4: 2 Rounds - 2.5 Sec	Draw Time:	Stage Time:	Score:
Stage 5: 2 Rounds - 7 Sec.	Draw Time:	Stage Time:	Score:
Stage 6: 1 Rounds - 2 Sec.	Draw Time:	Stage Time:	Score:
Notes:			**Total Score:**

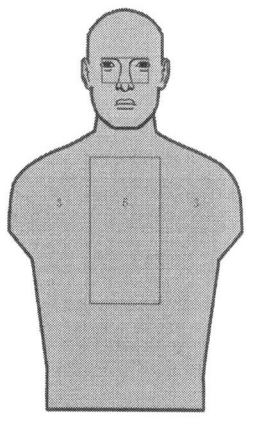

GUNFIGHTER PISTOL STANDARD 3

Date:	Location:	Holster: Concealed / Duty / Open	
Weapon:	Sights:	Ammo:	Day / Night
Stage 1: 2 Round - 8 Sec.	Draw Time:	Stage Time:	Score:
Stage 2: 5 Rounds - 5 Sec.	Draw Time:	Stage Time:	Score:
Stage 3: 5+1 Rounds - 7 Sec.	Draw Time:	Stage Time:	Score:
Stage 4: 2 Rounds - 2.5 Sec	Draw Time:	Stage Time:	Score:
Stage 5: 2 Rounds - 7 Sec.	Draw Time:	Stage Time:	Score:
Stage 6: 1 Rounds - 2 Sec.	Draw Time:	Stage Time:	Score:
Notes:			**Total Score:**

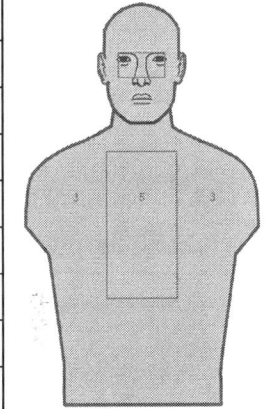

Passing score is 75 out of 85 points.

Date:	Location:	Holster: Concealed / Duty / Open	
Weapon:	Sights:	Ammo:	Day / Night
Stage 1: 2 Round - 8 Sec.	Draw Time:	Stage Time:	Score:
Stage 2: 5 Rounds - 5 Sec.	Draw Time:	Stage Time:	Score:
Stage 3: 5+1 Rounds - 7 Sec.	Draw Time:	Stage Time:	Score:
Stage 4: 2 Rounds - 2.5 Sec	Draw Time:	Stage Time:	Score:
Stage 5: 2 Rounds - 7 Sec.	Draw Time:	Stage Time:	Score:
Stage 6: 1 Rounds - 2 Sec.	Draw Time:	Stage Time:	Score:
Notes:			**Total Score:**

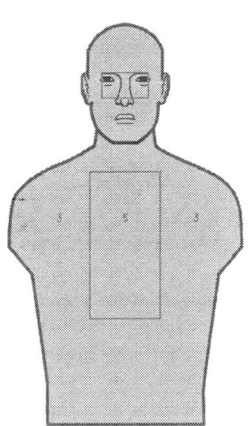

Advanced Pistol ©   Qualification COF - 3

GUNFIGHTER PISTOL STANDARD 4

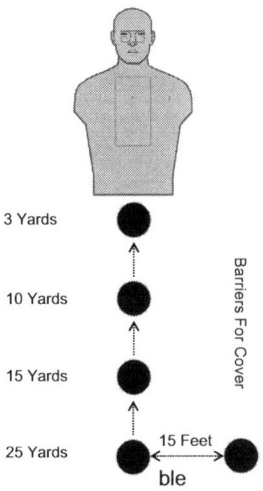

Target: JD-QUAL1

Distance: 25, 15, 10 and 3 Yards.

Par Time: 50 Seconds.

Extra equipment required: Shot timer, 2 pieces of cover, 2 or 3 dummy rounds, 2 or 3 pistol mags.

Loadout: 3 Magazines: 1st Mag: 2 Dummy Rounds. 2nd Mag: 6 - 10 rounds. 3rd Mag: Full with 1 dummy round within top 5.

Total Fired: 20 Rounds.   **Scoring:** As per target score. Subtract 5 points for any shot over par.

Goal: 80 Points under 50 sec par time.   Expert: 90 Points under 45 sec.   Gunfighter: 100 points under 40 sec.

Starting Position & Condition: Standing – Surrender/Interview. Weapon loaded with empty magazine and an induced dummy round dou-feed malfunction.

Description: At the 25 yard line, at the timer beep, attempt to fire, observe the double feed situation, move to the 25 yard cover, clear double feed by stripping the magazine, fire 5 rounds into the (5 point) A Zone body box using cover.

Stage	Distance	#Rnds	Position / Description *Reload and fix malfunctions as needed.
1	25 Yards	5	Clear type 2 malfunction behind cover. Any shooting position, 5 rounds to A zone BODY box from behind cover. Run to 15 yard line using L shaped cover movement.
	15 Yards	5	Any shooting position, 5 rounds to A zone BODY box from behind cover. Run to 10 yard line.
	10 Yards	5	Using only dominant hand, 5 rounds to A zone BODY box.
	10 - 3 Yards	5	While walking from 10 yard line to 3 yard line, 5 rounds to A zone BODY box.

GUNFIGHTER PISTOL STANDARD 4

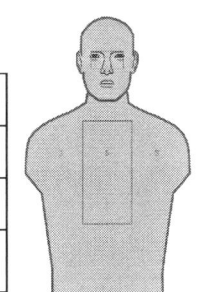

Date:	Location:	Weapon:
Sights:	Holster:	Cover Barrier Type:
Completion Time:	# In (5 point) Body A Box:	# In (3 point) Body:
Notes:		Total Score:

Goal: 80 Points under 50 sec par time.   Expert: 90 Points under 45 sec.   Gunfighter: 100 points under 40 sec.

Date:	Time:	Location:
Weapon:	Sights:	Ammo:
Completion Time:	Under Par: Yes / No	Shots Over Par:
# In (5 point) Body A Box:	# In (5 point) Head A Box:	# In (3 point) Body:
Notes:		Total Score:

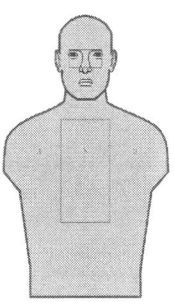

Date:	Time:	Location:
Weapon:	Sights:	Ammo:
Completion Time:	Under Par: Yes / No	Shots Over Par:
# In (5 point) Body A Box:	# In (5 point) Head A Box:	# In (3 point) Body:
Notes:		Total Score:

Advanced Pistol ©   Qualification COF -4

GUNFIGHTER PISTOL STANDARD 4

Date:	Location:	Weapon:
Sights:	Holster:	Cover Barrier Type:
Completion Time:	# In (5 point) Body A Box:	# In (3 point) Body:
Notes:		Total Score:

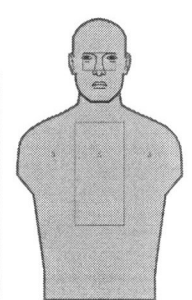

Goal: 80 Points under 50 sec par time.   Expert: 90 Points under 45 sec.   Gunfighter: 100 points under 40 sec.

Date:	Time:	Location:
Weapon:	Sights:	Ammo:
Completion Time:	Under Par: Yes / No	Shots Over Par:
# In (5 point) Body A Box:	# In (5 point) Head A Box:	# In (3 point) Body:
Notes:		Total Score:

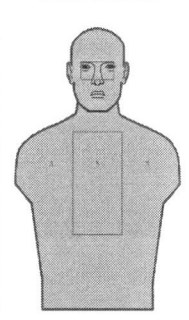

Date:	Time:	Location:
Weapon:	Sights:	Ammo:
Completion Time:	Under Par: Yes / No	Shots Over Par:
# In (5 point) Body A Box:	# In (5 point) Head A Box:	# In (3 point) Body:
Notes:		Total Score:

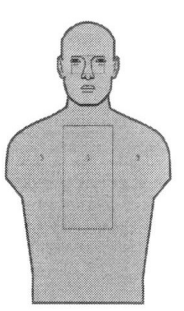

GUNFIGHTER PISTOL STANDARD 4

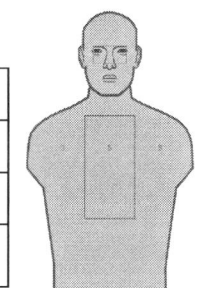

Date:	Location:	Weapon:
Sights:	Holster:	Cover Barrier Type:
Completion Time:	# In (5 point) Body A Box:	# In (3 point) Body:
Notes:		Total Score:

Goal: 80 Points under 50 sec par time. Expert: 90 Points under 45 sec. Gunfighter: 100 points under 40 sec.

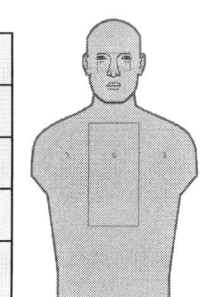

Date:	Time:	Location:
Weapon:	Sights:	Ammo:
Completion Time:	Under Par: Yes / No	Shots Over Par:
# In (5 point) Body A Box:	# In (5 point) Head A Box:	# In (3 point) Body:
Notes:		Total Score:

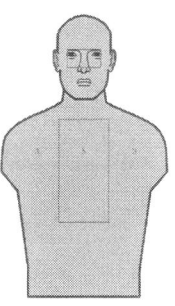

Date:	Time:	Location:
Weapon:	Sights:	Ammo:
Completion Time:	Under Par: Yes / No	Shots Over Par:
# In (5 point) Body A Box:	# In (5 point) Head A Box:	# In (3 point) Body:
Notes:		Total Score:

Advanced Pistol ©   Qualification COF - 4

NAME OF CUSTOM DRILL:

Purpose:

By:

Distance: Yards

Target:

Par Time: Seconds

Extra Equipment Needed:

Rounds per Repetition: Rounds

Total Rounds Fired: Rounds

Point Penalty:

Repetitions:

Starting Position & Condition: Start in the

Description:

Goals: Novice: Expert: Gunfighter:

Variations:

Custom Drill Name:

Date:	Location:	Weapon:	Sights:	Ammo
				Notes:
Date:	Location:	Weapon:	Sights:	Ammo
				Notes:
Date:	Location:	Weapon:	Sights:	Ammo
				Notes:
Date:	Location:	Weapon:	Sights:	Ammo
				Notes:
Date:	Location:	Weapon:	Sights:	Ammo
				Notes:

Custom Drill Name:

Date:	Location:	Weapon:	Sights:	Ammo
				Notes:
Date:	Location:	Weapon:	Sights:	Ammo
				Notes:
Date:	Location:	Weapon:	Sights:	Ammo
				Notes:
Date:	Location:	Weapon:	Sights:	Ammo
				Notes:
Date:	Location:	Weapon:	Sights:	Ammo
				Notes:

Custom Drill Name:

Date:	Location:	Weapon:	Sights:	Ammo
				Notes:
Date:	Location:	Weapon:	Sights:	Ammo
				Notes:
Date:	Location:	Weapon:	Sights:	Ammo
				Notes:
Date:	Location:	Weapon:	Sights:	Ammo
				Notes:
Date:	Location:	Weapon:	Sights:	Ammo
				Notes:

NOTES:

NOTES:

www.GUNFIGHTERSERIES.com ©

Training Classes Taken

Date:	Institute:	Class Name:	Weapon:

Notes about subjects covered:

___

___

___

Notes about equipment used:

___

___

___

___

Instructors Name:	Contact Info:
Instructors Name:	Contact Info:
Students Name:	Contact Info:
Students Name:	Contact Info:
Students Name:	Contact Info:
Students Name:	Contact Info:
Students Name:	Contact Info:

Training Classes Taken

Date:	Institute:	Class Name:	Weapon:

Notes about subjects covered:
_____
_____
_____

Notes about equipment used:
_____
_____
_____
_____

Instructors Name:	Contact Info:
Instructors Name:	Contact Info:
Students Name:	Contact Info:
Students Name:	Contact Info:
Students Name:	Contact Info:
Students Name:	Contact Info:
Students Name:	Contact Info:

Training Classes Taken

Date:	Institute:	Class Name:	Weapon:

Notes about subjects covered:
_____
_____
_____

Notes about equipment used:
_____
_____
_____
_____

Instructors Name:	Contact Info:
Instructors Name:	Contact Info:
Students Name:	Contact Info:
Students Name:	Contact Info:
Students Name:	Contact Info:
Students Name:	Contact Info:
Students Name:	Contact Info:

Training Classes Taken

| Date: | Institute: | Class Name: | Weapon: |

Notes about subjects covered:
_____
_____
_____

Notes about equipment used:
_____
_____
_____

Instructors Name:	Contact Info:
Instructors Name:	Contact Info:
Students Name:	Contact Info:
Students Name:	Contact Info:
Students Name:	Contact Info:
Students Name:	Contact Info:
Students Name:	Contact Info:

Training Classes Taken

Date:	Institute:	Class Name:	Weapon:

Notes about subjects covered:
_____
_____
_____

Notes about equipment used:
_____
_____
_____

Instructors Name:	Contact Info:
Instructors Name:	Contact Info:
Students Name:	Contact Info:
Students Name:	Contact Info:
Students Name:	Contact Info:
Students Name:	Contact Info:
Students Name:	Contact Info:

MY SAFE SPACE

Date:	B.Z.	Battle Ground:	Pistol:	Undead / Infected Human / Mutant
Max Z Box Distance:			**Max Distance Inside Head:**	Hostage Hit: Y / N
Date:	B.Z.	Battle Ground:	Pistol:	Undead / Infected Human / Mutant
Max Z Box Distance:			**Max Distance Inside Head:**	Hostage Hit: Y / N
Date:	B.Z.	Battle Ground:	Pistol:	Undead / Infected Human / Mutant
Max Z Box Distance:			**Max Distance Inside Head:**	Hostage Hit: Y / N
Date:	B.Z.	Battle Ground:	Pistol:	Undead / Infected Human / Mutant
Max Z Box Distance:			**Max Distance Inside Head:**	Hostage Hit: Y / N
Date:	B.Z.	Battle Ground:	Pistol:	Undead / Infected Human / Mutant
Max Z Box Distance:			**Max Distance Inside Head:**	Hostage Hit: Y / N
Date:	B.Z.	Battle Ground:	Pistol:	Undead / Infected Human / Mutant
Max Z Box Distance:			**Max Distance Inside Head:**	Hostage Hit: Y / N
Date:	B.Z.	Battle Ground:	Pistol:	Undead / Infected Human / Mutant
Max Z Box Distance:			**Max Distance Inside Head:**	Hostage Hit: Y / N
Date:	B.Z.	Battle Ground:	Pistol:	Undead / Infected Human / Mutant
Max Z Box Distance:			**Max Distance Inside Head:**	Hostage Hit: Y / N
Date:	B.Z.	Battle Ground:	Pistol:	Undead / Infected Human / Mutant
Max Z Box Distance:			**Max Distance Inside Head:**	Hostage Hit: Y / N

Z Fighter ©

PISTOL DRILL: **MERLE DIXON**

Purpose: Gain proficiency with 2 handed, then dominant and support hand only.

Distance: 3 Yards.

Target: KYL (Undead)

Rounds Fired Per String: 5 Rounds.

Total Rounds Fired: 15 Rounds.

Repetitions: 1 Rep of 3 strings.

Starting Position & Condition: Standing - Any ready position. Condition 1.

Description:

1st string: On your personal go, using a good 2 handed grip, fire 1 round into each dot in the middle column starting at the biggest on top to the smallest dot on the bottom.

2nd string: On your personal go, using left hand only, fire 1 round into each dot on the far left column starting from the biggest on top to the smallest dot on bottom.

3rd string: On your personal go, using right hand only, fire 1 round into each dot on the far right column starting at the biggest on top to the smallest dot on the bottom.

Goals: Meat Bag: 18 Points.   Survivor: 30 Points.   Z Fighter: 45 Points.

Variations:

⊕   Infected Humans: From 5 yards.

⊕   Mutants: From 5 yards. 2.5 Second par time per shot, staring in the low ready position.

Made in the USA
Middletown, DE
08 July 2022